WHO DESIGNED THE DESIGNER?

Michael Augros

Who Designed the Designer?

A Rediscovered Path to God's Existence

IGNATIUS PRESS   SAN FRANCISCO

Front cover photograph:
Twin Lakes, Colorado
by Zachary Repasky

Back cover photograph:
Kauai under the Stars
by Zachary Repasky

Cover design by Enrique Javier Aguilar Pinto

© 2015 by Michael Augros
Published 2015 by Ignatius Press, San Francisco
All rights reserved
ISBN 978-1-58617-969-4
Library of Congress Control Number 2014944005
Printed in the United States of America ∞

For my mother and father

Children have a friendship toward their parents as
to a good exceeding themselves, because their parents
are their benefactors most of all, since they are to their
children the cause of being and nurturing and instruction;
and such, too, is the friendship of man to God.

—Thomas Aquinas, *Commentary on
Aristotle's Nicomachean Ethics*

CONTENTS

HOW TO TAKE THIS BOOK

At a certain stage in their development, my children asked *why* about everything. Often this was just a stall tactic, as when my "Time for bed!" was followed by their "*Why?*" But every now and then they were expressing genuine curiosity. "Dad, why do our oak trees drop their leaves in autumn, but our pine trees keep their needles?" "Why does the moon follow us when we drive to Uncle Joe's house?" And my children could be tenacious. When I offered them an answer, they immediately wanted to know the why behind the answer, so that every question gave rise to another. Occasionally my wife and I were able to provide what should have been an ultimate answer, an answer worthy of standing on its own two legs with no need of further explanation—only to have our children ask us why yet again. Didn't they realize there must be things for which there is no why?

This endearing (if sometimes trying) property of children is human intellectual life in embryo. In its most mature forms of science and philosophy, the life of the human mind still consists mainly in asking why and in persisting in that question as long as there remains a further why to be found. Ultimately we wonder: Is there a first cause of all things? Or must we ask why and why again, forever, reaching back and back toward no beginning at all? Does every cause rely on a prior cause? Or is there something that stands in need of no cause, but just *is*?

At first this might sound like a very divisive question which separates us into various camps of atheism or theism. Not so. Not really. Almost everyone with a definite opinion agrees that there must be *some* sort of first cause. Most atheists, especially these days, believe in some underlying matter or energy or basic force that simply *is*, of which nothing else is the cause and which is itself the cause of everything we see. Believers in gods are surprisingly less unanimous about what the first cause is. Athena, for instance, derived from some sort of cause: she popped out of Zeus' head one day. Zeus himself was a son

9

of the Titan Kronos, who was the son of Uranos, the god of the sky. Uranos, in turn, rose up out of Gaia, the goddess of earth, and it is by Chaos (the "gap" between them) that these two became distinct gods and got married. In this cosmology, no single god was the first cause of all things, but instead some primordial god-containing soup lay at the beginning of it all. Meanwhile, the God of Abraham, Isaac, and Jacob simply *is*. So believers in gods also tend to think there is some primal cause or other, some making it a god and some not.

According to certain agnostics, it is beyond the power of the human mind to determine whether there is a first cause at all. Even the fundamental question whether there *is* a first cause of things may prove difficult. But let us assume, for the moment, that the question has been settled in the affirmative: There is (or are) some sort of first cause (or causes) of things. By far the more difficult business, and by far the more divisive, is the consequent question: *What is it?*

Is it, for example, something mindless and aimless, like inanimate matter or bungling chance? If so, why is the universe so beautiful, orderly, and coherent, and why do its basic laws appear to be a neat custom fit to the prerequisites of intelligent life?

Perhaps instead we should suppose the first cause to be intelligent. Then again, that seems to imply that the first cause involves some complexity of its own (maybe even in the form of a brain). But then wouldn't its intelligence have to be constituted of well-ordered components designed for thinking? If so, this intelligence would appear to need a cause every bit as much as the human mind does, and so it wouldn't be a *first* cause after all.

The purpose of this book is to put forward a solution to these vexing questions. Specifically, my intention is to show, by purely rational means, that there is indeed a first cause of all things and that this cause must be a mind. So far as that goes, this book is indistinguishable from a fairly continuous stream of "there is a god" books. So why bother with this one?

For five reasons:

1. This book takes a fresh, nonpolemical approach to the question of a designer.
2. It slowly and carefully develops a single proof for the existence of a mind behind the universe.

3. It does not call on you to trust in the observations or theories of others, such as scientists, but instead reasons exclusively from things you can verify for yourself.
4. It solves certain fundamental problems of theism, of which the atheists are aware, but which current theistic books largely ignore.
5. The certainty reached in this book is greater than that attained in science-based books for or against a designer.

Were I undertaking this experiment alone, I would not dare start with these high-sounding promises. Soon I will say more about the powerful help I intend to enlist, but first some explanation of each promise is in order.

1. The first distinctive quality of this book is its nonpolemical approach. God is not exactly easy for us to understand. There are real and formidable philosophical difficulties with the idea that the world has been produced by a designer, one of which was outlined earlier: Who designed the designer? If that is an unfair question, it is necessary to say why it is unfair and in a deeply satisfying way. Problems like these are understandably dealt with quickly or not at all in some of the more polemical books, focused as they are on highlighting the many deficiencies of atheistic thought. My goal is somewhat different. I do not aim to defeat the atheists, except secondarily and by the way. The spirit animating this book is not one of attack or defense or even persuasion as much as it is a spirit of wonder. More polemical books begin from the question "Is there a designer or not?" This one begins from what is more like common ground than a hotly contested question—namely, the need to admit some kind of first cause, whatever it might be. As we shall see, it is possible to decide that question without fretting over any of the details of evolution or the big bang, fascinating and important as those things are. That will leave us with a burning question: What *is* the first cause? Its very status as a first cause, we shall discover, is sufficient to reveal a surprising number of attributes that it must have, and others it must not have, bringing its identity gradually into sharper focus.

An advantage to the nonpolemical nature of this book is that you need no familiarity with the opposition in order to follow its reasoning. If you have never heard of Richard Dawkins or Stephen

Hawking or Christopher Hitchens, you can still read every sentence in this book with comprehension. On the other hand, if you *have* been reading a good deal about those thinkers, you will find their relevant thoughts present and accounted for in these pages. They do not get ignored. They get theirs. In the latter chapters especially, their names arise again and again. But this book is not *about* them. It *uses* them to the extent (and only to the extent) that they offer illuminating and worthwhile disagreement.

2. Another distinctive feature of this book is the care with which it develops a single line of thought ending in the existence of a god. You can find the same line of thought sketched out in a few other books, but only as one argument among many, each presented with a brevity sometimes bordering on the indigestible. Here you will find a meticulous, fully spelled-out investigation of the first cause, presented in the manner of a slowly unfolding story.

3. It is true that many science-based books that argue for a designer also focus on a single line of argument. But this book differs markedly from those. Books of that genre have obvious advantages. Everyone is impressed by science. Biochemistry or astrophysics can present cutting-edge evidence, stunning in its detail and gratifying to the human imagination. But these advantages come at the expense of seeing things for ourselves. When I read about the big bang or about the astronomical observations that are best explained by that model, I can (and do) believe these things. What I cannot do is see them for myself. I must take the scientists' word for it. When I read about the age of fossils or of the earth, or about the function and composition of a particular protein, I am in the same situation. Scientists themselves must trust one another's observations, calculations, and theories in order to make the rapid progress such a division of labor makes possible. Books for or against a designer that draw support from sciences such as astrophysics or biochemistry necessarily ask readers to place their faith in many things, to believe many things. Silly as it might be not to believe those things, some of us wish not only to believe that there is a designer, but to know this and understand it for ourselves, to see it as the necessary consequence of our own experience of the world. That is where this book comes in. As the argument advances, I will never ask you to believe in someone else's findings or observations. Instead, all the reasoning will begin from things you yourself can immediately verify. By the time you have finished reading this

book, you will truly be able to say that you see its conclusion for yourself. At any rate, that is my goal.

4. This book also explores questions usually left unasked by scientific books for and against design. The intelligent-design books of the last few decades for the most part attempt to show that living things and many of their useful adaptations could not have been produced by the known laws of physics and chemistry. What is the only alternative to these causes? A designer. The reasoning usually involves a calculation of the tremendous improbability that such laws could, as a freak side effect, produce the first living thing, or the first self-replicating molecule, or else some specific feature in an organism. Their main opponents (Richard Dawkins, to name but one) reply by saying the design thinkers have argued against a straw man. Few atheists today would say that living things and other seemingly "designed" features of the natural world are the fluky products of the known laws of physics and chemistry. They do not conceive of seemingly designed things, organisms, as the unlikely but possible results of sheer atom jostling and unforeseeable collisions. Many atheists instead maintain that organic things are the *nearly inevitable* products of the known laws and of things like atom jostling, albeit by as-yet unknown intermediate processes.

The probability that a crowd of atoms, even a universe full of them, will clump immediately into tigers and dolphins (or even an amoeba) here and there is either nil or the next thing to it, the atheists concede. But the same crowd of atoms might display a nearly inevitable tendency to form other things—such as stars and galaxies—which, in turn, are fated to churn out still other things—such as planets—some of which will almost inevitably feature the right physical characteristics and chemical endowment to cook up an amino acid–producing pond, and so on. If we ignore the intervening steps and instead calculate the probability of trillions of atoms immediately associating themselves into a duck or a street mime, unsurprisingly the odds are absurdly low. Allowing for intermediate steps, each of which is statistically likely, given the previous conditions, well, then we end up with a very different calculation. If we subscribe to this sketchy story, it is true that we are under obligation to produce the intermediate steps, or at least to expect their eventual discovery. So far as these types of thinkers are concerned, those who adhere to intelligent design effectively ignore their position, which is by all indications the mainstream among scientists.

It is partly for this reason that some have turned their attention to the fundamental physical constants, such as the strengths of the four basic forces that underlie all the statistical laws in effect in our universe. I mean gravitational, electromagnetic, and strong and weak nuclear forces. Are these basic forces themselves, then, the products of design? The fine-tuning books, kissing cousins of the biology-based intelligent-design books, argue that these forces possess, within extremely narrow tolerances, precisely those ratios required for living things to be possible at all. Mess with those ratios only the slightest bit, and stars will not be able to form, or they will all be too hot or cool to support life, or too few of them will churn out life-friendly planets, or else some other intolerable condition will arise. Since these are the basic forces, it is argued, there are no prior physical causes to explain their ratios; hence, the uncanny ratios must be explained by a nonphysical cause for whom the possibility of life is a goal. Enter the designer.

Opponents of this style of argument (Stephen Hawking, to name but one) point back one step further: before the basic forces underlying star formation is the basic stuff underlying universe formation, a stuff that is so nondescript that one might be tempted to call it "nothing" (except that it is so fertile it might give birth to as many as 10^{500} universes every morning before breakfast). This fertile nothing spews out universes quite randomly, and so the fundamental constants in them must represent nearly all possible quantitative variations. Most of them, presumably, do not allow life. But some of them inevitably will. And the fact that we happen to live in a life-friendly one is neither a matter of design nor a wild coincidence—*of course* the only universes in which we *would* come about must be those rare but inevitable ones in which we *could* come about. There you have a rough rendition of the anti-fine-tuning tale.

Which side has the particulars right? I do not intend to judge. The intelligent-design approach and the fine-tuning and big-bang arguments deserve serious attention, to say the very least. But there are plenty of excellent books out there on both sides of their empirical questions. And they tend to leave a deeper question unasked: What is so special about the designer that it needs no cause? Or, conversely: What is so special about matter (or the even simpler "nothing" from which our matter might have derived) that it *does* need a cause? We grown-ups might be right to chide our children when they demand a further explanation every time we offer one. But on a global scale, surely it is not child's play to know precisely when to stop asking why. What qualifies something to be an ultimate explanation? Or, conversely, what disqualifies something from standing on its own? How do we determine whether a cause needs a prior cause?

Tough questions. Compelling questions. Just the sorts of questions I mean to grapple with. How we answer these questions will decide whether we think there is a first cause and what we think it to be. And yet hardly anyone asks such questions nowadays. Certain philosophers do, but usually their work, excellent as it may be for its purposes, is too scholarly for a wide audience or too quick-paced for readers who seek in-depth understanding. This book is my attempt to fill the gap. Design haters and design lovers alike all too often presume without explanation that some type of thing gets to be the first thing, the thing that needs no cause, the uncaused cause. They differ only as to what this is. Some say "immaterial mind". Others say "mindless matter". But why the one rather than the other? It is not just a matter of taste.

5. I have also made another promise. The certainty this book aims to achieve is superior to the probabilistic results of science-based arguments for a designer. This is in part due to a difference in my method of reasoning, but mainly it is because the premises I will put forward differ qualitatively from those drawn from the empirical sciences. My method of reasoning is mainly deductive. By a *deduction* I mean a form of reasoning in which the conclusion must be true as long as the premises are. It is usually opposed to an induction, which is an argument for a general statement based on many particular instances, such as this:

Mushrooms are carbon based.
Flowers are carbon based.
Trees are carbon based.
Bacteria are carbon based.
Horses are carbon based.
Therefore, *All* living things are carbon based.

Notice that the premises are all true, but the conclusion is not necessarily true, even if the premises lead us to accept it. For all the argument shows, there might be living things outside our solar system that are silicon based and contain no carbon. The more representative of "all living things" the particular premises become, the more plausible the general conclusion. If we could include all instances of living things in the premises, or know that our way of listing them was somehow exhaustive, the truth of the premises would guarantee the truth of the conclusion, and the argument would be as good as a deduction. But as long as we remain uncertain of the exhaustiveness of the premises, their truth does not absolutely guarantee the truth of the conclusion. It is not a deduction then, but an induction.

Deduction is a rarer form of reasoning. But all of us use it from time to time. I remember my oldest son's first deduction. Max and his sister Evelyn were seven and five years old, respectively, sitting behind me in car seats as I drove them home from a play date. The conversation went like this:

EVELYN. Dad, are aliens real?
ME. Hm. You know, sweetie, I'm not really sure.
MAX. [*Indignant*] Dad! Of *course* aliens aren't real. Aliens are *monsters*, and monsters aren't real.

We might doubt whether Max's premises are entirely correct. But we cannot deny that if they are true, his conclusion is inescapable. The argument is therefore deductive. Empirical science, by contrast, frequently argues for a conclusion inductively by showing how it is the best explanation for a given set of facts. The conclusion doesn't follow necessarily from the facts themselves, then, since another "less likely" explanation might turn out to be the real one, having seemed unlikely to us only because we were as yet unacquainted with further relevant facts.

As I was saying, however, this book thinks differently from most others of its genre, not mainly by the form of its reasonings, but mainly by the character of its premises. To see what I mean, consider the following arguments, variations of which many pro-god and anti-god authors have proposed over the last twenty years:

General Premise: Everything made of irreducibly complex parts must have been caused by a mind.
Particular Premise: Cats are made of irreducibly complex parts.
Therefore, cats must have been caused by a mind.

General Premise: What was caused by natural selection need not have been caused by a mind.

Particular Premise: Cats were caused by natural selection.

Therefore, cats need not have been caused by a mind.

I have cast these two arguments as deductions. Notice that each argument lays down a general first premise, then adds a particular premise about cats (or, more exactly, about complex biochemical structures that make cats or other living things possible—I used cats just to make it quicker and easier to refer to these second premises). An author proposing the first argument would typically spend most of his time explaining his cat premise, devoting less attention to his more general first premise, which he would take to be fairly obvious once its meaning had been made plain. Conversely, in attacking his opponent, who proposes the second argument, he would mainly challenge its cat premise and spend relatively little time worrying about its first premise. The author proposing the second argument would likewise propose his first and general premise as if it were practically self-evident but would march in all kinds of evidence for his cat premise about natural selection. He would probably agree with the first premise of the first argument, and so he would attack his opponent's second premise (again, about cats) with gusto.

Why do these authors lay so much stress on their cat premises but relatively little on their more general ones? One reason is that they are often trained in the empirical sciences, which inclines them to pay special attention to those second premises. Checking statements such as "Cats were shaped by natural selection" requires painstaking work with microscopes, fossil data, X-ray crystallography, mathematical calculations, and the like. Scientists are at home with those premises and with the techniques required to establish them. The same authors depend also on premises such as "What was produced by natural selection need not have been produced by a mind", but they would rather agree about those, or not draw too much attention to them, since those generalities extend beyond their particular expertise.

This book is different. The reasonings in it will depend on principles even more general than the first premises in the two arguments above and will not introduce premises such as the ones about cats—premises, that is, that are the results of carefully procured and highly particular observations to which only a privileged few are privy. All of the premises in this book are meant to be verifiable without special empirical methods, convincing in themselves, and quite general. If, at the outset of *Darwin's Black Box*, Michael Behe was right to beg his readers for patience with the microscopic details he would be throwing at them, then I suppose I am obliged to warn mine of an unusually *un*detailed approach. The search for the first cause can certainly take advantage of such particulars as the ratio of the force of gravity to the electromagnetic force carried out to five hundred decimal places. But we can also conduct the search in a different way without that information or any information like it.

By focusing my attention on general connections among things, I am to some extent sacrificing the vividness of particulars. But there is something quite valuable received in exchange. That something is certainty. At first this sounds paradoxical. We often think that more general means less certain, more doubtful, as when we are making generalizations. When we make generalizations—that is, when we make hasty assumptions about the general case while relying entirely on an insufficient sample of particular cases—we are less certain of the general than of the particular. "*This* swan is white, *that* one is, and all the ones I've ever seen are white—therefore *all* swans are white." I am right in the particulars, wrong about the generalization (there are black swans in Australia). My reasoning was inductive, and I had not checked enough cases. *But not all general statements are generalizations.* I have not inspected every instance of the number six, yet I am convinced, and so is everyone I have ever met or heard of, that the general statement "Every six is even" admits no exceptions. I am not worried that someone in Australia has an odd six in his pocket.

How do we know when we have laid our finger on a reliable universal truth such as that? How can we be sure that we are not just making a generalization? A complete answer to that would be a book by itself, but a few quick indicators should suffice here. One way you can be sure you are not just making a generalization, that you are in fact holding a universal truth in your hands, is if the predicate is part of the definition of the subject. If you say "All bachelors are slobs" or "All bachelors are drunks", someone might take offense—how dare you make such sweeping generalizations? But if you say "All bachelors are unmarried", and somebody gets offended, have pity on that poor somebody, since he is an idiot. Another tip-off that a truth is a universal and necessary truth is that you can't deny it without somehow affirming it. Suppose you say to me, "There is such a thing as objective truth." "No, there isn't!" I reply. But in making that denial, I am insisting that what I say is objectively true. I cannot assert anything without also asserting, implicitly, that there is such a thing as objective truth after all, a sure sign that this is itself one of those universal truths.

There are general statements, then, that by themselves convict us of their truth independently of any particular cases that help us to conceive them. Once we conceive them, that's enough; our conviction is complete and does not increase when we see more examples of such statements. Unlike most statements of empirical science, there is a certainty in these statements that is immune to the influx of new experiences. Their very generality detaches these self-evident universals from dependence on any specific experience.

Many trails lead to the first cause. All include passage through universal principles. Some include trudging through minutiae and hairy details. Others do not. The path I take is of this latter type. To those who have never ventured down it, and who for the first time stand at the trailhead, it might seem a singularly unpromising path to take. It seems unlikely, when we first consider it, that general principles alone can really get us anywhere very interesting. Sure, we need those general principles, but don't we also need to roll up our sleeves and plunge right into the nitty-gritty of things? How can we arrive at any exact or important result from a bunch of generalities?

Usually we can't. But the interesting thing about the first cause of all things is that it is supposed to be, well, the first cause of *all things*. So even general things should lead us to it and tell us something about it, if there is such a cause. This would seem especially true if there is an intelligent cause of all things, who would presumably take particular interest in the intelligent inhabitants of the world, such as ourselves. It would be strange if the only way, or even the best way, to discover such a mind was by inspecting the components of a protein or the behavior of galaxies, or anything else known only to very few and only very recently. There is something fitting about approaching the idea of a first and universal cause (or causes) through the contemplation of general things.

I once read a description of general thought as the "high country of the mind". An apt comparison. In the foothills, we find rich forest life. Ascending a little higher, we see things beginning to thin out and dry up. Life gets scrubby and sparse. We start to suspect that higher up, life must disappear altogether—which is true eventually—but then we are surprised (and charmed) to find that before getting emptier, the terrain gets fuller again. As we climb, we discover that where one kind of life fails, another begins. We find new flatlands at the upper elevations, with new mountains of their own, and rivers and streams and forests, though sometimes of a very different, and otherworldly, quality. There is something like that in the life of the mind. The ascent from one's immediate particular surroundings and experiences to general ideas is at first still fairly particular. We are intrigued by some particular animals in our experience, such as giraffes. We study them and find there are many properties common to all giraffes. Our experience then widens to include horses and lions, and we discover, to our delight, that not only does each species have its properties, but common features and origins for mammals also exist. The general consideration of "mammal" in some ways presents less for us to think about than "giraffe" does, since "giraffe" adds certain things to "mammal". Nonetheless, in ascending to "mammal", there remains an intelligible content distinctive of that level of generality. If we keep stripping off more features, we might be surprised to see how slender, how general, things can become, while still supporting intelligible properties. This book takes full advantage of those high-elevation intelligibilities—like a trek along the tree line of a mountain, where dwell many things unseen anywhere lower down.

Though the path is promising and universally accessible, it will not be without its challenges. My students have taught me to appreciate the special difficulty of securing a refined notion of very universal things. When I ask them to define something fairly particular, such as *triangle*, they usually can manage it. They mention figure or shape in the definition—a more general thing, since every triangle is a figure but not the other way around. But how well, now, do they grasp this more general thing? They grasp what a figure is well enough to know one when they see one, and to see that it belongs in the definition of *triangle*. But if I then ask them for a definition of *figure*, the more universal thing, they don't fare so well. I get blank stares.

In their defense it could be said that we must eventually come to indefinable terms. We must come to things so readily conceived that they don't *need* a definition and to things so general that there are no more general categories under which to put them. That is certainly true. But *figure* is not so general that it cannot be categorized. It fits under the still more general category of "bounded things", since every figure is bounded by something (or is a boundary), but not everything bounded by something is a figure (a line segment, for instance, is bounded by its endpoints, but it is not a figure). It seems likely, then, that *figure* also admits of definition, although its definition is harder to find than that of *triangle* precisely because *figure* is so general, so elementary, that it contains very few defining notions. It is so close to being an elementary notion itself that it is a tricky business to discern the more elementary notions composing it.

The job I have lined up for myself will therefore have its share of difficulty. Most of the difficulty (for me) and excitement (for you) will emerge in the preliminary concept-refining stages of each chapter, not so much in the ensuing arguments based on those concepts. Once the preliminary concepts and premises have been ironed out, the actual reasonings will practically construct themselves.

Those same reasonings could look very silly, though, to anyone who reads them without first going through the prerequisite concept refinement. Here is an example of what I mean. We all have a sense of what we mean by the word *perfect* or *complete*. But we tend to be fuzzy about it, and we associate it with our own everyday purposes. When I am pouring wine into your glass and ask if that's enough, you say, "Perfect"—and you and I know what you mean well enough for me to stop pouring and for you to start drinking. Question: What is common to (a) the amount of wine in your glass and (b) an undamaged snowflake, which we might also call perfect? Unless we bother to think about it rather carefully, we might not be able to say. But there are people who have thought carefully about such things and who arrive at more exact notions of what we all fuzzily mean by *perfect*. And some careful thinkers adapt the notion of *perfect* to specific purposes. Mathematicians, for example, have a meaning of *perfect* that we do not use in ordinary life. A number is perfect when it is equal to the sum of its own factors less than itself; 6 is perfect in this sense since it is equal to $1 + 2 + 3$, the sum of its factors less than itself. That concept opens the mind to new truths. To anyone familiar with that sense of *perfect*, and also with the idea that a prime number has no factors other than itself and 1, it is immediately obvious that no prime number is perfect.

The statements at the heart of this book will be more difficult (but also more interesting) than "No prime number is perfect." The example nevertheless illustrates how someone might profoundly misread a book like this one. When Richard Dawkins reads Thomas Aquinas' fourth way of proving there is a god, he reads it as though no prior conceptual refinement of the word *perfect* were necessary to appreciate the force of its premises or to see what they are meant to apply to, and what they are not meant to apply to, and in what way. In other words, he reads the fourth way as though Aquinas had tossed it off in colloquial, inexact speech, ready to be absorbed by anyone who can read a gossip column. The unsurprising result is that the argument appears entirely ridiculous, even as the statement "No prime number is perfect" would appear silly to anyone who had not bothered to study the definitions of mathematics. "Perfect? Perfect for what purpose?" Joe Blow might say, "Any number is perfect for one purpose, dreadfully inappropriate for others. It is absurd to speak as though any number were simply 'perfect' for all occasions!"

Having mentioned Aquinas, I should take the opportunity to explain why I am able, without so much as a blush, to make all the promises I have made. Do I claim to have made some momentous discovery? Will I be presenting never-before-seen evidence of a divine being?

Not exactly. Most of what you will encounter in the upcoming chapters has been shamelessly stolen from Thomistic philosophy—that is, the philosophy of Thomas Aquinas. But for several reasons, that description of what I am up to is more misleading than informative.

One reason it is misleading is the word *philosophy* itself. Unlike science, *philosophy* in many circles has a bad name, and sometimes it deserves it. Some years ago I went to the dentist for a routine cleaning. The hygienist, making polite conversation, asked me what I do for a living.

"Cheecher", I said.

"A teacher? What do you teach?"

"Phiwoffophy."

"Philosophy?! *Huh*. Isn't that all just a bunch of opinions?"

She had recoiled just a little bit, and her tone was unmistakable. I was given to understand that no honest person would take a paycheck for peddling such disreputable stuff. Probably she had run into that brand of "philosophy" that tries to convince us that the chair we are sitting in might not really be there or that there is no real difference between right and wrong—the sort of "philosophy" that strives to achieve an expansion of the mind similar to that induced by LSD.

I solemnly promise not to indulge in any such mind-expanding techniques. I will not be asking you how you know your life is real and your dreams at night are not, and all that. As to "just a bunch of opinions", I must agree with my very sensible hygienist: much of what is called philosophy is just that—unsubstantiated opinions and assorted prejudices or even silly nonsense and meaningless verbiage. But how, then, shall we classify this very insightful statement that all those bogus ideas she regarded with suspicion are just a bunch of opinions? If that evaluation of hers is certain and true (and it is), then it is not itself a mere opinion or preference. Is it, then, an example of empirical science? Is it physics? Or chemistry? Biology perhaps? Of course not. It is in fact a shining example of a true philosophical reflection. It is an instance, however humble, of respectable and genuine philosophy. So it is not philosophy as such that deserves our contempt, but just the all-too-common quack variety.

Those who prefer empirical methods of tracking down the first cause are perhaps even better witnesses to the indispensability of philosophy in that search. While laying as much emphasis as they can on scientific evidence, even they cannot abstain altogether from philosophizing. Their cat premises won't cut it by themselves. They must also call on general premises stating which things need causes and which things do not. They can reach no conclusion for or against gods until they draw from the wells of philosophy.

The other reason it can be misleading to label this book Thomistic philosophy is the word *Thomistic*. There is too much of Thomas Aquinas in that. The implication is that the book in your hands will read like a medieval philosophy treatise. Nothing could be further from the truth. Aside from matters of style (Aquinas, bless him, had none), there is the important matter of a new and unified presentation. Atheists in the schools were not a big problem in Aquinas' day.

Today, they nearly control education. No surprise, then, that Aquinas always presented arguments for the existence of a divine being in summary form and never wrote his own book-length treatment of the question. He also did not bother to deal with objections from Darwinists or from modern physics and modern philosophy, for the obvious reason that he lived before all those things. What Aquinas has said in short form and in bits and pieces throughout his works I will say in more expanded form and in continuous logical sequence, while addressing the major sticking points likely to trouble any educated modern reader. The main substance of this book did not originate with me, then, but it is so largely unknown to people, so little made public, that the majority of its contents will come as big news to most readers.

The label *Thomistic* also falsely implies that there must be something peculiarly Catholic or Christian about Thomistic philosophy. Not so. Aquinas' philosophy, as distinguished from his revelation-based theology, was not his religion, not a confession of his faith, but an expression of his rational perception of the world, informed largely by the pagan philosopher Aristotle. Nor are the insights of his philosophy *his* in any important sense of the word. Universal truths are the private property of no man. There is nothing essentially Pythagorean about the Pythagorean theorem, even if Pythagoras of Samos did discover it or prove it for the first time; one could learn the truth of it without the least knowledge of or interest in who Pythagoras was, or when he lived, or what his views on other things might have been. Likewise there is nothing essentially Thomistic about Thomistic philosophy, and it is with a view to highlighting this important fact that I will for the most part ignore the man.

So much for the scope and modus operandi of this book. As for its target audience, I have in mind all educated readers with an interest in tracking down the first cause. If you number among the curious and the open minded, you may find here some of the answers you have been looking for. Are you an avid reader of the intelligent-design books? You can look forward to discovering in these pages an unlooked-for and complementary way of thinking about the universe and its maker. If you are a philosopher who holds Plato, Aristotle, or Aquinas in high regard, I hope you will rejoice to see familiar lines of thought given novel expression with more than customary clarity and concreteness, and even with a dash of spunk. Last but not at all least on my mind, if you are an avid and approving fan of all the Dawkinses out there, I have reason to hope that you will come away with a few hundred things to think about.

Well, that's enough prep talk.

On to business.

I

Common Ground; or, There Is a First Cause

> Evidently there *is* a first principle, and the causes of things are
> neither an infinite series nor infinitely various in kind.
>
> —Aristotle, *Metaphysics*

Mr. Monteith

There was a scary side to Mr. Monteith. He sported an unruly,
threatening beard, a balding dome with wild hair in the back, and the
general look of a survivalist Unabomber who had been writing his
manifesto in a cabin in the woods. He was the only man I had ever
seen wearing a pocket protector in a flannel shirt. While teaching he
would jump up on his desk and do a dance if he thought it would
illustrate a point. He would spin around in his chair and flail his arms.
He would throw things at you. And if he asked you a question, he
would stand right in front of you, arms akimbo, and stare you down
in your seat with widened eyes glinting under a furrowed and pro-
truding brow so you would be sure to know that the exactness of
your answer was a matter of life and death for you. He was intense.
But he was easy to understand. And impossible to ignore. My friends
and I knew he was the best teacher in our high school. And he
remains the best physics teacher I have ever had.

He knew just what the hard-to-grasp things were and how to boil
them down to brief, concrete, immediate ideas that would stick with
you for life. The distinction between mass and weight is always a
little tricky, since they are exactly proportional to each other. Monteith made it easy. Out in space, you can lift a barbell off the floor
of the shuttle much more easily than you can on Earth, because its
attraction to Earth is diminished at that distance. But you can't *roll* it

27

on the floor any faster than you can on Earth, because the mass does not change with distance from Earth. The barbell's weight is due to a certain attraction to Earth (the nearest significantly large body), but mass is a resistance to acceleration that belongs to the barbell in itself, independently of the barbell's location, and regardless of the direction in which you attempt to accelerate it.

"Weight is attraction; mass is shove resistance", he would say. (I could rattle off a bunch of those pithy one-liners that have helped me through my subsequent courses in physics.) When a fellow student of mine said he was still confused about the difference, Monteith's eyes bulged as he strode over to my neighbor's desk.

"Would you rather *lift* my car or *push* it if you had to do one or the other?"

"Pushing it is easier."

"Then mass isn't weight, is it? The mass of my car resists your *push*. The weight resists your *lift*."

It was around this time, when I was sixteen years old, that I first heard of the big bang. In the popular form in which the big bang had filtered down to me, it sounded like the big beginning of all visible things. But didn't a beginning imply a beginner? And since the beginner existed before all visible and changeable things, and hence independently of them, that beginner must be an invisible and unchanging thing—which sounds pretty near to a god.

I must have had some hunch that this was too simple. Or else I had a sense that Mr. Monteith would not agree with it—and yet I could not imagine how he would respond were he confronted with the thought. Would he deny that the big bang had happened? Would he dare to say he knew better than the physicists? Or would he dodge the conclusion by supposing that something could just begin without any reason at all? He was too reasonable to go down those paths. But then what would he say? I did not know. But I wanted to know. I wanted to know so desperately that I overcame my dread of Mr. Monteith's scary side and, for the one and only time ever, approached him with my question after class.

He took my question very seriously. He did not smile or pat me on the head. He mulled it over for some moments. Had I considered, he wished to know, whether the big bang was absolutely the beginning, or perhaps instead just the beginning of a new cycle in some endless repetition of explosions and collapses? In a star, nuclear forces cause an explosion of its matter, but gravitational forces counteract the nuclear ones and work to contract all its mass. If the nuclear reactions fail, gravity wins and the star collapses, perhaps into a black hole. If instead the nuclear forces win, the star explodes as a supernova, and its dissipated matter might someday be gathered up again by gravity to form a new star. Might the whole universe not be like that? An endless war between contrary forces causing now a rapid explosion, then much later a contraction, and later still another explosion? If so, the universe might never have had a beginning. It might have just always been.

That conversation with Mr. Monteith, almost thirty years ago, was a beginning for me—a kind of big bang in my mind. Although I continued to follow the evolving story of the big bang, I wondered most about whether one could prove there was a first cause of all visible and changeable things. I quickly found that great minds had grappled with that question for thousands of years. I discovered that although a handful had answered no or "unsure", almost all had answered yes. There was less agreement among the great thinkers about whether there are gods or whether human reason can even answer that question. But nearly all agreed there had to be a first cause or causes of some kind. Clearly that was a prior question.

Puzzles about the First Cause

Here I had an interesting problem. Nearly all great thinkers of the past twenty-five centuries have agreed that there had to be a first cause. And the big bang seemed to confirm the idea. And yet I could not for the life of me poke a hole in Mr. Monteith's scenario of a beginningless cycle of contractions and explosions.

How could I travel back in time to determine which was true? And why were the great thinkers so convinced about first causes when they could not travel back in time either and when they were without the benefit of modern science? Were they just making up stories?

Three reasons told me otherwise.

    1. Even the most ancient thinkers took great pains to distinguish themselves from the poets and mythmakers who invented fables

about the creation of worlds. Even if the thinkers did not always provide compelling reasons for what they said, they always provided reasons.

2. They were the *great* thinkers, not the sloppy ones. Had they been among the many sloppy thinkers of history, their names would have vanished long ago.

3. Twenty-five centuries' worth of great philosophers and scientists nearly all agreed that there was some sort of first cause. Had each simply made up his own story, there would not have been anything like this consensus among them.

So I had a problem. On the one hand, the big bang and the philosophers all pointed to a first cause. On the other hand, the philosophers had not known about the big bang, and while the big bang sounded like an absolute beginning, I could think of no reason why it had to be.

A year later, I read Aristotle for the first time, and my problem grew worse. Aristotle did not believe that the world had a beginning. According to him, this world had always existed more or less as we see it today. Before every chicken there was an egg, and before every egg, a chicken. And here was the mind boggler: Aristotle was part of the great consensus that there had to be a first cause. He believed in a first cause, but not in a beginning! To me that sounded like a patent contradiction. And yet I knew it could not be, since that would mean my seventeen-year-old self was smarter than Aristotle.

Fast-forward to my freshman year of college, in which I read Aquinas for the first time. He came as another shock. This gentleman believed the world had a beginning (he was a Christian), but he did not think it was possible to prove it. That the world had a temporal beginning was unknowable to the human mind and was a matter of religious faith. Now the shocking bit: he *did* think that the existence of a first cause could be and had been proved in many ways. Unlike Aristotle, he believed the world had a beginning. Like Aristotle, he thought the existence of a first cause was knowable apart from the world's having any beginning.

That same year another problem occurred to me. Suppose you have found a cause. Now suppose that this cause in turn has another cause. And so on, ad infinitum. Then there is no *first* cause in the series, and yet everything in the series has its own cause. The idea was so simple. No first cause was needed, since every cause in the infinite series already had a cause. There was nothing for a first cause to do.

But that nagging thought kept coming back. Was I really smarter than twenty-five centuries' worth of geniuses? Had I really outthought all those great thinkers who agreed that a first cause had to exist?

What First Cause Means—and Doesn't Mean

Fast-forward again about three decades. Dozens of courses and hundreds of books and thousands of conversations and plenty of teaching experience have seasoned me a little. Looking back, I can now see plainly that the main source of my confusion about the first cause was that I had failed to notice an important distinction. There are distinct kinds of priority in things. I had been thinking only about one— namely, temporal priority, as in "Breakfast comes before lunch", and "Chaucer came before Shakespeare."

But there are many other kinds of priority. Among them is causal priority. At first it was hard for me to see that this was anything other than an instance of temporal priority. The carpenter has to exist before he can build a house, after all. So the cause must exist before its effect in time. But wait. Was that quite true? When he is lying in bed asleep, the night before he is supposed to start building a new house, a carpenter is not having any effect (on the house to be). And if something is having no effect, is it really a cause? It is more like a potential cause, something that *can* be a cause but is not actually causing anything at the moment. It is only when a carpenter is actually building something that he is acting as a cause of something. And as soon as he is building something, there is also something being built; there is, in other words, an effect. So the acting cause and its effect are simultaneous.

It is possible for a cause to set something in motion and then stop acting, and for the motion to produce some intended effect later on. Imagine a terrorist planting a ticking time bomb and leaving the scene. The cause of the later explosion is the bomb, but more so it is the bomber, who is more responsible for that later effect, even though it happened after he had left the scene. Even in that case, however, his action and the dependence of its effects on him were entirely simultaneous, beginning and ending together. While he was placing the bomb, the bomb was being placed. While he was setting the timer, the timer was being set. There is no temporal priority of the acting cause to the effect's dependence on him and his action. And if an effect no longer *depends* on its cause, it does not seem to be an effect anymore, or at least not of that cause. Strictly speaking, when a cause is really acting like a cause, and an effect is really behaving like a dependent effect, cause and effect are perfectly simultaneous.

Does this mean a cause need not be prior to its effect? Not always in time, perhaps. A cause nevertheless exhibits a kind of priority to its effect, even if the two are simultaneous. The effect is *from* the cause, not vice versa. That irreversible order is itself a kind of priority, although not a temporal one. Leaving aside causes for a moment, consider a similar case of nontemporal priority. Pairs of eyes, like mine, normally come into existence simultaneously. Nonetheless, individual eyes have a kind of priority to pairs of eyes. My left eye can exist even if I cease to have a pair of eyes (by losing my right eye), whereas the pair cannot exist if the left eye ceases to be. The one eye has a priority in being to the pair, though not a priority in time. Similarly, the swinging of the carpenter's arm, though not prior in time, has a priority to the swinging of his hammer, since the motion of the hammer is from the motion of the arm, and not the reverse. The cause always has at least that priority over the effect, though not always a priority in time.

What does this have to do with the first-cause problem? It helps to solve it. Recognizing causal priority as distinct from temporal priority opens the door to a first cause of an *eternal* effect. *First cause* is a bit like the expression *first prize*. *First prize* does not usually mean the prize awarded first in time. In contests, third prize is often awarded first, second prize next, first prize last, to build excitement and avoid anticlimax. *First prize* means instead a prize that ranks before all other prizes in value or significance. Similarly, the great thinkers who all insist there is a first cause used the expression *first cause* not to mean (necessarily) a cause before all other causes in time, but a cause before all others in causal power. It meant a cause of other causes that does not itself depend on any other cause. It meant, in other words, something that exists and acts all by itself, without deriving its existence or causal action from anything else. And it meant not a thing stuck in the past, but a thing existing in the present.

The great thinkers who had puzzled me so much were right after all. They disagreed about whether the universe had a temporal beginning, but they agreed that it depended on some first cause—an uncaused cause, that is. If the world had begun, an uncaused cause (or some number of them) had begun it. If the world had always been, an uncaused cause was sustaining it and causing the motions and changes we see taking place in it. There had to be an uncaused cause no matter what.

What gave them this confidence? They were confident, first of all, that there are causes at work in this world. The cause of the oil painting's coming into being is the movement of the paint. The cause of the movement of the paint is the movement of the brush. The cause of the movement of the brush is the movement of the hand. Will this tracing back of effects to their simultaneous causes bring us to a first cause? To an uncaused cause, acting right now to produce the painting? The painter's brain, perhaps? If there is no first in such a series, there are two possibilities left: a circular series of causes, or an infinite regression of simultaneously acting causes.

Purely circular causation is obviously impossible. You can't be your own father, for instance. You can't give your own existence to yourself or receive it from yourself. Can two things cause each other? If so, that would be circular. Can A cause B while B is causing A? The answer seems to be that this is possible, but only so long as each gives the other something it does not receive from it. Two dominoes leaning against each other support each other by their opposite leanings, but neither receives its tendency to lean from the other, but from some influence outside either of them. Each domino forces us to look outside the circle to explain why each leans as it does.

Circular causation won't help us avoid a first cause then. Very well, why not go with the infinite regression? Why not say that every cause has another cause before it, making it to be a cause, and giving it its action? To exclude first causes in this way, we would have to say not only that an infinite regression of simultaneously acting causes is possible, but that it is necessary in every case. We would have to say that *no* series of causes comes to a stop, and *every* effect we see is being produced by an infinity of things acting on each other right now. Not a likely view. Really, though, it is much worse than that. It is simply impossible for any series of presently cooperating causes to regress without a first cause, and so we must admit the existence of at least one first and uncaused cause.

Particular examples will bring out the reason.

Why There Is at Least One First Cause

Suppose you are going to hang a lamp suspended by a chain. The power cord runs through the links, but it is the chain that will support the lamp's weight. The lamp itself will hang from something (the chain), but nothing will be hanging from it. The highest link on the chain might hang from a bit of hardware screwed into an electric box fixed to a ceiling joist, but the ceiling joist is not hanging from anything; instead it is sitting on the supporting walls, which sit on the foundation of your house, which sits on the earth, which does not need to sit on anything at all. To simplify things, let's suppose that the ceiling joist is a steel I-beam with a little hook on it from which the highest link of your chain is to be hung. That way the chain itself is hanging from something (the I-beam) that is not hanging but only sitting on something else. And now let's focus on the things that are *hanging* and on the things they are *hanging from*.

Every link in the chain hangs from something else and has something hanging from it. Every link is essentially a middle in that sense. There is something hanging after it, and there is something before it from which it hangs. And nothing could hang from any particular link if that link itself were not hanging from something else. If you unhang a link, you unhang whatever is hanging from it. The lamp itself is hanging from something (namely, the last link of the chain), but nothing is hanging from it. It is not a middle but rather the end of the line. The I-beam has something hanging from it (namely, the highest link in the chain), but it is not itself hanging from anything, so it is not a middle either, as far as hanging goes, but it is the beginning of the whole hanging business.

Notice that the whole chain, and not just each particular link, is also a middle. There is something after it, hanging from it (namely, the lamp), and there is also something before it, from which it hangs (namely, the I-beam). If the I-beam were to disappear, the chain and the lamp would come crashing down. Is this dependence on the I-beam for the suspension of the chain and the lamp due to the number of links in the chain? Suppose we had started with a ten-link chain. What if we were now to increase the number of links to a hundred? (We could make room for more links either by raising the I-beam or by shrinking the size of the links in the chain.) Nothing is changed. Clearly we still cannot hang anything from the hundred-link chain unless the hundred-link chain is itself hung from something else, such as the I-beam. We can add as many links as we like, but we will never produce a chain that can hang all by itself and suspend our lamp. That is just the way it is with chains.

Could we do away with the I-beam if we had a chain with an infinity of links in it? We could not. If there is nothing for that whole chain to hang from, it will not hang, and nothing can be hung from it. There is nothing about those links in themselves that makes them want to hang in space. A big chain, even an infinite one, would be much more apt to sit in a big pile than to hang in a straight line in some direction. Infinity does not have such a magic power, then, that it can make a chain hang without the chain's hanging from anything.

This pattern of relationships is not unique to hanging things and chains and lamps, of course. We find a similar relationship among moving things such as train engines and cabooses. The caboose is a part of a train that gets pulled (or pushed) by other railroad cars but does not itself move any other car in the train. It is the end of the line. The opposite is true of the engine, which moves another car but is not itself moved by any car. It is like the I-beam or the earth in the example with the suspended lamp. The engine can be immediately coupled to a caboose, but usually there are cars in between. A boxcar, for instance, gets pulled by a car but also pulls another car. Each boxcar is a middle in that sense, having a mover before it and something it moves after it.

You can probably guess my next question. Can we do away with the engine, and still get the boxcars to move? Obviously they will move if they are on an incline. But we want them to move not by gravity, which is outside the train, but of themselves, and in a direction of our choosing, which is what the engine had made possible.

Clearly two coupled boxcars will not suffice for that effect. They will just sit on the tracks or move in a direction determined by natural forces and not by an engineer. That is because each of our two boxcars is unable to move anything else except insofar as it is itself being moved by something. Neither one has anything in it to initiate motion. So each member of our boxcar couple is waiting for the other one to make a move, as it were. Neither one of them is a mover by itself. Each is only a would-be mover.

Is this because we don't have enough boxcars? What if we have five hundred boxcars all coupled together? Still no good, of course. They will still just sit there, going nowhere. Really, we have just increased the size of the middle, of the thing that cannot move anything unless it is moved by something before it. In fact, we now need a more powerful engine than we initially needed to move our two original boxcars.

What, now, if we have an infinity of boxcars on an infinite track? Will the infinity emancipate them from their dependence on an engine? Will they be able to move the caboose? Not a bit. Individual boxcars do not move anything except while they are being moved by something else. Consequently, a whole train of boxcars also does not move anything except while it is being moved by something else, regardless of the size of that train. That's just the way it is with boxcar trains. There is nothing about boxcars, even an infinity of them, that would incline them to move to the left on the tracks instead of to the right. Infinity does not have such a magic power, then, that it can make a train of mere would-be movers move anything.

Both the chain and the train are examples of series of simultaneously acting causes, each member of which receives its ability to cause from a prior member. In the interests of brevity, I limited myself to two examples. In the interests of making the examples as representative as possible, I chose one example to illustrate causes of rest (the hanging lamp) and the other to illustrate causes of motion (the train). But the point of the examples is, well, to *exemplify*. As interesting as lamps and trains might be, it is more instructive to discover something about causes in general. The lesson of the chain link is that it is impossible for things hanging from something else to be all there is. There must also be something *from* which things hang and which is not itself hanging from anything. The lesson of the boxcar is that it is impossible for things moved by something else to be the only kind of movers in town. There must also be something by which things are moved and which is not itself moved by anything. The general lesson is that it is impossible for things caused by something else to be self-explanatory. There must also be something by which things are caused and which is not itself caused by anything. The reason is the same in the particular cases and in the general one: the middle causes, when multiplied, just produce one big, fat middle cause. And it is not possible for a middle cause to be the whole story, since every middle by definition has something before it.

So we can now frame a general deduction of the existence of a first cause:

> If there were caused causes, with no first cause, they would constitute a middle with nothing before it.
> But it is impossible for there to be a middle with nothing before it.
> Therefore, there cannot be caused causes with no first cause.

It follows that *there is at least one first cause.* How many first causes are there? Neither the mere definition of *first cause* nor the argument above can tell us. Maybe all causal chains converge at a single first cause. Or maybe there is a whole committee of first and uncaused causes at the top of several independent causal chains. These are provocative questions, but they will have to be settled in the next chapter.

With the foregoing distinctions and arguments in hand, the original difficulties that plagued me as a young student evaporate. There is no need to go back in time to determine whether there is a first cause. In fact, that would not really help. A first cause that was first only in time and not in causation, even if it did exist in the past, might no longer exist today. If I see an enormous array of falling dominoes, I might be right to suppose that there had to be someone who tipped the first domino, but he might have died of a heart attack immediately afterward, long before the last domino fell. When I began this quest many years ago, I was not interested merely in a cause that triggered some reaction. I was after something else. I wanted to know whether there is any cause in existence right now that is a completely self-sufficient, self-existing, self-active thing, depending on no other cause whatsoever, whereas other causes depend on it. The foregoing argument has made it clear that there is indeed such a thing.

The same line of reasoning brought home to me the speciousness of an infinite regression of simultaneously acting causes. If we supposed such a series to exist, there would be no need for a first cause, it had seemed to me, since everything in the series already had a cause. What I had failed to see is that unless a first cause is admitted into the picture, none of the causes in the make-believe series can really be causes at all. The same is true of a circular series of causes. Why is A suspended six feet above the floor? Because it is being held there by B, which in turn is being held up by C, which in turn is being held up by A. Effectively, then, A is holding up itself, which is absurd. It does not help to say, "But everything in the circle has a cause: A has B, B has C, C has A." Really, *none* of the things in our hypothetical circle has a cause, since we have named no legitimate source of causal power for any of them. The same goes for the infinite series.

Aristotle said that even if we insist on an infinity of causes for some effect, there would still have to be a first cause. That idea astounded me when I first ran across it. He said it makes no difference if we assume an infinite series of caused causes; we will still have to admit a first cause of them all. The thinking goes like this. Consider any set of people of unequal height. There must be a maximum height among them, say, six foot two. Does the existence of a maximum depend on the number of people in our set? It does not. Whether we have ten people or a hundred or a thousand or a trillion, there must be a maximum height among them. What if you had an infinite number of people? As long as it is a definite set, not one we can add to or subtract from at will, and the heights are not changing, there must still be a maximum height among the people in it. (This has nothing to do with human height limits, incidentally. Suppose one fellow was infinitely tall. In that case, his height is the maximum.)

The same goes for a set of simultaneously acting causes in a linear series. Some are causes of more things, some of fewer, depending on each one's place in the series. And since the set is definite—it is the set of all things presently producing this one final effect—there must be a maximum among them. There must be a cause with the greatest multitude of effects in the series, whether that multitude be finite or infinite. This cause, which is producing the maximum quantity of effects in the series, cannot have any cause before it in the series. If it did, then *that* cause would be producing more effects than the maximum, which is a contradiction. The maximum cause, then, is the cause of all other causes in the series, and none are a cause of it. That makes it a first cause of our infinite series. Perhaps it cannot really be a member of the series, but an external and uncaused cause of the whole shebang. But an uncaused cause there must be.

Another, more radical objection to a first cause is that *maybe there are no causes in existence at all.* Not too many scientists take that idea very seriously. But the eighteenth-century Scottish philosopher David Hume proposed it, and some philosophers since his time have followed in his footsteps. If you are convinced that you have ever done anything or been truly responsible for anything at all, even the laundry or the dishes, then you disagree with Hume, and you need not worry about him. If, however, you are one of those unfortunate souls who have been educated into having his problem but were not educated back out of it, I invite you to read appendix 2 before moving on to chapter 2. Hume's attempt to cast doubt on the existence of causes is like Zeno's attempts to cast doubt on the existence of motion. You have probably heard some version of the famous dichotomy paradox of Zeno of Elea. You can't get out of the room, he would say, because in order to do so, you would first have to get halfway to the door and then go half the remaining distance and then half the new remaining distance and so on ad infinitum, and thus, to arrive at the door, you would have to traverse the *last* of these halfway points. But there *is* no last halfway point. There can't be. So it would appear that you cannot get out of the room, and motion is simply impossible.

Zeno proposed other motion paradoxes, too. His paradoxes are not easily solved. To solve them requires finding the mistakes in them, a thing easier said than done. But it is easy to see that there must be some mistake in them, even if it is not easy to identify it, since we all know we can make it to the door. Hume's attack on the existence of causes is like that, so it need not concern us here. The certainty of the existence of causes, like the existence of motion, is all we need to go forward.

How far have we come then? We now know that there is a first cause—at least one. It is by no means clear what the first cause is, though. *First cause* and *god* are not synonyms—not even if they turn out to be the same thing. "Joe's wife" and "my sister" are the same person, but those are entirely different descriptions of her, with quite different meanings, and someone who knows her under one of them might not have the slightest clue that she also answers to the other. Plenty of people think I have a sister without thinking, "Joe has a wife." Plenty of people think there is a first cause without thinking, "There is a god." That's because it is not at all obvious why a first cause has to be anything more than, say, some self-moving primordial glop, which, by the blind and basic forces inherent in it, has evolved into all the things we see, including us, but which itself has all the acumen of a speed bump. Such a lumpish first cause might deserve a lot of names, but *god* could not be on the list, since *god* always includes *intelligent* in its meaning.

Proving the existence of a first cause is therefore useful but insufficient for concluding that some sort of god exists. It is just the first, necessary step in the invigorating hike of the chapters to follow. In some ways, it's only a baby step. Most atheists are perfectly content to take it. Richard Dawkins speaks of a first cause and of a prime mover. In his own way, Stephen Hawking does as well. So that's settled. As long as there are causes at work in the world, we can rest assured that there is (at least) one thing in existence that simply is and is a cause of other things—a first thing with no cause of its own being that has the capacity to produce its effects without the assistance of any other cause.

2

The Tree of Being

> There cannot possibly be two things neither of which has a
> cause of its being.
>
> — Thomas Aquinas, *Summa Contra Gentiles*

Cousin Mike

When my wife and I were first dating, she was in college and working part-time at a movie theater. She and a certain usher who had
worked with her there for a few years shared the same last name:
Desrosiers. One day, out of the blue, Mike (the usher) drew attention
to their common last name. They had never talked about it before.
"I bet we're related", he said. Amy laughed at the idea. She did
not see much resemblance between herself and Mike. She had never
met him before working at the theater. And the common name was
shabby evidence; in any town in the northeast there are decent odds
of finding a Desrosiers or two in the phonebook. The next time they
were on break together, Mike asked Amy what her paternal grandfather's name was. His name had been Archille. "My grandfather had
a brother named Archille", he said. He had been doing a little family
research. Amy did some research of her own, and it turned out their
grandfathers had indeed been brothers. So Mike the usher became
Cousin Mike from then on.

Inquiries about the origins of similar names are not restricted to
family trees. Words themselves provoke the same curiosity. There
are plenty of obvious relatives, whether in the same language or in
different ones. The words *strip, stripe, strap,* and *strop,* for example,
surely have a common ancestor. And the French words *chat, doigt,*
and *vin* are either the origins of the English words *cat, digit,* and *wine,*

or else they derive from common origins. But it is the distant, unexpected relatives that delight us most. The words *army*, *arm*, and *art* are all descendants of an Indo-European root meaning "to fit together". The common ancestral root *sac-* or *sec-*, meaning "to split", seems to be the ultimate source of our words *section*, *segment*, *sex*, *saw*, and *scythe*. From a variation of that same root, *sci-* or *scid-*, meaning "to divide" or "to distinguish", derive our words *science*, *conscience*, *decide*, *chisel*, *scissors*, *scimitar*, *schism*, *homicide*, and *schizophrenia*.

Philologists are not content to trace individual words to their sources. They want to know the relations and origins of whole languages. Languages come in families, as it happens. There are Indo-European languages, such as Italian and Hindi. There are Sino-Tibetan languages, such as Mandarin and Vietnamese. Do language families like these form a superfamily? Do they all stem from a single mother language? Or are they just so many offspring of some number of utterly unrelated primitive languages that arose and evolved independently of one another?

The question I wish to ask now is similar, although the scale is somewhat grander. Are *all existing things* somehow related? Is there a single origin of them all? Or is there instead a quorum of first causes, an elite group that can never increase in number and that divide among themselves the labor of causing things or else contend with one another? I am asking, now, not about the first cause of people or things with similar names, or about the first language, but about the first cause of all things absolutely. In chapter 1 we saw that *among things from which other things hang*, there had to be a first cause of the hanging of a lamp. And *among things that pull other things*, there had to be a first cause of the pulling of a train. But it is also true that some things derive their being from other ones. The argument of chapter 1 works at that general level, too. *Among things that exist*, there has to be at least one that is a first cause of other things existing but needs no cause for its own existence.

At least one. But could there be more? With such a mind-boggling variety of things in existence, it is difficult to conceive how they could all have been produced by a single cause. How could any single entity be capable of bringing forth this endless torrent of diversity?

On the other hand, any number beyond one smacks of the arbitrary and demands explanation. What, are there forty-two first causes?

Then why not forty-three? If there were only one, it might not be fair to ask, "Why not two?" A first cause might be an unrepeatable thing, much as an even prime number has to be two and can't ever be anything else. Also, no first cause could produce another, since producing it would mean causing it. So it's unclear how there could be more than one. Besides, despite the tremendous diversity in things, there is also a deep and remarkable unity somehow binding them all. The reduction of many effects to one cause seems to be a pattern in the whole universe. Similar effects have similar causes, if not one cause; hence the great trend toward unification in physics. Where we see similar physical properties, we suspect a common cause. Rocks fall on Earth and also on Mars due to one force, not to special Earthly forces and quite distinct Martian ones. Causal unification happens so often that even when we find strikingly disparate effects, we tend to suspect that a deeper underlying unity will eventually come to light. This has happened with heat, light, sound, and motion, which are all forms of energy, and again with matter and energy, which are somehow equivalent. Countless millions of shockingly different chemical compounds are the offspring of about a hundred elements, and these in turn come out of a handful of subatomic particles.

Perhaps the most amazing unification story of all, if it is indeed true, is that all living things have descended from a single common ancestor. What diversity from that original unity! Biologists, noting the flexibility of certain species in the hands of breeders, first became convinced that distinct yet recognizably different varieties of some plant or animal, living in close proximity to one another in the wild, must have the same ancestors. Next they began to suspect that even many animals of quite different species, or exhibiting still higher-order differences, could be traced back to the same progenitors. Today, the general similarity of being organisms at all is fast becoming a sufficient reason for inferring that two living things derive ultimately from the very same origins or at least from origins of the very same kind. If being an organism is common to two distinct things, some one reason underlies this, even if we haven't the faintest idea what it might be. Maybe one of them is the offspring of the other. Maybe they are the descendants of a common ancestor. Maybe they evolved on different planets altogether, but due to prior similarities in the chemical foundations of life and in the survival trials with which their ancestors were faced, they turned out like two peas in a pod. As far as the general many-from-one pattern is concerned, it makes no difference which of these turns out to be the case. Experience has taught us not to be complacent with multitudes of things; there is always some underlying unity. It is a recurrent theme in reality—in art as well as in nature, and even in logic and mathematics.

This sense of the unity of all things has been commonly recognized for ages. The very word *universe* comes from the Latin for "turned into one", perhaps from the geocentric notion that everything we see appears to spin about a common center. While that idea is quite obsolete, the notion behind the other ancient word for the universe, namely, *cosmos*, is not, and it too implies a certain unity underlying all things. *Cosmos* is from the ancient Greek word for "order" but also for "ornament" and "embellishment" (we derive our word *cosmetics* from that source). Similarly, the Latin word for "world" was *mundus*, which first meant "personal ornament, decoration, dress", and later "the world". It remains a common perception today that the universe is somehow adorned and beautiful. The universe could not be beautiful, though, if it were an unintelligible mess. There must be some governing principle of order inherent in it, and an order is a kind of unity in things. But how would that come about if there were forty-two first causes, all existing and acting independently of each other? We would have a disjointed world. As things are, it seems as though all existing things are cousins.

The Lesson of the Snowball

At first, it might seem impossible to settle the question "How many first causes are there?" without yet knowing in detail what kinds of things first causes are. You can't count up the number of men and women in the room without knowing what men and women are. Fortunately, the absolute "firstness" of a first cause itself provides enough information for us to go on. In a similar way, we don't know what "all things" are in great detail, but that does not stop us from realizing that there cannot be more than a single "all": if there were really sixteen "alls", any one of them would not really be all, would it? The proof for there being just one first cause is a bit hairier than that, however. We must familiarize ourselves with a couple of principles first.

To begin, we must take full advantage of the universal negations implied in a first cause. There must be at least one first cause that is absolutely first, depending on no other cause whatsoever for its own causal action and therefore depending on nothing else for its existence. Those negations eliminate many suspects. No beast, tree, or stone can be the first cause, since these things all come about from prior causes. Their natures are not such as to have an existence and action that is altogether independent of other things. The stars themselves, seemingly immortal, are born and die and depend on causes that maintain them for as long as they exist. We humans, too, depend on causes not only to come into existence, but also to remain in existence.

I remember when I first began to realize that familiar things depend on causes to *keep* existing and not just to *start* existing. I was a boy making fortresses in the snow. On the coldest New England days, when the snow was most powdery, I could not make a snow fort or even a snowball. No matter how hard I tried to pack the snow together, it always just came apart in my mittens and blew away in the wind. If bringing things together were a sufficient cause of their staying together as one thing, I would have had no trouble making a snowball on those especially cold days. *Bringing* things together is simply not a sufficient principle of their *staying* together after you let them be. Even a humble snowball requires more than a mere shaper. It requires parts that can grab each other somehow. In the case of a successful snowball, then, there was another agency at work besides that of my hands.

So here is a simple but important rule: when something newly brought into being continues to be with some robustness, when it insists on its new unity even after the obvious causes of its coming to be have ceased to act, this is because of some other kind of cause at work.

I pour some wine into your glass, thus causing it to assume the shape of your glass. It continues to have that shape now, apart from any further effort of mine. Does the wine therefore persist in the glass shape of itself, altogether independently of any outside influence? Obviously not. The wine clearly depends on the glass and on gravity to continue in that shape, for as long as it has it. Sometimes a new combination of things persists due to causes of coherence acting from within, as in a snowball or a star. Other times, the new combination sticks together because an entirely external cause exercises some preservative action on it—as the wine and the glass shape stay together because of the glass, or as a prison population stays together because of the guards, locks, and razor wire. Either way, a combination endures due to the ongoing action of something that exists before the combination itself.

Every combination presupposes a combiner. Every combination that comes into existence depends on a combiner to produce it, and every combination that exists depends on a combiner to sustain it. But everything familiar to us is a combination of things. Nothing familiar to us is a first cause then, and so a first cause must be something quite unfamiliar. Is it some purely formless matter underlying all combinations? Or some entirely indivisible particle?

The principle I have been elaborating—that a combination of things implies a preservative combiner—is clearest in the case of combinations whose components dislike each other. If two magnets are kissing at their north poles, then something else is holding them together. If a house built out of heavy materials does not come down, something is forcing it to stay up. But it is also true that when things are merely *indifferent* to one another, the reason they are together lies in something other than them. What is indifferent to many alternative ways of being needs something other than itself to make it adopt one of them. A pile of oak planks, for example, in itself is capable of receiving any of a thousand forms of furniture; it never assumes those forms of itself, however, but acquires them only through extrinsic causes. And why doesn't it assume those forms of itself? Because of its indifference to them all. It has neither a necessary connection to any of those forms nor any active tendency toward them.

Once the oak is in the form of a dining table, it becomes independent of the human cause who brought it into that form. Is the oak table from then on independent of all causes whatsoever? Is it now a self-existing thing? We must not forget the lesson of the snowball. If the table holds together at all, exhibiting some persistence in its new unity, there are unifying causes at work. And they are causes of a kind that can exist and act independently of the table and that are working within the table, continuing its existence.

These rules are not restricted to artifacts. They are quite general. Every disease is an example of a combination. To have cancer is not part of human nature; otherwise everyone would have it automatically and by definition. Thus, cancer is found in this or that person because of something *added* to human nature by some cause or causes. Why is it that the four nucleotides thymine, cytosine, adenine, and guanine depend on a prior kangaroo or kangaroo cell in order to come together in the form of kangaroo DNA? Because those nucleotides, while capable of that particular arrangement, are equally capable of millions of others, and so in themselves they are indifferent to them all. And why do protons, neutrons, and electrons depend on so impressive a cause as a supernova (or else a particle accelerator) and certain specific processes in order to come together in the form of gold? Because they are capable of taking not only the form of gold, but also of lead, of hydrogen, and so on, and therefore in themselves those basic particles are indifferent to all such forms. There is no need to multiply examples. The general principle should be clear. It is not because of anything special about houses, or kangaroos, or chemical elements that they require prior causes to come into being and remain in it. It is because they all consist of combinations of things that are to some extent indifferent to their combination.

To sum up: When does something need a cause of its being? Whenever it needs something else to decide whether and how it will be, and this is when the thing itself is indecisive about the question. Shall the oak be a table or a chair? Nothing in the oak decides. It is indifferent. But when an indecision gets decided, there must be a decider—not necessarily an intelligent one, but a cause of some kind. Earth and stone can be arranged in an infinity of diverse ways; why this particular one that is called Mount Whitney? Because certain original mountain-forming forces decided the matter, and other presently acting forces are maintaining that ancient decision, while others alter it slightly over time. Whatever needs a cause of its coming into existence also needs a cause (perhaps a different one, or several) of its remaining in existence. That is the lesson of the snowball.

The Sullivan Brothers

The next principle we need reminds me of a job I once had. For years I worked with a remodeling company, first building and remodeling houses and later working in the company's cabinet shop. The owners were a pair of brothers, Jim and John Sullivan. I learned many things from the Sullivans—my own physical limitations, for one, and things useful for jobs around the house, too. I even learned many things useful for philosophy by working with them.

Most of the other employees were not educated beyond high school, if they had gotten that far. They had little interest in talking over the principles underlying their work. Jim and John, though, both held bachelor's degrees and loved nothing better than answering my questions about everything their business had taught them. Every now and then I could teach them something in return, not only about philosophy but about their own business. John and I were once constructing an in-ground fountain for a wealthy customer. The fountain was to consist of a concrete floor and walls in the overall shape of a hollowed-out cylinder. During the ride home on the day we finished installing the preparatory rebar, John was fretting about how much concrete to order for the pour on the following day. I got out a notepad and did some quick calculations. Using the formula for the volume of a cylinder, I calculated the volume of the fountain floor, since it was just a very short, flat cylinder, like a big nickel. Then I calculated the volume of the cylinder on top of it, where the water would be. Then I calculated the volume of the cylinder that included the water cylinder and also the concrete walls. Subtracting one from the other, I got the volume of the walls. Adding that to the floor, I came up with the total amount of concrete. John didn't trust the formula for the volume of a cylinder, thinking it must be a mere approximation. I assured him it was exact, but "just to be on the safe side", he ordered three extra cubic yards of concrete over my calculated quantity. The next day, after the pour began, we soon saw we had plenty more than we needed inside the fountain. So John had us frantically shoveling it out of the fountain before it set up, so that it ended up hardening on the patio around the fountain, and we spent the rest of the day jackhammering it off and carrying it away. That was his extra three cubic yards and his lesson in the precision of mathematics.

But for every lesson I taught the Sullivans, they taught me a hundred. Some of these I already knew in theory. Learning them in practice impressed them indelibly on my mind, however, and also provided me with wonderfully clear examples for future teaching. There is, for example, the law of diminishing returns. You can learn that law in the abstract. Or you can learn that if you spill a gallon of paint on the customer's carpet, and you can get 90 percent of it out in the first hour of cleaning, the next hour you will get only 5 percent more out and the next hour only 2 percent, and so on. Another important principle about the spilling of paint: if the homeowner sees you spill it, you have to get at least 99 percent out. If he doesn't see you, 95 percent will probably be good enough. Some of the most business-relevant principles concern how much time or how many guys it takes to do certain specific jobs. That is the art of the estimator and the job planner. Mistakes in that art can spell bankruptcy for a contractor. Some of the principles of the contractor's art of estimation are the following. If a job involves working from the top of a ladder and requires too many tools and materials to hold at the top of the ladder all at once, that's an "up and down" job and could take one guy a whole day. But if two guys work together, one guy fetching tools and materials and handing them to the guy on the ladder, it might take as little as an hour. On the other hand, if the job is in a tight spot, such as a very small bathroom, one guy might take all day to get it done, but two guys will take two days, since they will constantly be getting in each other's way. These things are somewhat obvious when you hear them, but it is the easiest thing in the world to forget them when you are actually planning a job.

What I learned from the Sullivans could probably fill a book. Many of the things I learned were about how older houses used to be built, and it is one of these lessons that is relevant for our purposes. Before plywood became a staple in house building (modern plywood was invented in the 1800s by Immanuel Nobel), the sheathing on wooden houses was typically a series of boards over which were applied tar paper and a siding material. Suppose you put one nail or screw through each end of each board into the stud behind it and applied the boards to the studs horizontally, as in figure 1. Is that structure rigid? No. Sideways forces can cause the whole structure to fold up or collapse, as in figure 2. But if you add a diagonal brace, as in figure 3, the rectangular structure will become rigid.

For that reason, diagonal corner braces were set into the studs in older houses, or else the sheathing was applied diagonally. The reason the diagonals provide rigidity is that they form triangles, and a triangular structure, even with just a single nail through each corner, as in figure 4, is rigid. That is, it cannot be folded over or have its shape changed without breaking the wood or shearing the nails, so that the strength of the structure reduces to the strength of its materials. It is because of the rigidity of triangles that you will see X shapes in scaffolding and in many bridges.

Rigidity in a square or rectangle can be achieved only by adding bracing. Not so the rigidity of a triangle, which just belongs to the triangle of itself, as a natural property of triangularity. The same property can sometimes belong to two different things, then, while depending on a cause in one case but not in the other. (By the way, it is usually best to ponder these matters *after* your workday, and not while staring off into space and holding a nail gun in your hand, with your fellow workers yelling at you in the background.)

It is not always fair to assume, then, that because something requires a certain type of cause in one case, it therefore needs it in every case. The rigidity of a square pattern of boards depends on an additional brace to cause it. The rigidity of a triangular pattern of boards does not. The triangular structure requires no further cause to make it rigid, as a square structure does.

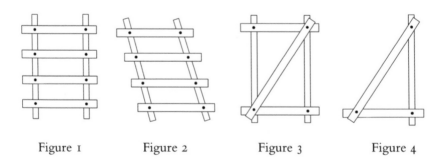

Figure 1   Figure 2   Figure 3   Figure 4

Triangular rigidity does depend on *some* causes, though. It depends on the hardness of the wood, for example, and on a builder to put the triangular shape into the wood in the first place. At first, it might even seem that this is true without exception, that any feature common to two things must belong to each through some kind of cause, even if not the same kind of cause. The form common to two pennies depends on the same kind of cause—a coining machine—to stamp it into the metal. Examples of the same kind of thing occur throughout nature. Certain features are common and necessary to all animals, for example, and taken all together these features might be called the nature of an animal. The nature of an animal belongs to this zebra and to that one and depends on the same kinds of causes—namely, parent zebras—in order to turn up again in this or that individual. On the other hand, the nature of an animal belongs not only to a zebra, but also to a cobra, and in this case the causes endowing each with an animal nature differ. The zebra depends on prior zebras, while the cobra does not. Nonetheless, the cobra derives its animal nature from prior cobras. By going through examples like these, it might seem that any feature common to two things must belong to each through *some* kind of prior cause, even if not the same kind.

That is not altogether clear, though. Existence belongs to water and also to matter, for example. Does it belong to each through a cause? In the case of the water, which is matter plus the form of water, we can see that a prior cause is needed, since matter is indifferent to the form of water. Matter *can* be in the form of water, but doesn't have to be, so whenever it is, that is due to some water-producing cause, such as the burning of a candle, and to some water-maintaining cause, such as certain bonding forces between the basic particles of matter. Water depends on prior causes to come into existence and to continue existing. That's our rule about the combination of a thing with another thing to which it is indifferent. That requires a combiner to initiate the combination and to sustain it. Matter itself, on the other hand, does not obviously involve any such combination. Maybe matter itself is perfectly simple, and just *is*, without any need for a prior cause. That is a question we will be getting into somewhat in the next chapter, but for now, it is enough to see that something (such as existence) might very well belong to one thing through special causes, and to another through no causes at all. The rigidity of triangles is such a case. The shape of a four-sided figure is determined by some cause outside the lengths of its four sides, because it can be rocked back and forth while still keeping the boards attached at the same intervals. But the rigidity of a triangle is independent of outside causes. Its shape is determined entirely by the lengths of the three sides themselves. The four sides of a quadrilateral are open to being an infinity of shapes, and something outside them has to decide which one they are to be. Any three sides that can form a triangle, however, decide the shape all by themselves.

Why There Is at Most One First Cause

After the considerations we have just made, we are ready to think about the number of first causes in existence. Could there be many first causes in the way that the Greeks thought there were many gods? Each Greek god was in charge of a specific domain. The sea belonged to Poseidon, love to Aphrodite, war to Ares, the afterlife to Pluto, and so on. Could there be two (or more) first causes if they are distinguished by being causes of different kinds of things in the universe?

Two gods could not be distinguished *only* by the distinction of the things they cause or govern. Those things are extrinsic to the gods themselves, and the gods must first of all differ from each other intrinsically. The governor of Maine and the governor of Arizona are different not just because the states in which they hold office are different. It is because they are already different people in themselves that they can be distinct governors of different places. If there were two gods, something in one or both of them would have to be the reason for their difference. Perhaps they could differ as the two governors do. The two governors have the same nature, human nature, but in different portions of matter—one in these materials here, the other in those there. Could our two gods differ like that? Could the common divine nature be stamped into two different parts of some receptive material, as it were?

Imagine two pennies again. The form of a penny requires a cause to stamp it on a metal that is indifferent to it. Just so would the form of a god require a cause to impress it on a material that is indifferent to being this god or that one. There is a cause, then, combining the nature of a god with the materials or features distinctive of a Zeus or an Athena or an Apollo. That was the rule about combinations needing combiners. It follows that whenever two things share a common nature and differ only by the addition of it to distinct hunks of some indifferent material, *both* will require prior causes. Neither of them can be a first cause.

It is not possible to get two first causes by combining their common nature with something to which it is indifferent—whether they are two pennies or two gods or two of anything else. That is one way to get two of something, but not a way to get two first causes. The combination of anything with something to which it is indifferent requires a prior cause, which knocks that combination out of the First Cause Club.

Can we have two first causes in some other way, without giving them a common nature? What if our two first causes were radically distinct things—for example, some kind of fundamental matter and a nonmaterial god? Would that work? Alas, it would not. Why not? Because even then they will have a common nature. Precisely because each one is supposed to be a first cause, each would have to possess at least the nature of a necessarily self-existing thing. A first cause cannot derive its existence from something before it, and so it has its existence of itself. That is a special nature. Many natures, such as the natures of cats and dogs, cannot be such a thing—a thing that, just because of what it is, is incapable of being produced by something else.

We can say more. Because a first cause must be self-existing, its nature cannot consist of things that might possibly be separate from each other, since in that case there would be some indifference between them, and so they would need a cause for them to be together. All these conditions for a necessarily self-existing thing, then, must be common to *both* our hypothetical first causes.

Nor can that be the whole story. In order to keep our candidates distinct from each other, we must suppose a positive distinguishing feature in at least one of them. For example, the material first cause would have dimensions, but the spiritual god would not. Or the god has an intelligence that is distinct from, and added to, its self-existent nature, whereas the matter does not have that. The distinguishing difference, whatever it is, cannot be something trivial, since it is the only way for our two first causes to be two and not just one and the same thing. And there is the kicker. Their common nature exists with the distinctive feature in one case and without it in the other. The common nature is therefore in itself *indifferent* to that add-on and hence enters into combination with it only through a prior cause, a combiner. Whichever of our first causes possesses this difference, and is distinguished by it alone, therefore, has its distinct existence only through that prior cause's having provided it with its distinctive feature—which rules it out as a first cause after all. Thus, there simply is no way to get more than one absolutely first cause.

The first cause has some features in common with other things. It has existence, for example, and unity and causal power. But it has these in a different way from all other things, namely, in an uncaused and self-sufficient way, much as a triangle has rigidity by its very nature while a square has it only thanks to the triangle. Other attributes are unique to the first cause, such as being first and uncaused and self-existing, and it cannot give these to any other thing, just as a triangle can give rigidity to a square but can't give it "self-rigidity".

In summary:

Two first causes would have to share a common nature.

They could thus be distinguished only by some addition to that nature in at least one of them.

That distinguishing addition, since the common nature is indifferent to it, would belong to its possessor through a cause.

Therefore, the possessor of the distinguishing addition would not be a first cause after all.

The force of these principles has decided our question for us. There cannot be two or more first causes. There is a single one at most.

Three Corollaries

Three corollaries immediately follow. The most obvious of these is that there is exactly one first cause, which follows thus:

There is *at most* one first cause (just shown).
There is *at least* one first cause (see chapter 1).
Therefore, there is *exactly* one first cause.

Another corollary is that all other things besides the first cause (whatever it is) have a cause of their being. There can be only one self-existing thing, as our reasoning has shown. All other things, then, have their existence by continuous dependence on a cause or causes.

The third corollary is that all things besides the first cause derive their existence from it. Anything other than the first cause has a cause of its being (by our second corollary); if that cause is the first cause, then we're done. If that cause is not the first cause, then it also has a cause of its being. And this cannot continue endlessly (according to the reasoning in chapter 1). This must terminate in a first cause. But there is only one of those. Therefore, all beings derive, whether immediately or through many intermediate causes, from the one and only first cause. All things are like a vast tree, whose leaves sprout from its twigs, whose twigs grow from its branches, whose branches extend from its main limbs, and whose main limbs stem from a single trunk. If both matter and some sort of god exist, then, it must be that one of them is the cause of the other. Only one or the other can be the first cause, not both.

We should stop to congratulate ourselves. The conclusion of this chapter has taken us light-years beyond the conclusion of the previous one. We have eliminated all but one thing as suspects in the great whodunit that is our search for the first cause. But there is still a long way to go. The conclusion that there is only one first cause of things, and that it is the cause of the being of all other things we can name, does not yet move beyond common ground with atheists and materialists. The reduction of all effects to a single first cause—matter—is the heart and soul of materialism, after all. The materialist view also fits with the idea that the first cause is responsible not only for things coming into existence, but for their continuing in existence as well. Nothing can exist even for a moment without the materials out of which it is made.

Is some self-shaping matter, then, the first cause? The impossibility of that will come into view after another bend or two in the road.

3

The Philosophy of the Axle

Most of the first philosophers thought that only causes of the
material type were the principles of all things.

—Aristotle, *Metaphysics*

Some Modern Myths

Intellectual history is haunted by certain myths. When I was in grade
school, I was taught that Christopher Columbus was the first person
to prove that the earth is round. I was also given to understand that
until he made his famous voyage in 1492, nobody believed his crazy
notion that the earth is anything but flat. He was alone in this scientific conviction, a visionary among scoffing primitives. I learned,
too, why ancient and medieval astronomers believed the earth was
at the center of the universe. My teachers explained that, before
the advent of science (circa 1492), it was a common conviction that
human beings are the most important things in the world. Therefore, people naturally thought the abode of humanity should be at
the center of the universe. It was also in elementary school that I
learned about Galileo. He was the one who really got science going
because he was the first person to propose checking our theories
against experience.

   These ideas possess a certain charm, and while they fib, they also
sprinkle in a few grains of truth. Perhaps that is why they persist. At
any rate, they are much more wrong than right. Well over a thousand years before Columbus, Ptolemy (to say nothing of his predecessors) gave very sound reasons for saying the earth was tolerably
spherical, and pretty much the entire educated world agreed on the

point. And Ptolemy's reasons for concluding that the earth sits at the center of a spherical universe derived from the apparent rotation of the heavens above us and the seeming stillness of the ground beneath our feet. His geocentrism had nothing to do with his belief in our pride of place as humans. In fact, he believed, like others of his time and long afterward, that mankind belonged to the inferior realm of destructible things that by their nature sink here to earth, the very pit of the world. The myth of Galileo is also half true. He deserves (and receives) oodles of credit for getting modern science off on the right foot. But he was by no means the first person to think experiments were useful. If Galileo taught us a new way to think, it was by showing us how to go beyond the constraints of our experience by imagining things in circumstances we have never experienced.

Another of these myths would have it that the ancient philosophers were all believers in immaterial souls and incorporeal deities, and that the history of human thought presents a more or less steady progress away from those primitive notions toward the materialism of modern science and philosophy. Materialism, as the story has it, is a sophisticated notion that could not occur to people until after they had taken a hard look at things in the cold light of mathematical physics. Nonsense. In both the East and the West, the most ancient philosophers thought the first cause was some sort of material underlying all things, endowed with certain self-motive properties.

Thales, considered by some to be the first philosopher (it is another myth that Socrates was the first!), said that all things were made of water. While this panhydrological notion is not very sophisticated by our standards, Thales had several reasons for proposing it. For one, there's lots of water around; it is an abundant raw material. Most of our world is covered with it. And water can assume a surprising variety of appearances. Even ordinary experience reveals that water, a liquid, can become a solid or a gas. All living things depend on it, both taking it in and "making water" later. It has no flavor or odor or color of its own, but seems to be ready to receive any of these qualities. All in all, water was a good first guess at the natural material underlying all things. Leaving aside any question of the quantitative laws governing its transformations, the all-is-water theory was more like than unlike the modern idea that all things are matter, or energy, or some such thing.

Later thinkers such as Anaximenes and Anaximander saw that water was too definite a thing to be the sole ingredient in everything. It had too many distinctive properties of its own that we do not find in all things; it's wet, for example. So they chose a different basic material, still more nondescript, such as air or even "the indefinite". Still later thinkers, such as Heraclitus and Empedocles, saw that it was insufficient to name as the cause of all things something that passively becomes all things and into which all things eventually corrupt. There had to be a reason why it moved or changed or became anything at all, and why it became now this and now that; they saw the need to introduce a motive cause. The mere susceptibility to undergo a change, to serve as the material for a product in the making, did not explain the making. The woodpile can be made into a house but does not make itself into one. Many materials are simply unable to explain the changes they undergo.

Ah, but *some* materials seem to move themselves! Magnets attract each other without our assistance. Heavy bodies fall to the ground without having to be talked into it. Living things move about of their own accord. There must, then, be some most basic material in things that is not just passive but also active and has motion of itself, and this (they thought) will be the first cause we seek. Water splashes about, perhaps, but it also sits stagnant. That can't be it.

So it was that Heraclitus introduced *fire* as the basic constituent in things; it was the basic material and the prime mover in one. Fire could turn itself into all things, and all things could turn back into fire. "All things are exchanged for fire, and fire for all things", he said. Commenting on this theory, twentieth-century theoretical physicist Werner Heisenberg once wrote that "modern physics is in some way extremely near to the doctrines of Heraclitus. If we replace the word 'fire' by the word 'energy' we can almost repeat his statements word for word from our modern point of view."[1]

In the East, the Taoists spoke of the Tao, which was not something above or outside the world of change, but underlying it, and which was responsible for the movements and changes we witness,

---

[1] Werner Heisenberg, *Physics and Philosophy: The Revolution in Modern Science* (New York: Harper & Row, 1962), p. 63.

and which it was wiser to cooperate with than to fight. It too was both mover and material in one.

Possibly this sort of thinking lies behind the old expression *Mother Earth*. To early human experience, things appeared to sprout up out of the earth more or less spontaneously—grass, trees, lava, even mountains and volcanoes themselves. It seemed as though all familiar things came *from* the earth, both in the sense that they were made *of* it (as statues come from the marble) and in the sense that they were made *by* it (as statues come from the sculptor). There was no clear distinction between the material and the maker in this way of thinking. Toss in just a smidgen more sophistication, and we see that really it is not *the* earth exactly that is responsible for all these things, but *earth*, or less poetically, *matter*, together with all its active properties and inherent laws of movement. So it is that the very word *matter* comes from the Latin *mater*, or "mother". A mother brings forth her child both as an active producer and as a provider of materials from her own body. And yet an expectant mother is not really the productive cause of her developing child once he has been conceived and has begun developing. The causes of development are within the body of the embryo itself. The mother is just supplying materials and a safe environment. Could it be that the most basic underlying material of all things is like the embryo—both the subject of the changes we see and the active cause?

In this general conception of a self-moving matter, we have our first serious candidate for the first cause of all things. Many a modern scientist is satisfied with it. Communist philosophers have talked it up. And it would appear to fulfill the requirements of the last two chapters. If we suppose there is some single, bottommost material in the world, and if we allow it to have just the right inherent tendencies to motion and change, would we not have found the first cause of all things? It would be a cause of the coming to be of all the outwardly manifest shapes and varieties and modes that come and go within it. It would produce all these by the motions and changes within itself. It would also be a cause of the being of things, as long as they endured, as the brick and mortar sustain the existence of a house. And the bottommost matter itself, involving in itself no combinations of forms, but only underlying all such things, could simply be, without need of any cause for its existence.

Matter Is Not the First Cause

The truth is otherwise, however. Matter is not the first cause. It is impossible for it to be so. Matter is subject to motion. The first cause, on the other hand, is not.

That matter is subject to motion is obvious. In the modern sense of the word, matter is anything that has mass (or "shove resistance") and takes up space. Anything of that description is capable of undergoing a change of place. Among philosophers, the word *matter* has also an older sense that is more like what people mean by *materials*. The lumber pile is matter for a house. Proteins are matter for a living thing. Generally, *matter* in this sense means an underlying thing that can assume new forms and thus persist through the changes from one thing to another. Sometimes the matter is purely passive in relation to the final product—as lumber is passive to the form of a house and does not produce it. Other times, the materials are not only receptive to the new form, but their active properties are conducive to it. Proteins, for example, not only get made into things, but even do some of the making themselves. In either sense—the scientific or the philosophical one—*matter* means something that can have motion in it.

The first cause is another story. It cannot have any motion whatsoever. To see this takes more doing.

It is easy to see that the first cause cannot *be* a motion of some kind. Every motion is the motion *of* something. This waving motion is an act of my hand, and that falling motion is an act of that stone. The thing the motion belongs to is called the subject of the motion, or the mobile, and it is plain that no particular motion can exist without the particular mobile to which it belongs. So every motion is the kind of thing that can exist only if something else exists—namely, its mobile. That cannot be true of the first cause. It is not the sort of thing that can exist only if something else exists. It is a self-existing thing. The first cause consequently cannot be a motion of any kind.

It is also true that the first cause cannot *have* a motion of any kind. That is a bit trickier to see. We have already made an inroad, however. Since the first cause cannot be a motion, it follows conversely that every motion is something other than the first cause. But everything other than the first cause is an effect and is caused by the first cause, according to the corollaries in chapter 2. So every motion is an effect that is caused by the first cause (and usually by other inter-mediate causes too, but at least by the first cause). That is helpful, because now we know that *if* motion could belong to the first cause, the first cause would be causing this motion in itself. It would be moving itself. This gives us something we can sink our teeth into. Is the first cause a self-mover? That is what the whole question boils down to.

The thing about self-movers is that they necessarily have a mini-mum of two parts—one part moving the other. This is clear enough in experience. You can move yourself about in various ways, but whenever you do so, one part of you is moving another part. Your leg carries your foot in front of you as you step forward. The same foot, once planted, moves the leg forward, pressing back on the (more or less) immobile ground. If the ground weren't there, pushing you back as you push on it, you would go nowhere. Even a self-mover seems to depend on an external mover then. But the more import-ant point for the moment is that the self-mover cannot move itself by the whole moving the whole. We are not like Superman. In the cartoons I used to watch as a kid, Superman seemed to "will" himself from point A to point B without so much as flapping his arms. He just soared from one place to another and hovered there. (Even in his case, though, his body did not move itself as much as his mind moved his body.)

It would be impossible to run through all the examples of self-movers and their parts to verify the general truth that they move themselves by one part moving another. No problem. There is no need. There is a general reason why no self-mover can move itself as a whole and why it must instead comprise distinct parts, some of which move others. The reason is this. To move something is to give it motion. To be moved by something is to receive motion from it. And it is not possible for the same thing both to give and to receive the very same thing at the very same time. I can give myself a hair-cut, but really one part of me gives it and quite another receives it. It is therefore impossible for something to give and receive its own motion to and from itself. It is not possible for something to move itself, then, unless there is a real distinction in it between what is causing the motion and what is only receiving it but not causing it. A thing can move itself only in the sense that something can scratch

itself; there must still be some distinction between the scratcher and
the scratched.

Could the first cause be like that? A self-mover, with one part
moved by another? Let us try to suppose this is so and see what happens. Let there be a part of the first cause that is in motion. Call it A.
Since this motion is an effect, and all effects are produced by the first
cause (see chapter 2), and yet A cannot give its own motion to itself,
then let it be moved by B, another part of the first cause.

Now, is B also in motion? If so, it too is receiving its motion from
another part of the first cause—and not from A, lest we lapse into
an impossible causal circle. Very well, suppose B is being moved
by C. And C by D. And so on. By the argument of chapter 1, there
must be a first cause of the motion of A. Call it G. This G, then,
cannot also be in motion, since if it were, it too would be receiving
its motion from a prior cause, and hence, there will be yet another
absolutely first cause besides G, which is impossible, according to the
results of chapter 2. Moreover, G is the first cause of the motion of
A, and A through F are not. Well, *blast it*. That means G is the only
real first cause in the bunch. And it is not in motion. There simply
is no way to get the first cause to have any motion. It can't even
move itself.

This brings out that all motion and mobile things must depend
on something immobile. To some extent, that is true even on a less-
than-global scale. The shoulder rotates in an immobile socket. And
Lao-tzu observed that "to turn a wheel, although thirty spokes must
revolve, the axle must remain motionless; so both the moving and
the non-moving are needed to produce revolution."[2] This reasoning
sounds the death knell for the theory that matter is the first cause.
Matter, energy, and fundamental particles are all subject to motion.
The first cause is not. So none of these, and nothing like them, is the
first cause. It follows as an immediate corollary that they are instead

---

[2] *Tao Teh King*, trans., Archie J. Bahm (Albuquerque, N.Mex.: World Books, 1986), p.18.

caused by the first cause. Matter itself is a *product*, receiving its very existence from the action of something before it.

Giving Motion While Having None

Whenever I go through this business with students, there are always a few (usually the brighter ones) who cry foul. They don't tend to have any particular complaint about the argument. It's the conclusion itself—that the first cause is a mover that itself has no motion—that bugs them. That sounds impossible. The first cause of all things must be the cause of motions and changes; but then if it does not have any change or motion of its own, how can it impart any? How can anything give what it does not have? You can sue me all you want, but you will never get a million dollars out of me, for the very good reason that I haven't got it. So too it would appear you can't get motion out of something immobile.

Really, though, that is like saying a calculus teacher cannot cause his students to learn unless he too, at the same time, is learning precisely what he's teaching. Or again, one might as well say he can't cause students to have an incomplete understanding of the textbook unless he too has an incomplete understanding of it. He can't give what he doesn't have, right? So if he *gives* an incomplete understanding, he must also *have* an incomplete understanding. If he *gives* only half the answer, he must *have* only half the answer. Of course, that's silly. He can give an imperfect understanding precisely by imparting some share in, but not the entirety of, his own perfect understanding. It is possible for a cause to impart *less* than what it has, something incomplete. An effect sometimes receives only a limited or partial version of the attribute found in its cause. Consequently, a name appropriate to the limitations in the effect might not apply to the cause, since the cause need not suffer from the same limitation or incompleteness.

Motions and changes are a case in point. They are essentially incomplete things. As long as I am walking home, it is false to say I have walked home, and as soon as it is true to say I have walked home, it is no longer true to say I am walking home. When the change is complete, it's also gone. Motion is therefore one of those effects that can in principle preexist in a cause in some form other than a motion. Motion can come from what has no motion but has instead something more complete. It is not universally true that what causes X also has X. The carpenter causes the "being built" of the house, but he himself is not being built at the same time. If the effect in question is something incomplete, it can happen that some more complete principle can produce it.

These results throw a little light on the action of the first cause. When we first think of action, we think of motion. But not every action is a motion. When you stand still while holding an eighty-pound bag of cement, you are not moving, but you are acting as a support, and you feel the action taking something out of you. The action of the first cause is also not a motion, at least not a motion taking place within itself. Its action quietly sustains the being of other things, such as the things familiar to us that are subject to motion, and it gives being to the tendencies and forces of nature themselves, which in turn produce motions in bodies.

First Implies Unchangeable

We have seen that the first cause cannot undergo any change of place. It is also immune to every other kind of change.

Obviously it could not have come to exist, for example, since that would require a prior cause. The first cause could not have caused itself to come to exist, since a thing has to exist before it can do anything. And if anything else caused it to come to exist, then *that* would be the first cause.

It cannot cease to exist, either, since nonexistence is not an option for the first cause. If it were, it would be like the dodo— a nature capable of existing, but also capable of not existing, and so the nature itself is undecided about the matter, and hence, something outside the nature must decide whether it is to be or not to be. That is not possible for the first cause. So it must be that existence is necessary to its nature, and nonexistence is simply impossible for it, just as existence is simply impossible for a square that is also a circle. The nature of the first cause, consequently, is such that it is impossible to create and impossible to destroy it.

Those who believe that matter is the first cause of all things corroborate this result. They too say that the first cause of all things can be neither created nor destroyed. The great thinkers, theists and atheists alike, agree that whatever the first cause is, it must be something necessary and eternal.

The first cause must also be altogether unchangeable. We have just seen that it cannot come to be or cease to be. But neither can it come to be green, or come to be hot, or come to be bigger or anything else. Why not? In order to acquire any new actuality, such as "green" or "hot" or "bigger", the first cause would have to be both at the giving end and at the receiving end of the same thing at the same time, which is impossible.

I have just used the word *actuality* in a way that might deserve some clarification. By an *actuality* I just mean a way of being in contrast to what people call a potential. There is an obvious distinction between the things that are (such as cats and stars) and the things that are not (such as my future grandchildren and world peace and lengthless lines and dragons). But among those that are not, there is also a difference. Although none of them exists in fact, there are some among them that *can* exist (such as my future grandchildren and maybe world peace) and others that *cannot* exist (such as lengthless lines and maybe dragons). The things that are not but can be are called potential things. That is a way of being, in some sense—at least, we say that someone is potentially a great artist or baseball player and that the marble *is* potentially a statue and that someone asleep is potentially awake, whereas a dead person or a stone in no sense is awake. By way of contrast to these, the things that just are, without the added qualification *potentially*, we say *actually* are. The sleeper, now roused, is actually awake. The marble, once carved, is now actually a statue. And so on.

Almost everything familiar to us seems to be in part actual and in part potential. This fellow is actually a carpenter, but he is also a potential musician. It is obviously impossible to find a purely potential thing—a potential thing that is not right now any actual thing. Whatever is potential in one respect must be actual in some other respect. If it were potential in every respect, it would not exist at all. For example, a potential physician must be an actual person. So every potential belongs to something actual. Is the reverse also true? Could it be that everything actual must also have certain potentials mixed up with it? Actualities and potentials are always commingled in the things of our ordinary experience. But if this is universally necessary, the first cause would have to be not only actual; it would also have to have some potential. Is that possible? In addition to its actual existence and action, does it also have some sort of potential to become or receive new actualities it does not already have?

The revelatory question is "Where would it get them?" It would have to get them from itself, since all effects come from it, whether mediately or immediately. So it would have to receive the new actuality while at the same time already having it to give—a vicious circle; a flat-out, jumping-up-and-down impossibility. So the first cause cannot possibly receive any further actuality beyond that which it already has. It is therefore entirely and in every sense unchangeable. There is no sense, then, to saying it has any potential. It is just actual. It is already as actual as it can ever be—or rather, it is as actual as anything can be, since all actualities come from it.

This fits with the very idea of a first cause, a first active producer of things. What is changeable or has potential always depends on something before itself, something already actual in the specific way required in order to cause the change and actualize the potential. Before everything buildable there must be a builder. But there cannot be anything before the first active cause. So *first* implies unchangeable. And that alone is enough to distinguish the first cause from the water of Thales, the Tao of the Taoists, and the matter and energy of the modern physicists. The first cause cannot be the same as any of these, nor can it be anything like these or anything dependent on these. More than that, matter seems to be the furthest thing from the first cause. A primary and fundamental matter, at least in the philosopher's sense of a material out of which all other things are made, must possess the maximum potential and the least actuality. A first cause, a primary active producer of things, must have no potential and be purely actual.

Let's tally our new results, shall we?

1. The first cause is not in any way movable or changeable.
2. The first cause is not matter (since matter is changeable).
3. The first cause has no potential of any kind but is purely actual.
4. Motion and everything subject to motion requires a cause.
5. Before anything self-moving there must exist an external mover.

Not bad for one chapter. We have now gone beyond the materialists but still not quite beyond the atheists. Someone could accept all the results of these first three chapters, and still believe in an immobile, primal cosmic force that is the cause of all things but has no awareness of anything, no intelligence. For that matter, someone could still think the first cause has shape and size and a particular location—just an unchangeable location and an unchangeable shape and size. Next task: to see why the first cause must be acquitted of these charges as well.

4

Beyond Imagining

> The occasion of all these errors was that those thinking about divine things were misled by imagination, by means of which it is impossible to form anything but the image of a body.
>
> —Thomas Aquinas, *Summa Contra Gentiles*

Twenty Questions

When my children were little, they loved to play twenty questions. And at first they were incredibly bad at it. When it was their turn to ask yes-or-no questions in order to guess what I was thinking of, their first question would be something like "Is it a Gila monster?" I'd say no, and the next question would be something like "Is it a coral snake?" "No." "Is it a crocodile?" They'd burn through their twenty questions in this way and be amazed when it turned out I had been thinking about a banana. Eventually they learned that *no* was not simply "un-information" but could be very informative in direct proportion to the generality of the thing negated. "Not a Gila monster" told them very little. "Not an animal at all," on the other hand, and therefore either a vegetable or mineral, would have been a better beginning. (Eventually they caught on.)

The same rule applies in the search for the first cause. So far, we have learned mostly negative things about it. The negations have been pretty far-reaching, however, and therefore very informative in their way. The first cause is certainly not a Gila monster or a crocodile or a banana, since it cannot be anything mobile at all. And it cannot be matter, since it has no potential to acquire any new attributes. The next step is to negate another very general thing. Almost everything we know has dimensions—length, width, or depth. If something has all three of these, and therefore has a kind of completeness to it, we call it a body. (Some people say there are more than three dimensions, but we need not get into that.) What has only two dimensions is the surface of a body. What has only one dimension is the edge of a surface, or a line. The first cause, we shall see, cannot be a body and can have no dimensions at all.

The thought is not an easy one to think. Thomas Hobbes even called the phrase *incorporeal substance* a contradiction in terms. He is not alone in rejecting the notion. Once a friend of mine took part in a philosophical discussion that his pious old aunt happened to overhear. She was horrified to learn that her nephew believed that "God does not have a body." She pronounced him an atheist on the spot. To her mind, a God without a body was as good as no God at all. Another woman I know used to teach catechism to the children at her parish. One day, she was explaining this same idea, that God does not have a body. One of the kids said, "Wow. Just a head, huh?"

For us mere mortals, a nonbodily thing is not a natural thought. By our senses we seem to be aware exclusively of visible or tangible things, which are all bodies—dimensional things existing in specific places. I never bump into anything devoid of size, shape, and location. It is hard to see what that would even mean. To think that all real things are bodies, then, is not some cockamamy, ad hoc refuge for atheists. It is the default setting of the human mind. We cannot become convinced of nonbodily realities except by reasoning from the bodily reality we all acknowledge. One of my former colleagues (we'll call her Edith) used to call herself an empiricist, by which she meant that she believed in nothing but what she could see and touch. She had no time for what she called spiritual entities. She took her empiricism so far that she was not always sure she believed in things like atoms and electrons. (I have never known a more independent thinker than Edith.) I recall many discussions over lunch with her in which I tried to convince her that her empiricism was unreasonably narrow, that she had to admit the existence of at least some things that she could never see or touch. Years later, after she had passed away, a mutual friend had found among Edith's things an interesting scrap of paper on which she had jotted down a kind of personal creed, and it came into my hands. "I am an empiricist", it began. "I believe only in what I can see and touch." It went on to explain why she had never accepted various Christian doctrines. But the paper was obviously quite old, and she had evidently come back to it several times over the years, adding things in the margins in assorted colors of ink. Off to the right of the opening line, "I believe only in what I can see and touch", she had added, in small print, "and also in what can be *proved* from what I can see and touch". I like to think I had a hand in that. The amended rule might still be too narrow for a variety of reasons, but at least this much is quite true: the human mind cannot, by dint of its own ingenuity, grasp the existence of nonbodily things except by reasoning from what it knows about bodily ones.

Such reasoning is possible, however, and in the present stage of our investigation into the first cause, it is actually the easy part. Putting together positive proof that the first cause cannot be a body and cannot have dimensions is a piece of cake, really, given all the results of the last three chapters. We can afford to leave that business till the end of this chapter, since it will take little effort. The hard part is disentangling ourselves from the specious reasons for believing that everything in existence must be a body or that the first cause in particular must be one. They are the following.

Reason 1: Objector 1 begins by observing that if we can imagine something, then it can exist. "Can you imagine anything that cannot possibly exist?" he demands to know. "Can you imagine something impossible and self-contradictory, such as *a triangle that has no sides*? I confess I cannot, and I do not suppose you are any different. Very well, then. If we can imagine something, it must be capable of existing. That seems to make the imagination the measure of the possible. And that means if we *cannot* imagine something, then it *cannot* exist. We cannot imagine, for example, a thing without size, shape, and location. Therefore nothing like that can be." That is the first reason to think only bodies exist.

Reason 2: Objector 2 concerns himself with the first cause in particular, and he argues like this: "The simpler a thing is, the simpler our idea of it is. That means the simplest thing of all must correspond to our simplest idea. What is the simplest thing of all? The first cause, of course. It can involve no combinations within itself, since every combination requires a combiner, a prior cause, whereas the first cause has no prior cause. It is perfectly simple then. Our idea of it, too, must be the simplest of ideas, which means it comes to us easily and without lots of complex thinking. Ideas of nonbodily causes, on the other hand, come to us with great difficulty, and they are complex ideas, involving many negations. And we certainly cannot imagine things like that. The first cause accordingly cannot be a nonbodily thing, since that idea is too complex. Some sort of simple body, a fundamental particle, perhaps, must be the first cause." Richard Dawkins[1] seems to be thinking along these lines when, in *The God Delusion*, he calls it a beautifully simple idea that all things are made of a few kinds of fundamental particles.

Reason 3: The ancient philosopher Epicurus and his greatest admirer, Lucretius, give us a third reason to conclude that the only real things are bodies. Whatever is real must be capable of acting or of being acted on. If it cannot do anything or have anything done to it, then it is indistinguishable from what does not exist. The first cause, especially, must be something capable of acting. Nothing acts on anything else, though, except by contact with it. Everything active and real, therefore, is capable of contact with other things, and this means it must have a surface at which it can come into contact with other things. This means it is a body. Nothing can exist that is not a body, therefore, and especially not the first cause.

I see no quick way to dismiss these three arguments. They are mistakes, but they are subtle ones that contain important elements of truth. They demand careful and separate treatment if we are to sort out each one properly.

Human Imagination Is Not the Rule of the Possible

The first objector's starting point was that the imagination is the rule or standard for what is possible, because, if we can imagine something, then it can be. Let's start there. Is it true that if we can imagine something, then it can be? A statement like that does tend to strike a chord in the breast of every hopeful and industrious person. No doubt imagination was a necessary ingredient in discovering such possibilities as skyscrapers and moon landings. On the other hand, many grand schemes go flop, turn out to be impossible, and probably

[1] Richard Dawkins, *The God Delusion* (New York: First Mariner Books, 2008), p. 176.

a great many more fail than succeed. The alchemist's dream of turning lead into gold by chemical changes is now known to be quite impossible, despite the ease with which we can imagine ourselves boiling lead, adding various ingredients, and stirring it until it turns to gold. Imagining things can be a necessary step toward determining whether they are possible. But it is not always sufficient. To imagine a bunch of shapes, colors, and movements in some pattern might prove that it is possible for such shapes, colors, and movements to exist together outside the mind—say, on a computer monitor. At that superficial level, it is quite true that whatever we can imagine can be. But if these shapes, colors, and movements are supposed to depict certain kinds of underlying things that have definite properties and behaviors, it might be that what they are depicting is something entirely impossible. Suppose a film documents a house exploding or a person contracting cancer and then dying. Play the movie in reverse, and you get a bunch of colors and movements, but they depict a series of entirely impossible events, such as the dead being spontaneously raised to life and living life backward, and flying debris spontaneously coming together into the form of a house. It seems that the statement "If we can imagine it, then it can be" is true only about visual patterns and the like.

That is enough to hobble reason 1 for supposing that everything real is a body. More can be said, though. Suppose we granted that everything imaginable is possible without any restrictions. It still would not follow that everything unimaginable is impossible, which is what the objector wants to say next. Obviously everything visible is possible, but it hardly follows that everything invisible is impossible. Air is invisible. It is not therefore impossible. Again, it is indisputable that everything existing right now is possible. But it still doesn't follow that everything not existing right now is impossible. So even if we grant objector 1's initial premise that everything imaginable is possible, it still won't follow that everything not imaginable is impossible.

Not only does it not follow, but the statement "If we cannot imagine it, it cannot exist" seems to be entirely false. Certainly there are many things that fit both descriptions. A triangle with no sides cannot be imagined, nor can it exist. The mere "unimaginability" of something, however, does not prove it cannot exist. One common illustration of this goes back at least as far as the French philosopher René Descartes, who observed that it is not possible for us to imagine a 1,000-sided regular polygon, or at least not in a way that is distinct from our image of a 1,001-sided one or from our image of a circle. There is nevertheless nothing impossible about a 1,000-sided regular polygon. Other examples come to mind, too. I cannot imagine this wood's potential to be carved into a statue of Venus. Whenever I try, I imagine the outline of an *actual* statue of Venus floating around somewhere inside the block of wood. That is not the same thing as the wood's potential, since the potential statue is not the same as an actual statue. I cannot imagine the potential without making it actual, which is exactly what it isn't. And yet the potential is quite real. The wood really has the potential to be carved, and the air in the room really does not. I also cannot imagine what is common to all triangles. I understand very easily that being a three-sided plane figure is common to them all. I cannot form an image of anything common to them all, however. I can only imagine particular triangles with definite shapes that are *not* common to all other triangles.

These examples and many others like them prove that what is unimaginable can often be real or possible and also possible for us to understand. At the same time, these examples give the objector some credit for a certain truth implicit in his argument. The truth I mean is this: whenever we understand something that is unimaginable, we still have to imagine something, and the something we imagine must be relevant to the unimaginable thing. I cannot imagine a 1,000-sided polygon, but neither can I understand it if I don't imagine *something*, such as one side of it at a time or a circle. The images I form in my imagination when I conceive of something are not always images of the thing I am trying to conceive; sometimes they are images of the opposite of what I am trying to conceive, or images of something related to but distinct from it. When I conceive of the ductility of copper, I cannot imagine the ductility itself, but I can imagine copper actually being drawn into wire through a die. Similarly I can conceive of the ability of the wood to be carved into an infinity of different statues, although I cannot imagine that as such; instead, when conceiving it, I imagine several statues the wood might be carved into. And when I say, "A thing that is not a body", I imagine, of all things, a body. I form an image of the body being negated, rather than an image of the nonbodily thing itself. This need of ours to imagine something as an aid to our understanding is an important insight into ourselves and the inner working of our mental equipment. It explains why we naturally tend to think that all real things are bodies and why the idea of a nonbodily entity comes only with difficulty.

Simple Things versus Simple Ideas

The second objector suggested that the first cause must be something that is easy and simple for us to conceive and even imagine, such as fundamental particles. We already know that can't be true, since such things would be mobile, whereas the first cause is not. And anyone who supposes that real subatomic particles are easily imagined or simple to conceive should take a moment to thumb through a graduate-level textbook on the subject. Why, the dratted things defy imagination, as it turns out. The physicists can't agree as to whether they are waves or particles, or both or neither, or sometimes one and other times the other. The majority agree that no single model is entirely accurate, and the things cannot be properly pictured. Whatever the case, it is certainly not true that these simple things are simple to imagine or understand.

Particles were only the objector's suggestion, however. The objection itself was independent of that idea. It began with an apparently innocent rule: "The simpler a thing is, the simpler our idea of it is." But is that a good rule? Is it true?

Not always. Counterintuitive as it sounds, we sometimes find when we compare two things that the simpler thing must be understood through a more complex idea. In geometry we find a pair of things fitting this description: point and line. To anyone who took high school geometry in the decade I did, this will probably sound wrong at first. A line was defined for us as an infinite set of points, and a point was left undefined. Given these definitions, *point* is so simple an idea that it really needs no definition, and *line* includes *points* in its definition, so that the line—the more divisible and less simple thing—corresponds to the more complex idea, just as we would expect. But there is something amiss. My teachers always insisted that a point is *not a dot*. It has no size at all. If you think a point is just a teensy-weensy dot, then geometry will not be exact anymore. Besides, if you think a point has a tiny smidgen of length to it, then the ends of its length will be points, so that our "point" will have two endpoints. Ridiculous.

There is another problem. How can a line be just a set of points, if these have no length? If the points were all sitting there like ducks in a row, then if we pick any point on the line we please, there would have to be a *next* point right after it. How could that work? The next point could not sit right on top of the original point we chose, since on that showing they would be just one and the same point after all. Nor could the next point sit a little way off from the original point, since in that case we could draw a tiny line segment connecting them, and then an infinity of points would lie along the new line segment drawn between the original point and the supposedly next point. Quite absurd. So it does not seem feasible to define a line as a set of points, infinite or otherwise.

Years later, in Euclid, and in a number of more recent textbooks that have returned to definitions like his, I came across another set of definitions that made more sense. According to these definitions, a line is "what has length but no width or depth". A point is "what has no length and no width and no depth". It is essential to say that a point has no dimensions. If it had any, if it were like a tiny black circle, that would wreak havoc on all the theorems of geometry. Here, now, is the surprising thing. Although a point is a simpler thing than a line, its definition is actually a little bit more complex than the definition of a line. A line is something in space with length, no width, and no depth, whereas a point is something in space with no length, no width, and no depth. *Point* adds one more negation to the definition of *line*. It is also possible to define a point as the end of a line segment, in which case the notion of *point* is clearly more complex than that of *line*, since *line* is mentioned in the definition of *point*, and not the reverse.

Sometimes, then, it happens that the simpler of two things requires the more complex idea. Odd. Or perhaps not so odd. If I have not yet exhausted your patience with this illustration, I would like to make one more observation about the point and the line that might shed some light on why their definitions have this unexpected relationship. A point is harder to imagine than a bit of a line or a curve. I can imagine a curved line without imagining a point, as in the case of the circumference of a circle. But I cannot imagine a point without imagining it as the end of a line segment, or the corner of a cube, or the tip of a cone, or as a microscopic dot that is not truly a point at all but is really a tiny surface. The simple point cannot be imagined without imagining other things that are less simple than it. It is *too* simple for that. Precisely because it is so simple and indivisible, a point is less easily imagined than a line or a surface or a solid. It must be imagined together with lines or surfaces or solids. Little wonder, then, that it must also be defined through them, since our understanding of things depends upon their relationship to our imagination.

Returning, now, to objector 2. In the course of his reasoning, he asked us to grant that the idea of the simpler of two things is simpler. In many cases it is. Consider words and sentences, for example. A word is a simpler thing than a sentence, since every sentence is made of words, but no word is made of sentences. *Word* is also a simpler idea than *sentence*, since *word* is in the definition of *sentence*, but *sentence* is not in the definition of *word*. A sentence is a series of words expressing a complete thought, or something like that. A word is any vocal sound significant by human agreement, so *cat* counts as a word, although there is no idea of a sentence in that.

The same goes for water and hydrogen. Hydrogen is a simpler thing than water, since all water is made up of hydrogen and oxygen into the bargain, but no hydrogen is made up of water. *Hydrogen* is also a simpler idea than *water*, since *hydrogen* is in the chemist's definition of *water*, but *water* is not in the definition of *hydrogen*. In these examples, however, the simpler thing is actually a component or ingredient of the more complex one, and for that reason the simpler thing must enter into the definition of the more complex one. That is not the case with *point* and *line*, as we saw. The line cannot really be a set of points, although we can introduce points into it by dividing it. The point is simpler than the line, then, not because the line is made up of points, but because, unlike the line, the point has no parts—it is completely indivisible. Hence the definition of *line* need not include the definition of *point*, since it is not made up of points. And so the definition of *line* need not be more complex than the definition of *point*. More than that, we can imagine a hydrogen atom without imagining water, but we cannot imagine a point without imagining it as the end of a line segment or as a feature of some other divisible thing such as a cone or an angle. If anything, then, we must define *point* by *line* (as in "a point is the end of a line segment") or by *length* (as in "a point has no length"), so that the less simple things are components of the simplest thing's definition.

Which of these two kinds of examples, now, is the first cause more like? The first cause is simpler than any of its effects, but not because it is a component of them, as hydrogen is to water or a word to a sentence. That would make the first cause a kind of material capable of assuming different forms, which chapter 3 proved impossible. No, the first cause is simpler than any of its effects for the purely negative reason that in itself it involves none of the combination, potency, and mobility we find in all its effects. That is like the case of the point, which involves none of the combinations of line segments constituting a line and is not itself a component of a line either. The first cause is even less a part of its effects than a point is of a line, since a point can be the end of a line segment, whereas the first cause cannot be some feature or property of any other thing.

Objector 2 has made the mistake of thinking that our idea of the simpler of two things is always simpler. That is true when the simpler thing is a component of the more complex one, but otherwise it need not be true. And the first cause is not a component of anything, and consequently our idea of its simplicity must come from negating the kinds of complexity we find in all other things. It is too simple for us to imagine or for us to understand first and by itself. We must understand it by distinguishing it from all other things of which it is the cause, which requires a series of negations.

The Fallacy of the Elephant

The third reason for supposing that every real thing must be a body was founded on the idea of acting by contact. This reasoning commits a logical fallacy called begging the question, or assuming the very thing to be proved. Egocentric elephants might try to prove they are the only animals in existence by a similar argument. They

could say to themselves, "There can be no animals other than us elephants. Why not? Because all animals must make a living somehow,
which demands action. But action requires gripping things with one's
trunk. And only we elephants have trunks. Therefore ..." Ah yes,
but "gripping things with one's trunk" is elephant specific, whereas
other animals besides elephants might have other modes of action
not requiring the use of a trunk. The argument will not work, then,
unless we first assume there are no animals in existence besides elephants. And that is assuming the very thing we are trying to prove.
Likewise, acting by means of body contact is body specific, and there
might be other things besides bodies, and they might be causes in
their own way. The argument will not work, then, unless we first
assume there are no things in existence besides bodies. And that is the
very point in dispute.

Anthropomorphism

There was once a philosopher named Xenophanes who lived before
Socrates and who made some rather astute observations about our
anthropomorphic tendencies. We humans, believers in gods and dis-
believers alike, are prone to understand each thing by imagining it.
That becomes a cause of error when the thing we try to imagine
happens to be unimaginable. Imaginable things are akin to us, somehow, because they are accommodating to the modus operandi of our
mental faculties. It is not always a mistake to say that something else
accommodates us in this or that way, of course. But to make things
resemble us or correspond to us just because that is the default setting
of our minds, well, that is dangerous. By itself it is no guarantee of
truth. Here is Xenophanes on the subject:

> Mortals think that the gods are born, and that they have clothes and
> speech and bodies of their own.
>   Ethiopians declare that their gods are snub-nosed and black, Thra-
> cians that theirs have pale blue eyes and flame-colored hair.
>   But if oxen or horses or lions had hands, and with their hands could
> draw and make things as men can, horses would draw the forms of the
> gods like horses, oxen like oxen, and they would make their bodies
> like the bodies they have themselves.

There is one god, the greatest among gods and men, not at all similar to mortals in body or in mind.

He stays always in the same place, moving not at all. Nor does it befit him to go elsewhere at another time.

The whole of him sees, the whole of him thinks, the whole of him hears.

Aloof from hard work, he sways all things by the thought of his mind.[2]

If it is anthropomorphic and without rational foundation to suppose that gods, if they exist, must produce their effects only with effort and must have bodies that resemble ours, might it not be anthropomorphic and without rational foundation to suppose they have bodies at all? Why, after all, do we presume that what is real must be a body, if not because we ourselves have bodies, find ourselves surrounded by bodies, and know bodies first and best?

Why the First Cause Cannot Have Dimensions

At the outset of this chapter I promised that the argument showing that the first cause has no dimensions would be a quickie. So here it is. The first cause has no mobility or potential (see chapter 3). But every body has both mobility and the potential to be newly qualified in various ways and cannot cause anything independently of mobility in itself and other things. Therefore, the first cause cannot be a body. Voilà. Other arguments could be given, but brevity is a virtue, and so I will content myself with just this one.

The first cause is incorporeal then. It is not a body—not a thing of three or more dimensions. Much less is it a thing of fewer dimensions, like a surface or an edge, since that would make it a property inhering in a body, depending on it to exist, and mobile together with it. No. It is altogether distinct from the dimensional world.

My dear old friend Edith, had she come this far, would have said that the first cause must be one of those "spiritual entities". But I hesitate to assert that just now. The word *spirit* is not a synonym for

---

[2] Xenophanes, fragments DK14, DK16, DK15, DK23, DK26, DK24, and DK25. My translation.

not a body, since it has positive content as well. It implies emotion, or will, or thought and meditation, as in "a spiritual person" or "a spiritual experience" or even "a spirited discussion". But we have no reason yet to attribute thought or will to the first cause, and to say it must have a mind just because we do—well, that's anthropomorphic again. There are also meanings of the word *spirit* not tied to thought, but none of them is appropriate to the first cause. Hard liquor is called spirits, maybe because it can lift our spirits or make our conversation more spirited, but most probably because its vapors are volatile (hence *mineral spirits*). But the first cause is not spiritual like a vapor or a fume. It is not thin, invisible, dimensional stuff, flying about. It is not dimensional at all. And it has no motion at all.

The first cause is also nondimensional in a way different from a geometrical point. If points can exist outside the mind at all, they exist in bodies. That means they are in some way mobile—as the point at the tip of a cone moves along with the cone. The first cause, however, is in no way mobile, and it cannot depend on bodies or on the human mind to exist. The first cause is not a point.

But enough negation. The first cause is not material, not mobile, not dimensional. Not, not, not. What *is* it? It is time to start thinking positive.

5

The Most Intensely Existing Thing

The business of an animal is not only to reproduce (which is
common to all living things), but they all of them also participate in a kind of knowledge (some more, some less, some
very little indeed), because they have sense-perception, which
is a kind of knowledge. But the worth we assign it hinges on
whether we look at it compared with intelligence or with the
class of lifeless things. Compared with intelligence it seems
like almost nothing to have a share of touch and taste alone,
but compared with the absence of all sensation it appears a
great thing. For even this form of knowledge would appear
a precious thing compared with lying in a state of death or
of nonexistence.

—Aristotle, *Generation of Animals*

"No Better Than a Worm"

The year was 1995. It was my last year of graduate school and my first
year as an instructor for two introductory courses in philosophy for
undergrads. The practice of having grad students teach undergrads is
widespread, although it is often unpopular with parents footing big
tuition bills from private schools. But tenured faculty love it; they
get lighter teaching loads and more time for research. Administrators
love it; grad students are cheap labor. The undergrads have various
reactions. Some love green teachers because their youth increases
the odds that they will be hip or good-looking. Others, like their
parents, resent the idea that their teacher is wet behind the ears and
does not hold a doctorate. But teachers have to learn how to teach
sometime, somewhere. And there is nothing magical about the con-
ferral of a degree that endows its recipient with teaching ability. That

comes mainly with experience. Maybe we should institute teaching schools like teaching hospitals, with lower tuition rates and faculties composed of rookies. Anyway, many of my grad-school peers heard complaints from their undergrad students about their age: "How old are you?" "Are you really a professor?" "Aren't you dating my room-mate?" I had no such problems. My first gray hair appeared when I was in seventh grade. By 1995, my hairline was in a deep recession, and what hair I had left was as much salt as pepper. My students probably thought I was in my late forties. In reality I was as green as anyone can be, and I remember my teaching blunders at that time quite vividly. It is one of these I must now relate.

On this particular day, I was supposed to present various famous arguments for the existence of a god. One of these was the fourth way of Thomas Aquinas, one of his famous five proofs for the exis-tence of God. It was a tough argument loaded with odd statements that have accumulated objections through the centuries. While pre-paring the night before, I reviewed all the scholarly objections I knew of, in case my students should happen to think up anything like them and wish to discuss them. They didn't. Instead they objected to the one premise to which I had given no special attention—the seem-ingly innocent statement "Some things are better than others." One young woman in particular (I'll call her Catherine) raised her hand and wanted a clarification.

"That just means some things are better *to you*, right? Because other things might be better *to me*. 'Better' is subjective, isn't it?"

Looking back now, I am amazed I hadn't seen that coming. Still, I was quick enough on my feet. I steered the conversation away from ethics and art and parked it squarely in the natural world. Surely she would grant that living things were "objectively" superior to non-living ones, for example, and that among living ones those endowed with sensation were superior to those without it? No such luck. She cocked her head to one side and squinted with the classic expression of skepticism.

"I thought Darwin disproved that", she said. "Doesn't 'the sur-vival of the fittest' mean every species is well adapted for its particular survival? Do you just mean some species survive longer than others?"

Well, no, that *wasn't* all I meant. I meant that one kind of thing could be nobler and better than another, regardless of how long either one survived.

As Catherine continued pursuing the Darwinian line, I noticed my other students' facial expressions and body language. They were all leaning in, enjoying the show. I suppose it was fun to watch their classmate wipe up the floor with a professor in his late forties. When Catherine pointed out that preferring one species to another was subjective and not a matter of objective truth, their eyes positively sparkled with mischievous pleasure.

But I was not yet at a loss for words.

"Really?" I said. "You wouldn't admit any inequality among species besides the lengths of time they have been around? I mean, you think that your mother is a better creature than a worm, don't you?"

Until that moment her classmates had been staring at me. Now all eyes were on her. And I will never forget what happened next. A distinct blush appeared in her cheeks, climbing right up to her ears as she said, loudly and clearly, "*Objectively* speaking, my mother is no better than a worm."

I was stunned. To judge by their faces, so were her classmates. And I was mortified. I felt as though I had unintentionally played a cheap trick on this poor young woman, who certainly had not gotten out of bed that morning with the idea of saying any such thing. How did this happen? Why was she willing to bite the bullet and say what she said rather than qualify her previous statements or at least pause a moment to think? She was not a stubborn or willful person. She was not incapable of amending her view. In subsequent classes, to my relief, she remained her cheerful and talkative self. No harm had been done. She did not hate me or my class. But what she had said stuck with me. She obviously had not wanted to say it. And yet she had somehow felt she had to.

Natural Superiorities and the Democratic Principle of Equality

I have told this story because in this chapter we will secure our first positive attribute of the first cause beyond the mere fact that it is a first cause and it exists. This new attribute is *supreme being*. By *being*, here, I don't mean an intelligence—not yet—just a thing that has being, a thing that exists. By calling the first cause the supreme being, I mean that among all existing or possible things, it is the best, the most complete, the noblest, the most perfect. That is what I hope to show. But before doing that, circumstances oblige me to clarify my meaning further and to address certain common concerns about superiority and inferiority.

I first learned that lesson from Catherine, and I am grateful to her. Looking back now with the benefit of much more experience, I think I have an idea of what was going on in her mind. If she had been a bio major, I might have diagnosed her with what is called scientism, an excessively and inappropriately scientific outlook on the world to the detriment of good common sense. That can sometimes result from hyperspecialized training coupled with a lack of exposure to other disciplines and methods. But she had not been a bio major. I cannot swear to it, but I think she was an English-lit major. It was not a case of scientism then. Something more common had motivated her. I now think it was a cultural phenomenon. True, scraps of Darwinian thinking had filtered into her mind, but they were not the real cause of her condition. They merely confirmed ideas that had been sown in her mind long beforehand.

We modern democratic spirits don't care much for "superiorities". We don't usually look for them in the world, much less hope for them, and generally don't care for them when we meet them. Now, I am no different. I am no closet aristocrat or monarchist, and I have every reason to think that had I lived in an aristocratic time and place, I would have found myself permanently situated among the have-nots and at the service of the haves, much to my chagrin. My life, I am certain, is better because of the democratic evolutions and revolutions that preceded it, and I find myself with a certain amount of education and even leisure that I would otherwise almost certainly never have come by. I also believe, as most people do nowadays, that there is a deep-down equality among human beings and that all decent treatment of our neighbors and every just form of government must respect that truth in one way or another.

Nonetheless it is possible to take the principle of equality too far—to take it outside the political realm altogether, for example, and to suppose that the whole universe is founded upon the principle of equality, as though it were a giant democracy and any pretended superiority of one entity to another must be a foul lie and must be put down. Alexis de Tocqueville, in his *Democracy in America*, explored at length the tendency of democratic peoples, and of Americans in particular, to see all things through the lens of equality. Many of his observations, while not always flattering, seem to be even truer and more relevant today than when he made them in the nineteenth century. There are, of course, many inequalities that even we democratic souls find undeniable—inequalities of height, wealth, strength, education, and so on. But the more these things are conceived as add-ons that any of us might achieve (so long as we are provided with an equal opportunity), the more they fall in line with the basic principle of equality and the less they bother us.

It is the rock-bottom inequalities we don't like. They smack of aristocracy. If one fellow thinks he's just *better* than another, by birth, as it were, and not just because of certain things he has achieved that the other fellow also might achieve if only he applied himself—that stinks of aristocracy. If that one man thinks himself a better kind of being, with a nature permanently outranking that of the other, and to which the other and his ilk ought not even to *aspire*—that is contrary to the principle of equality. The principle of equality makes human beings all of one basic nature, although sharing unequally in advantages and disadvantages as fortune and history would have it. When we are talking about human beings, the principle of equality, thus understood, rings true. I do not regard myself as existing for the sake of making life better for the haves, for my superiors, any more than I conceive of others as existing to make life better for me. And although I must countenance many inequalities among human beings, I see none that would justify segregating them into castes in which the lower lived purely for the happiness of the higher.

There is much more merit than this in the principle of equality, but right now I am concerned with certain distortions that an undiscerning worship of equality can introduce into our thinking. One of these, of particular relevance to what follows, is to suppose that it is not just human beings, but all animals, even all living things, that are fundamentally equal. That, it seems to me, is arrant nonsense. I do not mean it is obvious that plants and animals exist for our sake—although I do not deny this, and I lose no sleep over slapping a mosquito on my neck. I only mean that our human lives are richer and more complete than the lives of any animals or plants. Since I will be arguing from that sort of inequality momentarily, I cannot proceed without first addressing the common prejudice against it.

Are You Better Than a Microbe?

If A is superior to B in some respect, our democratic instinct is to look for some other respect in which B is superior to A, as though everything is basically equal, after all—as though the very respects of comparison might not themselves be unequal! A man is better than a cockroach at composing epic poetry, granted, but a cockroach is better than a man at scuttling into small places and eking out a living under the most trying of circumstances. Harvard biologist Stephen Jay Gould was fond of saying that by the only objective standard— namely, success at surviving—microbes win the superiority contest hands down. They outdo us by far in how long they've been around, how long they will be around, how many of them there are, and how much biomass they constitute.

This view has a certain appeal and even some truth. It is appealing because it gives off the pleasant odor of humility. And we can't help but feel good about ourselves for being modest enough to make such admissions as "The microbes have bested us." And there is truth in such observations. In a quantitative way, microbes and many other things, living and nonliving, surpass us. I once took my two boys to Sequoia National Park. I had heard about the awe the giant sequoias tend to inspire. Somehow I did not think I would feel it. I was wrong. Those solemn creatures filled me with admiration, even emotion. Here was a magnificence, a longevity, a primal beauty that we fragile humans cannot hope to enjoy in this world. And yet, just in this very acknowledgment, we can also see that we *do* enjoy these attributes of the giant sequoia. In fact, we enjoy them more than the sequoias do themselves. I would rather be little and short-lived me and rejoice in the ancientness and grandeur of much-admired General Sherman (that is the present name of the largest sequoia) than trade places with him. I do not truly envy his three thousand years of life. I would rather live thirty of mine than thirty thousand of his. And why is that? It is because my life includes his, somehow, but his does not include mine. Old Sherman is a part of me, now that I know him, but he is oblivious to me and even to himself.

The quantities of life are not unimportant. There is a dignity, and something divine, in living for thousands of years or in towering over other things. But these superiorities are of a lesser kind. To rank them ahead of qualitative superiorities is to turn things upside down. If we took as our principal measure of dignity how much space and time things take up, we would get the inverted pyramid Gould endorsed. Intelligent life would be simply inferior to nonintelligent life. For that matter, life would be inferior to nonlife, since nonliving things can be much bigger and older than Sherman and are far better at continuing to exist in diverse environments that we would consider extreme.

The glaring truth, however, is that "how good it is at enduring through tough circumstances" is not an objective standard of the intrinsic merit of a certain type of life. So too "how good it is at multiplying its numbers" is an entirely extrinsic standard. These are measures of survival power and reproductive power but are no measures at all of the worth of the thing surviving and reproducing. Absurd myths, errors, and superstitions often have a way of perpetuating themselves and sometimes become more commonly believed than the truth; it does not follow that the errors are therefore, objectively and simply speaking, superior things to the truth. Survival itself, in fact, is never desirable unconditionally, not even for the survivor. It is desirable only on condition that the life of the survivor is somehow worth living.

For my part, I would rather be me for a short life than a tree for a long one. I would rather live just fifty years with all my faculties than be deaf, blind, stuck in one place, and paralyzed for three thousand, like old Sherman. Similarly, the superior survival power of one species over another does not prove the superiority of what is surviving. What is it that survives, anyway? If we are talking about survival for millions of years, the only "it" that survives is the species. It is not really a living thing at all, but a mere commonality found in diverse individuals. It is more like a mental construct than a reality. All that really ever exists or lives and acts is the individual. And if we compare the individual microbe with an individual human being, all of a sudden we find that the human wins even when it comes to taking up time and space.

A truer and more principal measure of the dignity of things is to see how rich they are capable of becoming within themselves and how much they are masters of their own actions rather than the instruments of other things. That is to look to what *being* and *living* mean, to what they consist in, rather than to some extrinsic measure, such as how many instances there are of it or how long it exists. But I will not insist on this. If anyone acknowledges the qualitative superiorities of one kind of being over another, I will not demand a further acknowledgment that this kind of superiority is superior to the quantitative kind. The main thing is to see that both kinds exist and that among familiar things there is roughly an inverse relationship between them. The creatures that exist for the longest time are also the ones with the most superficial existence. The stone outdoes the man in quantitative terms, but the man outdoes the stone in quality of existence. That is the sort of thing I want to elaborate on now.

The vegetable is superior to the mineral by quality-of-existence standards. The plant takes action for itself, using minerals as instruments for making its living. It does not know that it is doing this, perhaps, but it does it nonetheless. It is an entity that can draw other things into itself, quite literally, and make them parts of itself. A tree can take in its surroundings, in some sense, bringing things outside itself into itself, incorporating them into its own substance, its own life, and making them do its bidding, as it were. By its roots it takes hold of the earth, grasping something other than itself to its own advantage. It absorbs water, minerals, gases, and sunlight and puts them to work. It makes them partakers of its own internal actions, by which it persists, and increases itself, and multiplies its kind. No stone can do the like.

A stone is just a stone, incapable of bringing anything outside itself into its service or internal action. It resists the world, excludes it, and keeps it sharply outside itself. It might get taken in by something else, but nothing else gets taken in by it. Nothing ever gets conscripted into the business of being the rock. We might suppose that a sedimentary rock, which is built up slowly by addition of layers, takes things to itself. But really this is the attachment of things to the outside of what is already there, not an enrichment of its interior, as it were. It is an accretion. The same can be said for crystals, which in some sense grow, but what is added is added to their outside, not drawn within and actively dissolved and assimilated.

The plant is therefore a nobler entity than a stone—it more truly "does" things than the stone, more truly acts for itself, and its parts are more truly united in a common enterprise, regularly bearing each other's burdens toward the promotion of the whole.

The animal is a quantum leap up. By *animal* I mean something that, besides all the assimilative aspects of the plant, has also sensation, however rudimentary. And by *sensation* I mean any sort of interior awareness of the here and now. This is not a "performance" definition of sensation, as in "a capacity to respond in a definite way to specific stimuli", by which definition a thermostat or even a mousetrap is "sensitive". It refers first of all to the kind of thing we each experience directly in ourselves: seeing, hearing, smelling, tasting, feeling warmth, and anything else of the kind that connects us to things seen, heard, smelled, tasted, and felt, without erasing the distinction between ourselves and those objects. These impressions are our windows looking out from ourselves to the other things in existence. And I cannot take seriously those who suppose only we humans have experiences such as these, while all the things we call animals are mere robots with no interior experiences of their own. Dogs, cats, and horses also have a share in sense life, and they clearly have pleasures and pains.

The animal surpasses the plant, then, in being alive in this heightened way. Beyond the plant, the animal enjoys an additional form of interior existence, a sense life, into which it can draw things from the outside without ceasing to be itself and without destroying them and sometimes without even affecting them. It is not like Vegetable 2.0 but is an altogether novel thing. The animal has sensation, at least the sense of touch, by which it can bring other things into itself in a subtler way than the tree does. It has an awareness of them, and forms interior impressions of the world around it. The tree can take things in only in a spatial sense; the things must themselves enter into the tree bodily, as it were, and they must cease to be "out there" where they had been before being taken in. But by the sense of sight you can take in the stars and take in the mountains and take in the sunset and any number of other things without their entering into your physical constitution. Certainly they affect your sight by means of light, which must enter your eyes in a spatial sense, but by means of this you are put in touch with the things "out there" that remain "out there" and don't get pulled into your body. They become parts of your inner life, but you leave them be.

It is not always obvious, of course, whether an organism is endowed with sensation in the sense in which I now intend it. Dogs, cats, and horses obviously have it. Worms, too, though they obviously have less of it, and what they have they have less obviously. Amoebas are tougher, and what about Venus flytraps, and the uncanny ability of climbing plants to wind themselves around specific objects? Do they have the sense of touch, or are they just chemically responsive to external stimuli in self-serving ways? When an oak tree is attacked by some destructive insect, it releases chemicals that other oaks receive, stimulating them to produce compounds that the bugs don't like to eat; even oaks that have not been attacked by the bugs respond in this way. Is this communication? A sign of thoughtful strategy? Probably not. At least, a stimulus-specific response is not sufficient proof of interior awareness. But if the response is specific enough, and beneficial, it can mimic what sensitive creatures do for themselves through sensation. A scanner has no interior awareness of a barcode as we do by sight, but it can react to one as though it did. The wine glass shatters when the singer reaches the right pitch. But this is not because the glass heard the singing and deplored it. It was vibrated by the pulses in the air and shaken apart. Without being plucked, the strings on the guitar play a note along with your humming, if you hit the proper note. But that is not because the strings hear the tune and wish to hum along. So it is possible for nonsensing things to react much as sensing things do, yet without truly sensing. Among living things, similarly, there seem to be many that produce specific responses, even self-beneficial ones, without any awareness of what they are doing. And it is these that have traditionally been called plants.

Among the animals, there are many that it would be difficult or impossible to rank in terms of a superiority of life. Which is more alive, a fox or a dog? Maybe neither one has more life, more interior richness, than the other; maybe they merely have diverse adaptive means for supporting that life within, while the degree to which they can be called alive is more or less the same. It is not important for the present. But there can be no doubt that there are inequalities. If some animals, such as the sponge, the hydra, the coral, and maybe the amoeba, have no sense other than certain types of touch or taste, these are clearly inferior to animals endowed with more senses, especially the sense of sight. A horse, for example, can see and in some sense recognize others of its own kind, can spot an enemy at a distance, and can take in its surroundings all at once, in stunning detail, in a way that the sense of touch could never compete with. There is a much larger part of the world at large inside a horse than inside an animal confined to the sense of touch. Thanks to its enviable mobility, the horse can roam about, taking in many more environments than an animal that is for its lifetime glued to a particular rock in the ocean. More than that, the life of a horse seems to involve more than mere survival. It appears to delight in its senses and in its interactions with others of its kind. Horses and dogs can have a social life. Puppies play—or at least this is a plausible understanding of them—whereas it is incredible to suppose that oysters or corals play with one another. A dog or horse has a much richer life than an amoeba does. The horse lives in a much larger world—the amoeba is more closed in on itself, to say nothing of the plant. The world inside a horse's mind, while limited, might look almost recognizable to us, if we could form an inkling of it.

Even the horse's world is a tiny, contracted thing, however, compared with the world inside a full-grown, healthy, educated man. I suppose I could quote Shakespeare praising the godlike reason of man. I will restrain myself. It should be enough to say that a man can have in his head stars and galaxies whirling about and the possibility of alien life and of gods; and that he can think of the remote past and of the remote future and about all species of living things he encounters. The horse, meanwhile, noble beast that it is, does not even seem to notice that there *are* stars. At least, I have never caught one gazing up at them in wonder.

This preliminary sketch should be sufficient to lend color and depth to several of the premises in the arguments now to follow.

You Can't Get Blood from a Turnip

Mineral, vegetable, animal, human. These kinds of beings form a ladder of sorts. Ascending from one rung to another, we find something more capable of including other beings within its own being. That

was the point of the preceding reflections. We are not now trying
to work out all the distinct rungs of the ladder, however. We want to
identify its highest rung. What has the most being? Out of all things
in existence, which one is most all inclusive of the various forms
of being?

The answer is the first cause. It, and it alone, contains all other
beings, all modes of existence whatsoever, in its own being. The first
cause, in other words, is the supreme being. The proof of this rests
on a fundamental axiom. That axiom, like many others, appears to
admit of exceptions, but once we consider it carefully enough, we
can see that it really does not. For that reason, I will spend this section discussing the axiom I have in mind before applying it. It is this:
"Nothing gives what it does not have." One popular version is more
colorful: "You can't get blood from a stone", or, as another variation
has it, "You can't get blood from a turnip." That's because (surprise,
surprise) a stone (or a turnip) has no blood to give. The expression is
most commonly employed in money matters. As I mentioned a couple of chapters ago, try as you might, you can't get a million dollars
out of me, for the excellent reason that I haven't got it.

Clearly the general version of our axiom—"Nothing gives what it
does not have"—is not limited to money. It applies to anything that
can be said to give something. Causes, for example. A sculptor gives
the marble a new shape. A teacher gives information to students. A
fire gives off heat. To be an active cause is to give an actuality to
something. That means a cause must always possess in advance the
type of actuality it gives. We could call this the turnip axiom.

My brightest students have taught me that even axioms—or especially axioms—can look as if they admit of exceptions when we
descend into particulars. The general statement "Nothing gives what
it does not have" appears self-evident enough. But now say, "No
cause gives what it does not have", and apparent counterexamples
leap to mind. Fire blackens paper but is not itself black. A five-foot
man can have a six-foot son. A chemistry book confers knowledge
of chemistry while itself having none. A murderer brings death to his
victim but is not himself dead. All kinds of things appear to give what
they do not have!

Not a single one of these is a true counterexample, however. The
fire does not really "give blackness"; it gives heat, which destroys the

chemical composition of the paper. The blackness is just the natural property of the resulting compounds. The five-foot father does not exactly give his child his height, but, together with the mother, confers a set of genes that enable the child (with sufficient nourishment) to reach a height of six feet. The parents by themselves are not sufficient causes of the height attained and therefore don't have to have it fully themselves. The chemistry book gives knowledge to readers only by striking their eyes with word patterns that signify the concepts in which the science of chemistry consists. So really it does have what it gives—namely, the signs of certain concepts—but it neither has, nor gives, the understanding of those signs. The murderer is a slightly different story. A murderer who stabs me in the chest with a knife gives me a new concave shape I did not have before, the same shape the knife has (although in a different way—namely, convexly), and this shape in me is incompatible with my vital functions. He causes my death, in other words, not by "giving me death", but by giving me other positive things that are incompatible with my life. You can see how it often happens that an axiom is more readily grasped as an abstract generality than in its concrete application. But it remains that no cause can give what it does not have.

Must the cause possess an actuality in the same way its effect will receive it? Sometimes that happens, but not always. When a teacher has finished teaching, his student might understand the matter exactly as he does. But the plan of a house exists in the carpenter quite differently from the way it exists in the house itself. One fire produces another just like itself. But friction can produce heat or an electric charge, even though friction is itself neither of these things.

If these differences between cause and effect are possible, is there any rule at all about the manner in which the cause must contain the effect? There is. The cause must contain the same type of actuality to be conferred upon the effect, either in the same way or else in a superior way. It is possible for the cause to give exactly what it has. But it is also possible for it to give something less than what it has or a part of what it has. The teacher can communicate all his knowledge to the student if the student is able to receive it all. But the carpenter cannot communicate all that is in his mind to the materials for a house. He has many house plans in mind, but the lumber pile is capable of receiving only one. The carpenter is also a human being who is more than just a carpenter, so he will have many other things in his mind besides plans for houses, most of which the lumber pile cannot receive at all. The form of a house, as we find it in the house, limits its recipient to having just the form of the house and nothing else. As it exists in the mind of the carpenter, the form of a house does not limit him to having just that one form. In this way, the house plan in the mind of the carpenter has a mode of existence superior to the one it has in the house. The same form is found first in the mind of the carpenter and later in the house, but its mode of being is less constricting in the first than in the second. That is one way in which the actuality of the cause can surpass that of the effect.

The actuality in the cause can also simply be more intense than it is in the effect. The fire is hotter than the water it boils. The motion of the hands rubbing together is more unified and organized than the far more random motions, known as heat, which it produces among the molecules of the hands.

And it is always true that a cause possesses its actuality more self-sufficiently than its effect does, as long as the cause is actively causing.

So in one or more of these ways, the actuality in a cause can exceed the corresponding actuality in its effect, for the simple reason that a thing can give less than it has, but no more.

The Supreme Being

The relevance of all this to the first cause is straightforward. The first cause produces all actualities in things. Therefore, by the turnip axiom ("nothing gives what it does not have"), the first cause possesses in itself all types of actualities found in things. And that makes the first cause the supreme being, the most intensely existing thing. A stone is nothing but a stone and does not possess anything beyond that single nature. The tree not only has its own nature, but it also grasps the stone with its roots and uses the stone for its own treeish ends. The tree "has" the stone, has actively appropriated it and enlisted it in its service. The bird does the tree one better. It not only uses the tree, but sees it, smells it, feels it. The bird takes in many things through its senses. The eye of the eagle is even all encompassing in its way. The aquiline outlook does not have room, however, for the expansion of the universe.

Among animals, it is a uniquely human privilege to take hold of the universe itself, however imperfectly. Man is a microcosm—all things writ small. And yet his assimilation of things remains incomplete. The human imagination misses many things, and for the human intellect countless questions persist. No single creature, not even a human being, actually possesses all forms of things in itself, except maybe the universe, if it is right to call it a single thing. Even it does not really pass muster. It once contained dodos and T. rexes but no longer. Those one-time actualities have sunk back into the ocean of potentiality. Perhaps the universe contains the potential for all things, but it certainly does not contain them all in an actual way. By the foregoing argument, however, the first cause must possess every actuality in itself, not potentially, but actually. (The first cause, remember, is in no way potential.)

This conclusion is the deathblow to pantheism. The pantheist makes the supreme being the sum total of things or else the stuff underlying them all and persisting through their comings and goings. But that grand collection (as much as its underlying stuff) is changeable, increasing and decreasing the number of natures actually represented in it. It cannot, then, possess all actualities at once. But the first cause does. And so it is a superior being. Besides, the universe is the continuous effect of the first cause, and so the first cause must contain whatever actuality is found in the universe, but the universe need not—cannot—represent the full actuality of the first cause.

Even if we supposed the universe contained all particular natures in actuality, not just in its potential, it would not do so in the manner of the first cause. The universe contains all things only as a multitude of actualities somehow united in one order. The unity of the universe is merely the connection between distinct actualities; it is not a single, indiscriminate actuality. But the first cause is a single, indiscriminate actuality. There is only one first cause. And it cannot consist in the connection of distinct things, since every connection presupposes a connector, whereas the first cause presupposes nothing. The first cause is not a vast collection of things. It has to be a single, separate actuality, containing other actualities not as its parts or components, but in the way a single cure can contain all the benefit of a multitude of merely palliative treatments, or as a single proof can contain all the power of a multitude of merely plausible arguments.

This understanding of the manner in which the first cause contains all the actualities it causes in things avoids a number of absurdities. For example, the first cause is the cause of catfish. Is it therefore a catfish? Is it by parity of reasoning winged and four legged? Does it possess a nose? A beak? A trunk? A proboscis? Mandibles? Leaves? And since it is the cause of all qualities in the world, must these qualities also belong to the first cause itself? Must we say that the first cause is sweet, hot, loud, circular, and green? And if so, why not say that it is sour, triangular, and red while we're at it? All these notions, apart from being rather ridiculous in themselves, run afoul of what we already know about the first cause—namely, that it has no body, no magnitude, no dimension.

Where, then, does this reasoning go wrong? It goes wrong in assuming that the actuality in the cause always deserves the same name as the actuality it produces in the effect. We first saw the flaw in that thinking back in chapter 3. The cause of a thing's changing can also be changing, but it doesn't have to be. Why not? Because change is always an incomplete and unfinished business, as long as it is going on, as the act of learning something is an incomplete version of the act of understanding it. Understanding can cause learning without being an instance of learning itself. Similarly, any particular being that is limited, that has its own peculiar actualities but is lacking others, can be caused by something having a fuller share of the actualities of things, something that therefore differs from it in kind and does not receive its name. A house, for instance, need not be produced by another house—heck, it can't be; it is produced instead by a carpenter.

And what about actual rottenness or ugliness or lopsidedness? Are those qualities to be attributed to the first cause? Is it blind and lame and stupid? Richard Dawkins, in *The God Delusion*, with his usual charm and humor, raises this sort of difficulty in the middle of his critique of Aquinas' fourth way to prove the existence of God. First he paraphrases (rather than quotes) the argument of Aquinas, and then he deals the would-be coup de grâce:

> *The Argument from Degree.* We notice that things in the world differ. There are degrees of, say, goodness or perfection. But we judge these degrees only by comparison with a maximum. Humans can be both

good and bad, so the maximum goodness cannot rest in us. Therefore there must be some other maximum to set the standard for perfection, and we call that maximum God.

That's an argument? You might as well say, people vary in smelliness but we can make the comparison only by reference to a perfect maximum of conceivable smelliness. Therefore there must be a pre-eminently peerless stinker, and we call him God. Or substitute any dimension or comparison you like, and derive an equally fatuous conclusion.[1]

This is supposed to force us to admit either that certain incongruous particularities belong to the first cause or that certain degrading attributes must belong. I have already dealt with the incongruous particularities (such as "winged" or "four-legged"). As to the degrading attributes, something more needs to be said. "Stinky" might be a particular actuality just as much as "aromatic". And we have already dealt with particular, limited actualities. But what about "bad" or "evil"? That seems no more particular than "good" or "perfect". So why attribute only *good* qualities to the first cause? Why not bad ones? And if it cannot have both at once because of their contrariety—although we have equal reason to say it has both—then shouldn't we say there are two first causes, a good one and a bad one? That would explain the presence of evil in the world rather neatly. And so it is that many people have gone down this road.

But it is a dead end. We have already seen (in chapter 2) that there cannot be more than one first cause. Besides, there is no need to posit a cause of defects as there is a need to admit a cause of positive actualities. This is the main thing Dawkins overlooked in Aquinas' fourth way—namely, that it was precisely about things that need productive causes. It was about perfections only, not defects. Stinkiness is therefore quite irrelevant.

Defects or deficiencies are not really actualities existing in the world as much as absences of actualities that could, but don't, exist in certain places and things. Physicists don't look for a cause of darkness, for example, except in the sense of finding a body that is absorbing or blocking light. There is no notion that there is some source in the universe that is emanating darkness for the obvious reason that

---

[1] Richard Dawkins, *The God Delusion*, p. 102.

darkness is not a *thing* to be emanated. It is just the absence of a thing—namely, light. Similarly, blindness consists in the absence of sight, and although we speak of causes that are productive of blindness, the only positive thing they really produce is certain other qualities (such as cataracts) that replace the ones on which sight depends. Any deficiency involves an absence, and the name of the deficiency chiefly designates that absence. Illness means the absence of health. Poverty means an absence of wealth and the goods it affords. But there is no active cause of the absence as such, since nonbeing does not really require a positive cause. There are only two ways in which something might be called an active cause of absence or nonbeing: (1) by being the active cause of the being of something and then withdrawing its action, as when a song stops because a singer stops singing or a light goes out because it is switched off, or (2) by being the productive cause of some positive thing incompatible with another one, as when the factory-made cubical shape of the clay departs because someone gives the clay a new shape. In neither of these ways does the productive cause actively produce the absence itself. In the first case, the cause *stops* acting, and the absence ensues. In the other case, the cause acts, but in order to produce something *else*, on which the absence of another thing follows as a side effect. Even if the absence were the very thing intended, as when a murderer aims to deprive someone of life, the cause cannot accomplish this simply by actively producing the absence. A murderer cannot "make death" or give his victim death without giving him anything else. He can only produce other positive things that are incompatible with the life of the victim.

The same goes for all defects or undesirable attributes. Lopsidedness consists in the absence of symmetry where it ought to be present or where someone wants it. Stinkiness consists in some sort of imbalance or disagreement with certain olfactory receptors. These absences, while they might have an explanation of one kind or another (as my students usually do for their absences from class), never require an active cause producing the absence itself. The absence is always the side effect of some other positive thing (such as my students' enjoying a day at the beach), not the actual product of an active cause.

Since defects as such need no productive cause, they do not come forth from the first cause, and so there is no reason to attribute defects to it, as there is a reason to attribute positive perfections to it. Someone might still wonder what sort of explanation can be given for the defective things in the world. Why are certain animals deformed or less than optimally adapted? Why is the natural world apparently run on dog-eat-dog principles? Why do bad things happen to good people? But these are distinct from the present matter, so I will take them up later (a little bit in the next chapter, in fact, but more at length in chapter 9).

What about intelligence? The first cause is a cause of human intelligence. Does it therefore have intelligence? Or is intelligence like motion, which can be caused by something having no motion? Can the sufficient cause of intelligence have no intelligence? Intelligence also seems fairly particular, since it is found in very few things, so is it like fire, which can be sufficiently caused by things other than fire?

This question merits a chapter of its own.

6

The Ear of Whittaker's Daughter

Art is older than nature.

—Plato, *Laws*

Which Comes First: Intelligence or Unintelligence?

Just over half a century ago, Whittaker Chambers wrote an autobiography entitled *Witness*. The book recounts his life as a Communist spy, his subsequent rejection of Communism, and his testimony against Alger Hiss. His repudiation of Communism coincided with his conversion to Christianity. Among the many episodes that lent impetus to his conversion, one in particular stands out for being surprisingly commonplace and for producing an effect on him seemingly out of all proportion with the event itself. Here is the story in his words:

> I date my break from a very casual happening. I was sitting in our apartment on St. Paul Street in Baltimore. It was shortly before we moved to Alger Hiss's apartment in Washington. My daughter was in her high chair. I was watching her eat. She was the most miraculous thing that had ever happened in my life. I liked to watch her even when she smeared porridge on her face or dropped it meditatively on the floor. My eye came to rest on the delicate convolutions of her ear—those intricate, perfect ears. The thought passed through my mind: "No, those ears were not created by any chance coming together of atoms in nature (the Communist view). They could have been created only by immense design." The thought was involuntary and unwanted. I crowded it out of my mind. But I never wholly forgot it or the occasion. I had to crowd it out of my mind. If I had

completed it, I should have had to say: Design presupposes God. I did not then know that, at that moment, the finger of God was first laid upon my forehead.[1]

Certainly there is more of gut feeling or divine inspiration than cold deduction in this narrative. The idea that "those ears ... could have been created only by immense design" is not proved, not concluded, but somehow immediately intuited. Still, it does not take a mystical experience to get the impression that the things of nature, such as "those ears", are the products of design. Richard Dawkins himself, prince of antidesigners, defines the subject matter of biology as "things that give the appearance of having been designed for a purpose". The principal task of biology, as he sees it, is to explain (or explain away) this ubiquitous oddity, and to this end he introduces causes that have no designs on things. He (along with many others) enlists self-replicating molecules, random mutations, natural selection, and so on. It is furthermore his contention that these causes, which he takes to be demonstrably and incontrovertibly responsible for living things as we find them, are quite sufficient. If living things are to be produced and fully understood, no designer need be hired for the job.

The sufficiency of the causes is demonstrated rather unsatisfactorily, however. "Give me these causes, and I'll give you those effects" is the way Dawkins argues in every case. This is why he laughs off the notion that the first cause might use evolution (of one sort or another) as a tool, as a means to an end. Evolution as he conceives it would, he thinks, leave the designer with nothing to do. According to him, if we allow that his causes exist and produce living things as we find them—things he presumes more than proves—then living things will result, and so no more need be said.

I could just as well argue: "Give me the materials for a house and all the tools moving in just the right ways, and *presto!* I can prove that a house must result. No architect is needed and no carpenter." That would be clever of me. I would have conveniently ignored the question of whether the tools and materials can move in just the right ways by themselves. Do they need to be caused to move in those ways?

[1] Whittaker Chambers, *Witness* (Washington, D.C.: Regnery Gateway, 1980), p. 16.

If there is need for carpenters, it is not because their hands will *replace* the hammers, but because the hammers cannot be effective except in their hands. The hammers are genuine causes, but the carpenters are causes of another order entirely: they cause the hammers to be causes. Similarly, if there is need for a designer of the products of nature, it is not because it will replace nature and her laws, but because nature and her laws themselves cannot *be*, and cannot be causes, except by the causation of the designer.

Can nature and her laws exist and act by themselves? That is the question. The deductions of the foregoing chapters have shown us the answer is no. The world of nature is a world of mobile and dimensional and imperfectly actual things, and such things require a cause for their being and action, so long as they are and act. There is only one entity that simply is and is the cause of being in all things other than itself, and I have been so far labeling this entity the first cause.

The question, then, reduces to what sort of cause the first cause is. Is it an unintelligent, blind, automatic force? Or is it intelligent? If the first alternative is the truth, then as long as we grant Dawkins' evolutionary premises, his concluding to undesign might well follow. If instead the second is true, then even if we were as generous with Dawkins as possible, conceding all the positive details of his account of the production of living things, his conclusion would not follow. In fact, it would certainly be wrong. If the first cause is intelligent, then all things are the products of its intelligence, and living things are just what they always appeared to be—*designed*. Dawkins would have mistaken the tools and materials for the principal and primary causes. He would not have looked deep enough.

Dawkins, Gould, and others also like to point out "bad design". It might be instructive to keep a log of how many things originally thought to be badly designed or useless have turned out to be extremely useful indeed, in ways we had not originally been wise enough to appreciate. Be that as it may, there is nothing particularly threatening to the notion of a designer, not even a perfect one, if the products exhibit defects. That might spell disaster for anyone who thinks a perfect, flawless, infallible mind produces living things immediately, without the use of secondary causes as instruments. As it is, we all acknowledge that animals give birth to new animals and find nothing particularly offensive about saying that their designer, if it exists, must be willing to use at least these instruments in order to bring about new results. And if the intermediate causes are not infallible, if they are defectible, then we might well blame them, rather than the first cause, for any flaws we find (or think we find).

This solution prompts another question, though: Why would a perfect designer make intermediate causes that are capable of failure? Probably that is just what material things must be—capable of success, if made sufficiently well, but also capable of failure, since they are made of materials that are able to be things other than what they are at present and are therefore able to be interfered with or damaged by interaction with other material beings. To make a material being is to make a being capable of failure. To ask, "Why make things capable of failure?" is to ask, "Why make material beings?" Perhaps the designer thought that even imperfect goodness, fallible goodness, was worthwhile. Well, then, why doesn't the designer make each product solo, rather than enlist these fallible workers? I suppose the answer must be that the whole point of making natural things is to let them *be*, to let them do their natural thing and exhibit their own degree of power and success, fallible though it might be. When I have my students translate Ovid or Virgil, there will be mistakes. But it is still better for them that I let them do so. Why bother with students at all if I am to do all the translating myself?

In his book *The Grand Design*, Stephen Hawking makes the move in physics that is analogous and complementary to Dawkins' move in biology. Even the very laws of physics as we know them, which Hawking calls "the apparent laws of physics", the ones we see in our universe, appear uncannily designed. They look purpose-made for producing a life-friendly universe. If Hawking were a student of Dawkins' style, he might have said that the subject matter of physics is "mathematical laws of motion that *appear* to be purposeful and directed to life, especially intelligent life". So the goal of theoretical physicists—those of Hawking's school—will be to expose these appearances as an illusion.

Hawking attempts to do so by saying it is possible for everything to come from nothing. What he means by *nothing* is not sheer nonbeing, but a multidimensional raw material, capable of undergoing change and endowed with gravity subject to the laws of what he calls M-theory—a rather dreary thing, to be sure, but not exactly nothing in the strict sense. He takes no pains, at least in the popular work just mentioned, to explain in detail exactly how this "nothing" can produce all the myriad universes he supposes it to have made, including our own; his story is even sketchier, if possible, than Dawkins' story about how life began. More importantly, though, his is again the same sort of argument: give me these causes, and I'll produce the effects. He is arguing against a designer who would *replace* the natural causes rather than *cause* them.

Perhaps there are plenty of people who believe in such a designer—that is, one that replaces rather than uses any other causes—and so these authors are not simply arguing against no one. Their arguments are nonetheless wholly ineffective against any designer that is a cause of nature itself. The target of their attacks is not an author of nature who gives it its very being and inherent tendencies, but something rather like a cosmic meddler who takes it upon himself to fiddle with some independently existing material that would rather be left alone. Nothing could be further from my mind than such a busybody as that. And I quite agree that nature depends on nothing of the kind.

The reality is that the first cause is productive of natural things, of dimensional things, of mobile things, hence also of this "nothing"—if it exists and even if it has always existed. As the last five chapters have established, even were it possible for this "nothing" to change into all things and in some sense to self-develop, its mobility precludes it from being the first cause, from being a purely self-existent and self-acting thing. Its existence and power would therefore continuously depend upon the first cause. Hence, if the first cause is intelligent, the game is up.

And that is the question to be settled in this chapter. For all our reasoning has shown thus far, the first cause might yet be a blind power behind all things—some sort of primal thrum. And there is some reason to lean toward that view. What, after all, is the alternative? Is the first cause a thinking, deliberating being? But thinking and deliberating are like movements or changes in a mind, aren't they? If all intelligence is like that, it is impossible for the unchangeable first cause to understand anything. Really, though, understanding and knowing are not the same thing as thinking about something or deliberating. We think about something before we understand it. We deliberate before we know what to do. And in any such process as thinking about or deliberating, we begin from things we already knew independently of the process. This means all our step-by-step thinking originates from things we simply and immediately understand without running through steps. Some of our understanding, in other words, is neither a mental process nor dependent on one. We human beings understand very little without reasoning—simple things like "Equals added to equals make equals." We cannot imagine a mind that could understand all things in that natural and effortless way, without any reasoning or learning. But we have seen many times now that what we can and cannot imagine is no sure guide to what can and cannot be. And the way our mental life must be is no standard for deciding how another kind must be.

Which comes first, then, intelligent causes or unintelligent ones? The answer is not obvious. Looking at familiar examples, we find the one before the other, and the other before the one. We sometimes find an intelligent cause before an unintelligent one, as when a man builds a machine. Other times we find an unintelligent cause before an intelligent one, as when nature builds a man; an unthinking zygote mindlessly develops a human brain.

Thus, we are thrown back upon natural causes, and we are left wondering what sort of cause they might depend on. They depend on the first cause—but what sort of cause is that? The priority of thoughtless natural causes to human intelligence, or at least to the human brain, suggests that unintelligent agency is simply prior after all. On the other hand, human intelligence can employ natural causes to do its bidding, whereas natural causes cannot use human intelligence to fulfill their own tendencies. Man uses his understanding to train dogs to guide blind people, whereas dogs cannot harness the full power of human intelligence to promote their canine agendas. Among familiar cases, intelligent and unintelligent causes have different types of priority to each other.

The Intelligence of the First Cause

When I was in high school, I read my first book about ancient Chinese philosophy. I do not remember the title or the author, but one of the proverbs always stuck with me. It went like this:

> The uncarved marble is better than the statue.
> It is all statues.

That got me thinking. "All statues" is better than "one statue", I had to agree. But the uncarved marble is only potentially all statues. It is actually none. It is not even potentially all, as though it could one day be all statues at once. It is potentially all only insofar as it is able to be carved into one statue and which statue it is to become has not yet been decided.

Time has not altered these convictions of mine, but it has added some things. What the ancient Chinese philosopher had said was not right when applied to what is somehow "all things" by its passive potential. But it is right when applied to what is "all things" by its active power or effectiveness. In a court case, for example, a single uncontested confession is better (from the standpoint of the prosecution) than all the prosecutions' other pieces of evidence put together, since the confession actually has all their convicting power and more. Back in chapter 5, we saw that the first cause is "all things" in this way. It contains in itself every actuality and perfection found in other things, but without their defects, their limitations, their multiplicity, and their mobility. This was because all actualities come forth from its active power, and nothing gives what it does not in some way actually possess. Does this mean we can argue now like this?

> The cause of intelligence must have intelligence.
> The first cause is the cause of intelligence (namely, ours).
> Therefore, the first cause must have intelligence.

Perhaps. But we must be careful. Not everything found in the effect is found in its cause in the same manner, and therefore its presence in the cause might not earn for the cause the same name as its effect. Doctors, for instance, produce health in their patients, and it is true that they do so by virtue of their possession of health in some way. Does it follow that every doctor is healthy? No. To cause health in their patients, they must have health in their knowledge, but not necessarily in their bodies. They might be afflicted with Parkinson's disease or arthritis, but not debilitatingly so, while continuing to heal other people. A doctor can "have health" in a cognitive fashion, yet not really be healthy. Could it be, then, that the first cause "has intelligence", but in such a peculiar manner that we cannot say the first cause is intelligent?

Let us recall the rule governing whether the description of some effect can also belong to the first cause. It is this: any name that necessarily implies limitations or potentials in its meaning must not be attributed to the first cause, and any name that does not imply these things must be attributed to it. That is because the first cause has all actualities in some way (see chapter 5), and therefore no real limitations, and it is purely actual and in no way potential (see chapter 3).

Let's apply the rule to some examples. The first cause is a cause of cats. It must possess in itself all the actuality contained in the feline nature. Does it therefore deserve to be called a cat? By no means. *Cat* includes not only actualities and perfections, but also mobility and limitations. According to my shorter Oxford English Dictionary, a cat is "an agile, partly nocturnal, quadrupedal carnivorous animal". Every word in that definition necessarily implies a mobile body. But the first cause has no mobility and is not a body, since it has no potential of any kind. So whatever it is, it cannot be called a cat except, perhaps, as a metaphor. If we conscientiously scrubbed the definition clean of all references to potency and mobility, we would not have anything recognizably feline left.

Next consider the word *olfactory*, as in "possessing the sense of smell". Is the first cause olfactory? Not if this means something *limited* to the sense of smell. Even the human intellect is not typically described as olfactory, since, though it is conscious of smells and knows a good deal about them and can even produce them by means of its knowledge of chemistry, it is not limited to knowing only smells. The nose is an olfactory organ because it knows smells and only smells and because it is affected by smells. The first cause contains in itself all the actualities of smells, but of course it is not a being somehow limited to smells, nor is it affected by smells, and so it should not be called olfactory.

Well, what about *intelligent*? If *intelligent* meant "capable of understanding by reasoning and by using a brain", that could not apply to the first cause. It is not mobile, so it does not progress from one understanding to another, as a reasoner does. It has no dimensions, so it has no brain. But that definition is more like a definition of *human intelligence* than a definition simply of *intelligence*. Suppose there was a being that was always understanding all things all the time with perfect clarity, with no need to reason and no need for a brain. Wouldn't we have to call it intelligent? There would be no better name for it. It would be infinitely more intelligent than we are, unhampered by the limitations of brain space and time spent reasoning. So far, that description fits the first cause.

Our analysis of intelligence included the word *understanding*. Does that apply to the first cause? What understands, as opposed to what hears or smells, is what in some way knows all things, not just some, and can know them independently of their physical presence or absence. All of that pertains to perfection, not limitation. And what knows is a thing whose own actuality is not limited to itself, but somehow within itself includes realities other than itself as well—again, not a limitation, but a magnification of being. The core significance of the word *intelligence* accordingly implies no mobility or limitations. Our rule therefore dictates that intelligence is one of those actualities that the first cause not only causes, but possesses in such a way as to be describable by it. The first cause is intelligent—unlimitedly so.

It follows that the natural world and everything in it is truly the product of understanding and intention. The ubiquitous appearance of design, from the lowest laws of physics to the highest living things, is no mere appearance, no grand illusion. It is simply the truth. Long before they came into being, eyes were meant for seeing; ears were meant for hearing. And the world was meant to produce living beings with eyes and ears. And the world was meant to be seen and heard. And this remains true whether eyes are irreducibly complex components or not.

The Intelligence of the First Cause Revisited

The image of the apple is in the eye of the person seeing it. The form of the statue is in the mind of the sculptor imagining it. Things known exist within the knower in some way. This fact suggests that the first cause must know all things, actual and possible, since all things exist in it in some way.

The matter is not quite so simple, however. The form of the thing known exists in the knower in a special way, not in any old way. An egg has the same shape as its fellow egg beside it. But it remains quite oblivious to the shape of that other egg and even to its own shape. How can we tell whether the way in which actualities exist in the first cause enables it to know them? What is distinctive of knowers, of the way they possess the forms of the objects they know? If we take a moment to reflect on some properties of conscious beings, we will see why all things contained in the actuality of the first cause must lie open to its understanding.

Things devoid of knowledge give us our first clue. A knower cannot know something devoid of knowledge by possessing its form in the same way the thing itself has it. The stone has a certain color and shape and is unaware of these qualities even in itself, let alone similar qualities in other things. To the extent that I have color and shape in similar fashion, I am no better off than the stone. As I lie fast asleep, I have shape and color only in an unconscious way, as a stone does, and not in the special way distinctive of a knower of shape and color. What is missing? Particular actions of various organs and the brain, surely, but what is it that these actions accomplish, so that I have knowledge while the stone does not? What is new about the manner in which I come to possess the shape of my hand afresh when I can see or feel or imagine it, and not just have it in my hand as even a statue might have that shape? And what is common to my act of seeing and my act of smelling—or even a dog's act of smelling or an amoeba's act of feeling—such that the resulting fresh possession of a shape or an odor blossoms into knowing?

The nature of the stone, as we find it in the stone itself, rigidly shuts out all other beings and their properties. The stone is only itself and has none but its own qualities. It is, you might say, profoundly self-absorbed. It is not even right to say that it lives in solitary confinement, since an inmate in that condition is at least able to reflect on himself and reckon his situation a painful deprivation. The stone has no reflecting pool in itself, no repository for the forms of other things besides itself. If the shadow of the tree beside it falls upon the stone, it receives this form only as a new property of its own, without any interior reference to the principal owner. The stone has no room in itself for any other being. It is too small a being, you might say, to contain other things besides itself.

Of course, the opposite, a knowing being, is not closed off to other things besides itself, but embraces them in itself somehow.

There are some philosophers who would deny this. Some have said none of us has any connection to any reality outside his own head or no certainty of such a connection. But they themselves cannot live in accord with that theory. They theorize in one world and live in another. Nor can they speak in accord with their theory—especially when they presume to be speaking to other people besides themselves, attempting to convince them of their theory. Some of the philosophers who propose this sort of theory are hacks. But not all of them. There are genuinely interesting and worthwhile difficulties about how we know even the most ordinary of things. In the end, though, they are just that—difficulties, not proofs that we don't know things. They are like Zeno's famous motion paradoxes, which prove that motion is hard to understand, not that it doesn't exist. Such difficulties need not detain us here. Just as the existence of motion in the world is self-evident, so too is the existence of our knowledge and of our connection with realities outside our own minds. Sometimes we are mistaken, of course. Sometimes we hallucinate. Some of us have phantom limbs. Life is strange, things are not always what they seem, and we are not infallible. But neither are we imprisoned in ourselves.

The mere fact that things *seem* to us at all means that we are beings capable of contact with realities outside ourselves. Not so the stone. To be a knower, then, is to be the sort of thing that can somehow possess at least some forms of other beings. It is to be a thing whose own form is not incompatible with all other forms but is open to some of them at least, so that the knower can have the being of other things in having its own, without detriment to itself. What this openness to foreign forms consists in might differ from knower to knower, and even from faculty to faculty in a single knower. How the form of another being exists in a knower, how it "gets there", might also vary. The specific manner in which this is done (which is in all cases mysterious to me, and I dare say to everyone else, too) does not affect the root difference between knower and nonknower.

This nonopposition to other forms that is peculiar to knowing beings is the cause of another property distinctive of them. Things that are opposed to each other in a piece of purely unconscious matter become less opposed when they exist in a knower. A sheet of paper cannot be both black and white at the same time and in the same way. Those two qualities evict each other from the paper. Where the paper turns black, white gets kicked out, and vice versa. The same goes for straight and curved, and any number of other opposites. To some extent this opposition remains when things enter into our vision. When one part of my field of vision is seeing white, it cannot also be seeing black at the same time. But the opposition between them is already mitigated somewhat. When I see black and white side by side, seeing the black helps me see the white better. I have trouble telling which sheet of paper is whitest if I see them only one at a time. When I see them together, each helps me to see the other better. One opposite does not help the other *to be*, but *to be seen*.

The reconciliation of opposites in a knower becomes more pronounced in proportion to the knower's knowledge. Ascending from pure sensation to imagination, for example, we find that imagination is both more cognitive than the senses and also more capable of embracing opposites. It is more cognitive, because whatever I can see or hear I can also imagine, but not vice versa. Things are also less opposed in the imagination than in the external senses—the sense of sight and the sense of hearing are opposed to each other in their respective sense organs (the conditions of the eye prevent it from smelling, and similarly the nose cannot see), but they are reconciled in the imagination, which is able to present the objects of all the senses, as when we dream.

Human understanding is another step up again. It is more cognitive than either the senses or the imagination. Anything I can see or imagine I can also think about and understand and compare and contrast. But there are many things I can understand that I cannot see or imagine—the number 10^{5000}, for example, or the relationship between premises and a conclusion. And the unity of opposites is also greater in our understanding than it is in our senses or our imagination. To see or imagine exactly where one color stops, it can help to see or imagine the contrary color right next to it. But that is not entirely necessary. I can see white without seeing any other color, let alone its contrary, black. But in the intellect, it often happens that understanding one opposite is impossible without understanding the other. I can form no concept of *whole* without thinking of *parts* at the same time. I can form no idea of *sickness* without putting *health* in its definition. Two opposites not only help each other to be understood; sometimes they must both be understood together or not at all.

The more cognitive something is, the less opposed opposites become when present in its knowledge. This fits with the nature of a cognitive being—a thing whose form does not exclude all forms of other things but accommodates at least some of them without compromising their identity or its own. The knower's nonopposition to outside things diminishes their opposition to each other, insofar as they exist within the knower. The degree of nonopposition between forms existing in a thing is therefore a measure of its own nonopposition to outside things—which in turn is a measure of its capacity for knowledge.

Since the supreme nonopposition of forms is to be found in the first cause, in which all forms and actualities exist in a single actuality, the knowledge of the first cause must be supreme. All things that exist in it without opposition, the manner of existing unique to knowers, will lie open to its knowledge. But all things exist in it in this way. So it simply knows all things.

Giving *Mind* a New Meaning

Among our own cognitive acts, most imply definite limitations. The sense of smell is the ability to know only smells, not colors and sounds. The imagination knows only things of which an image can be formed, nothing else. But the mind can understand all things, at least in a general way—and so it alone can form the conception "all things". Given the options, a mind or an understanding is the least inappropriate name for the first cause. I say least inappropriate because its knowledge must differ profoundly from ours. Recalling the conclusions of previous chapters, we can begin to see that it has a knowledge very foreign to us indeed. Since there is no change or motion in the first cause, and no deficiency, there can be no transition in its thought, no beginning in ignorance followed by learning, no deliberation, no discourse, no argumentation, no laborious pondering. Instead, it naturally understands all things all at once with perfect distinctness and clarity by comprehending its own all-containing and all-causing substance. That is already a tad foreign to us. But there is more.

Most objects we know seem somehow to produce likenesses of themselves in us. We form an idea of hippopotamuses only after we encounter them, and they make an impression on us. But the first cause cannot be acted on and informed. So it cannot possibly get its knowledge from the things it knows. Quite the reverse. The forms of things exist in its understanding first and are distributed to exterior effects afterward, as tables and chairs that a woodworker might build exist first in his mind and afterward in the products themselves. And there is still more.

In our case, there is obviously a distinction between us and our various acts of understanding. I cannot be the same as my act of understanding what a triangle is—if I were, I would cease to exist as soon as I stopped thinking about triangles. So I am one thing, and my various acts of understanding are additions to me that I am capable of. Understanding this or that is something I can do but am not always actually doing. No such distinction can exist in the first cause. The first cause includes no composition within itself, no difference between understander and act of understanding. If these were distinct in it, then the understander considered in itself would be something potential to the act of understanding, whereas there is no potential in the first cause. Even old Xenophanes, the pre-Socratic philosopher, dimly grasped this unique simplicity of the first cause when he said: "There is one god, the greatest among gods and men, not at all similar to mortals in body or mind. The whole of him sees, the whole of him thinks, and the whole of him hears."[2]

The first cause is a subsisting act of understanding. That is its very substance. To imagine it as something else that is conducting that act of understanding—as we ourselves differ from our own act of understanding—is a profound mistake. Worse still to think of it as a being that makes great efforts to figure things out.

The Harmony of the Beautiful and the Intelligible

The intelligence of the first cause of all things explains the look of design everywhere in the universe. But it also explains other ubiquitous facts about the world. One of these is beauty.

[2] Xenophanes, fragments DK23 and DK74. My translation.

Here is an odd fact: the universe is beautiful. It is beautiful not only overall, as a grand entirety; it is beautiful in nearly all its parts. Not only a galaxy, but speckish earth is beautiful. Not only the whole panorama of life, but the elegance of one lone eagle in its flight stirs the soul. Not only the outwardly sensible appearances, but the intelligible laws and relations inherent in the structure of the world—in a solar system, in an isolated star, in a snowflake—excite our fascination and wonder. The hardheaded physicists themselves, even the atheists among them, are frequently moved by nature's graces to abandon their accustomed modus operandi and to adopt instead the language of the poets, as if on fire to win for nature new admirers.

This is surely a very odd fact. It is as if the whole universe turns out to be just as one would have hoped, or rather much better. What were the odds? Charles Darwin saw that he could not hope to explain the beauty of most animals by his principles. To insist on the sufficiency of his principles, then, he had to deny the reality of beauty, which is just what he did. If it seems an odd fact for the whole universe to be revolving around us at the center, perhaps one can explain this by denying it is a fact: the motion we so easily attribute to the heavens actually belongs to ourselves. Likewise, if it seems an odd fact for the whole universe to be so pleasing to us to behold, both with the eyes and ears and also with the mind, perhaps one can explain this by a similar Copernican revolution: Is the beauty we so easily attribute to the universe perhaps nothing else than our subjective reaction to it, some side effect of our own evolution? Is beauty something unreal, merely a subjective human response to a world that is not really beautiful at all?

Not likely. For beauty to be something real, no more is required than for us to admit that certain realities are such as to please the human eye or the human mind in the mere beholding of them. It has long been popular to say that beauty exists only in the eye of the beholder; witness our disagreements about what is beautiful out there. But our disagreements are usually about subtleties and about human things like faces and fashion and art where our other feelings tend to cloud our judgments. When it comes to the beauty of the world, however, we humans agree far, far more than we disagree. The human eye and the human mind have pronounced preferences. They do not find all things equally beautiful, and universally they find some just plain ugly. Few have praised the tapeworm for its aesthetic qualities, disgusting to contemplate both in appearance and in its manner of making a living. It is well adapted for its line of work, like other organisms, and there is a sort of elegance in the coordination of its parts for the benefit of the whole—a magnificent piece of engineering, one might say. But it is still a nasty sight. We are not, then, simply programmed to gape in awe at everything we see. Nor are we usefully drawn to beautiful things, so that the attraction could be neatly explained by natural selection. Poison dart frogs are magnificent. They even look good to eat. In fact, many of the most beautiful animals and plants are also the most deadly. The humble potato, by contrast, is very useful indeed, but that lumpy tuber provides little inspiration to painters. Thundering cataracts, even were they not deadly, are not particularly useful for us to stare at. Rainbows even less. It is simply incredible that any tale of utility told in terms of natural selection could be an adequate explanation of the beautiful. It could only sweep beauty under the rug. Besides, all that is fable making. It is much more honest to take the beauty of the universe for a reality than to try to dismiss it as a subjective quirk of the human brain in order to safeguard the sufficiency of our preferred ideas. If someone is an ardent admirer of the form of the tapeworm, he might well be the subject of a quirk, if not mental illness. If someone shrugs off the stars with indifference, we safely label him a trousered ape.

If we face the odd fact of beauty, it is only natural to wonder what its cause is. It is not just our good luck. It nearly permeates the world and its fabric. And the beauty of a single thing consists in a million ingredients cooperating toward an overall pleasing effect. One tiny detail gone wrong can wreck the whole thing, like an otherwise beautiful face missing its nose.

Why is beauty just about everywhere? Most things are beautiful, both in particular, and in their mid-scale and large-scale associations. But if all things were beautiful without exception, we might think it was a condition of existence—nothing can *be at all* without being beautiful. Instead, not all species of animals and plants are beautiful. It is almost as if most of them are, in order to make the world as a whole beautiful, but just enough of them are not, in order to make it clear that the beauty is an added grace and not just de rigueur.

The intelligence of the first cause harmonizes very nicely with our oddly beautiful world. What other kind of cause, if not an intelligent one, could be intent on producing beauty as such, rather than as a side effect or an accident? The beauty of the world is the signature of an intelligence—of someone's taste and generosity, one might say. It is so much underscored by our experience that the word *cosmos* comes from the Greek for "adornment", as we had occasion to note before. If its beauty were not produced by a mind that delights in things seen, it would not truly be an adornment. And then it would not be what it seems. And that would make the beauty of the world an ugly thing after all—an illusion.

Richard Dawkins demonstrates much good taste in his admiration for the beauty of the universe. But he feels no need to explain it. In *The God Delusion*, when he takes the "argument from beauty" to bits, he considers only the beauty of certain manmade things, such as sonatas and paintings and sonnets. He is quite right to say that the musicians, the painters, and the poets are causes of these beauties. But he does not offer any reason to suppose they are the first and only causes of them. Is the human mind itself, for instance, due to any external cause—and not just a formerly existing cause, such as natural selection, but a presently existing and sustaining action? And why are natural things, not just paintings and poems, beautiful? Could paintings and poems be beautiful if the natural things from which painters and poets draw inspiration, and which they represent in myriad ways, were ho-hum? These questions did not occur to Dawkins, it seems. On one of the first pages of his book, he quoted his departed friend Douglas Adams, asking, "Isn't it enough to see that a garden is beautiful without having to believe that there are fairies at the bottom of it too?"[3]

Presumably this is meant to resemble an argumentative question: "Isn't it enough to see that the universe is beautiful without having to believe that there is some sort of unusual intelligence responsible for it?" Well, frankly, no. Composite beauty, ephemeral beauty, transcendable beauty, beauty that did not need to be and yet came to be, that requires many things to go right, and that disappears when any one thing goes wrong—no such beauty as that is intelligible on its

---

[3] Dawkins, *The God Delusion*, p. 7.

own or capable of existing by itself. And that is the only sort of beauty we ever find in our universe. It bears every sign of being an effect, a work—one might even say an *expression*.

On the other hand, perhaps Adams' remark is not meant to be an argument, but just a bit of scolding along these lines: "What sort of spoiled children are we, not to be content with the beauty of this garden we call the universe, but who would rather look for something more beautiful and amazing still? Such ingratitude!" Hm. I don't know. It seems to smack more of ingratitude not to bother wondering whether there is anyone to be grateful *to*.

Dawkins also quotes the famous quip of Bertrand Russell, who, when asked what he would say were he to find himself face-to-face with the Almighty, inquiring why he had been an atheist, replied: "Not enough evidence, God, not enough evidence." But the evidence is all around us. One may, but need not, peer through a microscope or a telescope to find it. One may find it in commonplace things, such as "the delicate convolutions" of the ear of Whittaker's daughter.

7

Who Designed the Designer?

> Everyone says "Nature is great, and yet it is simple!" But
> nature is great *because* it is simple.
>
> —Lao-tzu, *Tao Teh King*

By the Way, There Is a God

I remember the first time I began to think seriously about the meaning of the word *god*. It was 1985. I was at the mall helping a friend pick out one of those newfangled CD players. He had sufficient funds to make such a purchase (they were prohibitively expensive for most people back then), and I was eager to hear the new sound of those iridescent little discs, supposedly superior to vinyl and in a purportedly indestructible format to boot. Somehow or other (I really do not recall how) we got to talking about god, and my friend, who was from a family of atheists, turned to me with a bemused smile and said, "Do you really believe in a giant superman in the sky?"

I hardly remember any more of the conversation than that, I'm afraid. I know there was no ill will on either side, or else it would have stuck with me better. What did make a lasting impression was his conception of god. I thought it very silly, but it seemed to operate in the minds of many people. The gods of the polytheistic religions were thoroughgoingly anthropomorphic and hence difficult to tell apart from modern superheroes. There even seems to be some overlap—Thor, for example. And what exactly did I mean by *god* anyway? A first cause of all things was not quite enough, since my atheist friends all believed in that; only they called it matter. Intelligence was the missing key ingredient.

Richard Dawkins began his critique of the "God Hypothesis" (in *The God Delusion*) by defining it as defensibly as he could conceive, not tying it up with the peculiar offenses, real or perceived, of this or that religion. He defined it thus: "There exists a superhuman, supernatural intelligence who deliberately designed and created the universe and everything in it, including us."[1] By calling this a hypothesis, Dawkins betrays his misunderstanding of many of his opponents. He can call it a mistake if he likes, even a delusion, but to call it a hypothesis is to ignore the logical status it had in the minds of Plato, Aristotle, Aquinas, and most other heavyweight theists. It was never intended by them as a mere explanation for us to adopt until a better one might happen along. That hypothetical mode of thinking characterizes empirical science and detective work. It is also the way of thinking most familiar to Dawkins. But that is not the only sort of thinking. It is not the sort of thinking that mathematicians do, for example. Nor is it the sort of thinking behind the conclusion that there is a being such as the one Dawkins here describes—at least, not as outlined in the last six chapters. That thinking began not from hypotheses, but from self-evident and necessary truths such as "Nothing can give what it does not have" and "The same thing cannot both give and receive the very same thing at the very same time" and a long list of others like these. The thinking was not probabilistic, but deductive, drawing out the inevitable consequences of these self-evident starting points.

At the moment, however, I am more interested in the definition of *god* implied in the formula above than I am in Dawkins' description of it as a hypothesis. According to his statement, *a god* must mean "a superhuman, supernatural intelligence who deliberately designed and created the universe and everything in it". If that is what a god is, then one way to state the conclusion of the last six chapters is to say that there is indeed a god. On the other hand, there might already be a little dose of Judeo-Christian influence in restricting the meaning of the word *god* to a first creator of all things. The ancient Greeks called Athena a god (or goddess), but they entertained no notion that she had deliberately designed and created the whole universe and all things in it. By awarding her the

[1] Richard Dawkins, *The God Delusion*, p. 52.

name goddess, they meant only that she was an immortal intelligent
being. The Dawkins definition is more like the definition of the *one
true god* or the *principal deity*. Be that as it may, it clearly applies to the
first cause, according to chapter 6.

I will put off speaking of *god* no longer then. But I will imitate
Christopher Hitchens' habit of spelling the word with a lowercase *g*.
My reasons differ from his. He did it to express contempt and to
retrain our supposedly misguided sense of awe. I do it because I wish
to avoid confusion. Capitalizing the word *God* suggests that we are
speaking of the first cause not just as a being we can discover by
careful thought, but as someone within the context of a particular
historical interaction. *God* with a capital *G* refers to someone who has
spoken to some of us mortals in some definite time, place, and manner. I do not deny that such a thing has happened. But the types of
arguments I have made in this book fall far short of establishing that.
There can be no doubt that if the God of Abraham, Isaac, and Jacob
exists, then he must be a god in the sense that Dawkins has been so
good as to define for us.

But the reverse does not follow. It is a logical possibility that god
has never intervened in human history nor had any special dealings
with the Jews. Many people look upon arguments such as those in
this book and then complain when the conclusion "God exists" is
drawn. "Where is the proof that this being came down as one of
us, born of a virgin?" some would demand to know. "And that he
was circumcised? And baptized in the River Jordan? And crucified
under Pontius Pilate? And that he cursed a fig tree? And all the rest
of it?" In short, the meaning of the word *God*, for such people, is
nothing less than "the subject of all the divine predicates in the enormous book called the Bible [or the Koran or the Book of Mormon,
and so forth]". If that is what the word means, so that "God exists"
effectively means "all the statements in the Bible are true", then it
has been by no means proved in this book that God exists. Nor has
any intelligent person ever thought it possible to prove that God, so
defined, exists. But the word *god* (or its equivalent in other languages)
existed before Christianity, before Judaism, before the Bible. And the
word had a meaning. And there is no other word I know of (except
for evident synonyms) to signify an immortal, intelligent being. That,
and more than that, has been proved to exist in the preceding pages.

So I hope I will not be misunderstood when I say god definitely exists, but I must for the purposes of this book leave aside any question about God.

I have also been referring to god as a he. But really, since god (as god, now, and any thought of incarnation aside) has no body, clearly also god has no sex. Consequently it would in some way be preferable to refer to god as an it. The only problem is that an it always implies something devoid of understanding. It doesn't take much to qualify as an it. A brick or a speed bump is an it. No one of us would feel particularly flattered in being labeled an it. The neuter pronoun is inappropriate to god, then, not because it is sexless but because it is impersonal. God is intelligent and is therefore a who rather than a mere what. An it is something beneath stupid. That leaves the personal pronouns. I could ignore pronouns and just say *god* over and over again. But then *I* would sound stupid. In English, I am left with no choice but *he* or *she* as a pronoun. (I cannot bring myself to resort to the monstrosity *s / he* or similar remedies. They repel any reader burdened with a sense of style.) The major monotheistic religions refer to god as a he, so I will from here on do the same, with no further apology than to say that I thereby imply no sexual characteristics in god and that if anyone finds the masculine pronoun offensive, in what follows I invite him / her to change *he* to *he / she / it* or whatever pleases him / her best.

Very well then: there exists a god. By itself, that is not a compelling reason for affirming or denying that god has ever intervened in human history or said anything to us in words. The conclusion is simply neutral on such questions. No doubt that is not a completely satisfying account of reality, and it invites a number of further questions. Thank goodness, though, my task is a more modest one. The New Atheists have undertaken to show that belief in a god, as Dawkins defined it, is a delusion. I have undertaken to show them wrong—no more, no less.

Richard Dawkins Objects

I have now drawn the main conclusion of this book. I have yet to face the main objections to it. We have all run into the question

"Who made god?" If instead someone asked "What caused the first cause?", the illegitimacy of the question would be obvious at once. Whatever else *first cause* means, it means something that needs no cause. We might wonder whether there is anything that needs no cause. And we might wonder what is so special about it that it needs none. But we can't really wonder what caused something that needs no cause. We saw back in chapter 1 why there has to be a cause that has no cause before it. And we saw subsequently that what is special about it, and what distinguishes it from all other things that need causes, is its simplicity. Every combination presupposes a combiner, and hence a cause. What needs no cause, then, is in no way a combination of things but is perfectly simple.

So far, so good. But the word *god* does not mean merely a first cause, but "an intelligent one". And it is not easy to see how to reconcile "intelligent" with "what is perfectly simple" and "what involves no combination of things". No one urges this objection more famously than Richard Dawkins. Dawkins objects that since the first cause has to be very simple—a point that has emerged in the preceding chapters of this book—it cannot be a mind, much less an extremely complex one. Any mind would have to be complex to such a degree as to require a prior cause. The first cause, then, whatever it is, would have to be mindless.

Dawkins has laid his finger on one of the great intellectual obstacles to seeing the existence of god. Most of the philosophers before Socrates had the same problem. They saw that simpler things enjoyed a certain priority to composite ones, but were also less perfect. Atoms can exist without people, not the reverse, but individual people can think, and individual atoms cannot. A person, not an atom, is a microcosm, a whole universe in a tight space. The person is better and smarter, but the atom is prior and more independent. After this initial survey of the gamut of things, the conclusion appears all but inevitable: the first cause or causes must be perfectly simple, and therefore imperfect and unintelligent.

That conclusion is too hasty, however. It is a verdict based on half the evidence. "Simple things come before composite ones" is true. But it is also true that "actual things come before potential ones." And the principal cause must always have what it gives to its product. The first cause of all things, then, must actually possess intelligence somehow, not merely as one of its potentials. We have already seen, too, that the first cause must possess intelligence in such a way as to deserve to be called intelligent, much more so than any of us.

What we are seeing is that a first cause must be both perfectly simple (so that it will need no cause before it) and perfectly actual (so that it will have everything to offer to its effects). The very nature of things compels us to unite these in one being. And yet we struggle to do so. It is no easy matter to see how "intelligent" and "perfectly simple" can be reconciled in one thing—the very word *simple* is sometimes used to mean unintelligent. There are three things in our experience that cause this difficulty: (1) our dependence on our brains, (2) our need to think things out, and (3) the nature of truth itself.

Our dependence on our brains in order to think makes it natural for us to suppose that any intelligence would require a brain. And a brain is plainly a complex thing with many interacting parts. To some extent, superior brain power goes hand in hand with greater neurological complexity. One animal or man is smarter than another in proportion to the number of circuits, programs, and places for data storage in its brain, to speak in crude analogies. But god has no body and hence no brain. And that gets us out of the first scrape. His intelligence is not brain based, and so he cannot fall under the rule that more intelligence comes with a more complex brain. This is not a cop-out. The nonbodily nature of the first cause, every bit as much as its intelligence, was a necessary consequence of self-evident principles, not something assumed ad hoc, at this particular spot, in order to squirm out of a pinch. For their part, Dawkins and others like him have no proof that all intelligence must be brain based. Why, it isn't even clear in our own case that our brain is actually doing our understanding. You cannot count what you are seeing without using your eyes—it hardly follows that your eyes are doing the counting. Likewise, if you cannot understand without simultaneously using your brain, it still does not follow that your brain is doing the understanding. Maybe instead it is just supplying images of things for you to think about, as your eyes supply things for you to count.

But that was only the first scrape. Our dependence on forming definitions, statements, and inferences can also get in the way of our understanding god's intelligence. Not only our brains, but our mental acts themselves involve complexity and combination. To understand what the Pythagorean theorem means, I have to combine a number of thoughts that can be expressed in words like these:

> In a right triangle the square drawn on the hypotenuse is equal in area to the sum of the two squares drawn on the remaining sides.

To see that this statement is true, I need to deduce it from a combination of several prior statements. Even the thought behind some of the individual words of the statement above is analyzable into a further combination of thoughts, as *hypotenuse* means "the side of a right triangle that is opposite the right angle". Our thought is jampacked with combinations. If we were forbidden to combine ideas, prevented from composing definitions and statements and deductions from these, it seems we could hardly think. David Hume, noting all this, drew the conclusion (in his *Dialogues Concerning Natural Religion*) that a mind that does no reasoning is no mind at all. But the first cause is perfectly simple and immobile, and so no reasoning process can exist in it. So Hume would force us to choose: either the first cause is intelligent and complex (and therefore needs a cause), or else it is simple but unintelligent (and therefore not a god).

The error in this thinking is not difficult to expose. It is impossible to form compound thoughts unless we also have elementary ones. Granted, I know the truth of the Pythagorean theorem by composing a proof of it from prior statements. But how do I know the truth of those prior statements? Perhaps by proofs composed of still more fundamental statements. But that cannot go on forever. If it did, I would need to know an infinity of prior statements before I could know the truth of the Pythagorean theorem—and then I simply could not know it. But I do know it. So the proofs must begin somewhere from statements so evident that they need no proof at all. These statements are the ones we call self-evident, such as "Equals added to equals make equals" and "Every right triangle has a hypotenuse." Every proof presupposes prior understanding that does not depend on proofs at all. Similarly, if I know what a hypotenuse is by composing a definition of it from simpler terms, and I understand those terms by putting together definitions from still simpler terms, that also cannot continue forever. Every definition presupposes a prior understanding that does not depend on definitions at all. All our composite thoughts, in other words, grow out of simple understandings that do not involve any combination.

It is simply untrue, then, that a mind that does no reasoning or combining is no mind at all. There could be a mind that simply understands without reasoning and stating and defining, even as our minds do in their most elementary grasp of things. It is true that our simple and unreasoned understanding of things is pretty poor stuff, and that our fullest understanding is the fruit of complex reasoning. But it is precisely because our first and simple understanding of things is poor that we need to combine and refine our thoughts in order to arrive at a fuller conception of reality. If there were a mind whose first and simple understanding of things was perfect, which included in itself every insight we humans can attain only by defining and reasoning, then this simple being would not be only a mind, but a mind much superior to our own.

Truth and Correspondence

There is still another way to cast Dawkins' objection to the intelligence of the first cause. This more challenging version begins from the definition of truth itself. It goes like this. Any true understanding of reality has to correspond to that reality. That's pretty much what *true* means. It is impossible, then, to have a true and distinct understanding of a bunch of distinct things without forming a corresponding number of distinct ideas about them. So now we have a choice. Either god has only a single idea of things, or else he forms a multitude of different ideas. If we say the first, then god understands only one thing distinctly, such as ducks; how sad for him that he has to spend his eternal existence dwelling on that one idea, since he can't change his mind, being immobile. If we say the second, then god has complexity in his mind after all, and he will need a cause as much as we do. We might try to get out of this tangle by saying god's single thought is not ducks, but being, which includes all things. That would be like saying I understand all animals by thinking "animal". That's true in a way. But when I think that thought, all I really have in mind is what is common to all animals.

I don't have "wombat" in there explicitly, for example. And there are many animals I don't even know exist just by knowing what an animal is in general. A single thought for many things ignores their distinctions. That kind of knowledge will not make for a very impressive god. If god eternally ignores the distinctions among all things—such as the difference between a cat and a dog—then he knows less than I do.

This business turns on one of those ambiguities that is hard to notice until someone points it out, but after you see it, you can hardly believe it passed you by. The whole problem rests on the notion that a true or correct understanding must correspond to the things understood. That is true in one sense, false in another. Exactly what sort of correspondence does truth require? A good photo of my wife is very like her in certain ways. It is also very unlike her in others—it sits still, and it is only two-dimensional. But those noncorrespondences don't make it a bad photo. My visual image of the mountain range outside my window is very like those mountains in some ways, but very unlike them in others—my image is in my eyes, but the mountain range itself is outside them and is much too big to fit into my eyes. But that sort of noncorrespondence doesn't mean I'm seeing the mountains wrong or getting a false idea of their size and distance. Likewise, certain noncorrespondences between my understanding of things and those things themselves will not mean my understanding of them is wrong or deficient. It is possible for an understanding of things *not* to correspond to those things in certain respects, while still being perfectly correct and adequate.

Imagine, for a moment, that a correct understanding of something meant that the understanding itself had to be in every way like the thing understood. Then a correct understanding of a stone would *be* a stone—and, conversely, every stone would be a correct understanding of itself. Pretty silly. A correct understanding of a nonunderstanding thing obviously has to differ from the thing in some ways.

So what is the rule? What type of correspondence does truth require, and what kind does it not require? Think of the photo again. Certain things in a photo are meant to tell us certain things about its subject, while others are not supposed to be representative. A photo of Abraham Lincoln says he was taller than other men and had a pockmarked face and deep-set eyes. It does *not* say he was two-dimensional and made of paper. Those are peculiarities of the photo itself, not the peculiarities it expresses about its subject. We find a similar distinction in our knowledge of things. There are certain things that our understanding attributes to the objects we know, and if our understanding fails to correspond to things in this regard, our understanding is wrong. But there are plenty of attributes that belong to our understanding itself that need not correspond to the attributes of the things we understand. For example:

1. My understanding of past things is something that exists in the present. But the past does not itself exist in the present—except in my understanding or memory. This discrepancy, however, is not of itself a falsification of my understanding or my memory. It is possible to have a *present* understanding of *past* realities without prejudice to the truth and accuracy of the understanding.
2. My thought about the location of the Statue of Liberty either has no physical location at all, or else it is in my brain. Either way, the location of my understanding is not the same as the location understood. That doesn't mean all geography is false. It is possible to have a true understanding of something *there*, even though the understanding is not itself there.
3. In my understanding, "what a triangle is" can be found without "equilateral", "isosceles", or "scalene"—namely, in my general concept or definition of "triangle". I can think "triangle" without thinking "equilateral triangle", but not the reverse. I can think "three-sided plane figure" without adding anything further about what the ratios of the sides are. But no triangle can *exist* that way. Any triangle that exists outside my understanding—even a triangle that exists in my imagination— must be either equilateral or isosceles or scalene.
4. I can form a *finite* definition of *infinite*. My concept of *infinite* does not itself have to be infinite to be a correct thought of what infinity is. The dictionary definition of *infinite* is not itself endless.
5. I can form *one* thought or definition of *many*. The thought of *many* does not itself have to be many to be a correct thought of what *many* means.

Many more examples come to mind. But the general point is now clear. A true understanding of some property of things need not itself have that property and can even have the opposite property. This fits with what we discovered about knowers in the last chapter—namely, that in them there is a kind of reconciliation of opposites. The knower can know things quite other than itself without becoming those things, without losing its identity. I can understand a stone without becoming a stone. My thought can embrace things stuck in the past without itself being stuck in the past. My understanding of one opposite, such as blindness, includes the other, sight, so that there is really one understanding of the two together in my mind, although they cannot exist together in the same eye. If I can reconcile two things in one thought, nothing prevents a greater mind from knowing a vast multitude of things without presenting any corresponding multitude within itself. And so it is with god. His understanding of all the complexities in the world is in itself perfectly simple.

As unimaginable as that might be for us, it actually makes sense with other things we know about knowledge even in ourselves. A stone exists in my mind very differently from the way it exists at my feet. All the more must an intellect, which differs in its nature from all other things, operate in a unique mode. All things will exist in it differently from the way they exist in themselves. In themselves, and as parts of the universe, stones and cats and trees are a multitude of diverse things. But god's knowledge of that multitude, true as it is to all their details and distinctions, is itself one simple idea. His causal power, too, consists in his single actuality but produces the whole diversity of effects in existence. It is fully competent to do so, since the multitudes of created things are just so many distinct ways of imitating and partially reflecting the simple actuality of the Creator.

Simplicity Comes in Two Flavors

Very well then. Perfect simplicity and supreme intelligence are not incompatible. But Dawkins and the pre-Socratic philosophers are right about one thing: greater simplicity often does go hand in hand with greater imperfection. The amoeba is simpler than the human—and also dumber. In god's case, though, greater simplicity seems to go hand in hand with greater perfection. Why is that? Is there any prec-edent for that in our experience? And if so, what is the rule dictating when simplicity will entail *im*perfection, rather than perfection?

Human experience provides some examples of greater simplic-ity entailing greater perfection. The mountaineer walks through the woods along a winding, lengthy path to reach his goal at the top of the mountain, but to soar straight there like the eagle is the bet-ter way. And it isn't the brighter student, but the less gifted one, who needs more explanations and more examples to get the idea. In mathematics, a simple proof that gives one universal reason applica-ble to all cases of a theorem provides us with a better understanding than a more complex proof that separately considers many particular cases. It often happens, too, that initially disparate and independently developed parts of science get unified, such as the respective theories of electricity, magnetism, and light. These were considered separate domains until a single, unified theory accounted for them all in sim-pler terms. The unified and simpler understanding of these things as variations on one theme is an improved understanding, not an impoverishment. In general, it is more simplicity, not complexity, that is the sign of a superior theory.

I suspect that everyone with expertise in some field could sup-ply examples of his own. My brothers tell me that in the program-ming world, sometimes a single, elegant solution will "losslessly" do everything that several more complex programs can accomplish. And certainly there is something like this in the world of literature. If someone wanted to tell a story about a poor fisherman, he might start by telling us a bit about the old fellow's character. Suppose this fisherman accepts some bait as a gift from a sympathetic young boy who has befriended him. Our would-be author might go on to say something like this:

> The old man was humble. But he didn't used to be. When he was
> young, he had been pretty impressed with himself. Not for his intel-
> ligence or education. He had always been a simple person. No, he
> used to think he was tough. That he did not need anything from
> anybody. But no longer. Something in his long experience had taught
> him humility, had taught him to see himself as a small and needy
> creature in a big and bountiful world. The funny thing is that he

could not have told you exactly when he had learned this lesson. He was not analytic enough to have noticed the change in himself when it had come.

Or, after the old man accepts the sardine bait from the boy, our story-teller could follow instead with this:

> "Thank you," the old man said. He was too simple to wonder when he had attained humility. But he knew he had attained it and he knew it was not disgraceful and it carried no loss of true pride.

The first version is by yours truly. The second is Hemingway's.[2] His is not only shorter (39 words to my 114), but it actually says everything mine does and much more besides. His is powerful, compact. Mine is diffuse.

Just from examples like these, drawn from human experience, we would expect the supreme knowledge to be at the summit of simplicity, not of complexity.

So what is the rule? When does greater simplicity imply greater perfection, and when does it instead imply greater *im*perfection? It all depends on the type of simplicity. Sometimes what is simpler just has fewer parts than another thing does, while the other thing has all those same parts as well as other parts, each of which brings something more to the table. In cases like that, the greater simplicity will imply greater imperfection. If we took out every other word from a sentence in Hemingway, for example, the result would be something "simpler" than the original, since it would have fewer words. But it would be less perfect, because the omitted words were doing things that the remaining words alone cannot do. That is an example of what we might call a deprived simplicity.

But something can be simpler than another in a different way. It can have fewer parts than the other thing, but superior parts or parts brought together more effectively, endowing it with all the advantages belonging to the more complex thing and more besides. Hemingway's 39 words are better words and work better together and are more unified than my 114. So his accomplish all that mine do and

---

[2] Ernest Hemingway, *The Old Man and the Sea* (New York: Scribner, 1952), pp.13–14.

more besides. That is an example of what we might call a concentrated simplicity, one that gives you more bang for your buck.

Deprived simplicity is more familiar to us and is easier to grasp. With only that type in our minds, we would be apt to stumble into the mistake of Dawkins. But once we see that the other type exists, our reconciliation of simplicity and perfection in god is complete. He is perfectly simple. The most concentrated and effective simplicity of all.

The Supreme and Everlasting Animal

If you are having difficulty conceiving of the divine mind—a single thought simultaneously grasping all things, past, present, and future, actual and possible, in all their nitty-gritty details—you are in good company. No one can fathom it. I certainly cannot. If I could, I would be able to form that potent single thought myself. And then I would be god. As it is, I have to form a distinct thought for each thing I want to understand distinctly. I can either think about all things in a vague and general way, gaining perfect simplicity of thought while giving up all detail, or I can think about them one at a time—first porcupines in particular, then triangles, then democracy, and so on, thus gaining detail and particularity, but at the price of having to change my mind all the time and of knowing at any given moment only one tiny thing in a very big world. Any single thought I form leaves out either most things or most differences between things. Any one thought I form is a poor thing by itself. God's one thought concentrates all the advantages of a whole lifetime's worth of my thoughts and more. So, as I said, his thought lies beyond my understanding.

But that does not mean I cannot know it exists. I have no idea what the next prime number after $2^{43112609} - 1$ is, but I am perfectly certain there is a number of that description, because I understand the proof that there cannot be a greatest prime number. Likewise, I can't form a distinct notion of god's thought or of what it would be like to be god, but I am certain that he exists and understands in the manner I have been trying to describe, thanks to the proofs of the last six chapters.

Does this mean we can form no conception at all of god's inner life? I think that is going too far. Beginning from the only kind of knowledge familiar to us firsthand, our own, we can form an inkling or two—provided we take care to tag and remove our own limitations from the picture. Our understanding of things becomes more complete and penetrating with time. God's is always complete. We work hard to understand and spend most of our time misunderstanding or trying to understand. God's understanding is error-free and effortless. Our conception of things is always to some extent general, lacking in detail, and abstract. God's understanding reaches every single thing, in all its specificity, in every place and time.

Even our experience of sensation can help us to understand god better, it seems to me. In many of those respects in which our intellectual life disappoints, our sense experience delivers. I strain to understand the stars. But I can see them without effort. And my eyes don't see just stars in general, in concepts; I see those particular stars out there, all at once, pricked out in the night sky. The difference is not lost on my students. With their eyesight they can see beauty much more easily and vividly and continuously than they can with their insight. They are always begging me to hold class outside in the gorgeous California sun. They don't like squinting at things with their minds. They prefer gazing on things with their eyes. They like to take it all in, all at once, without work. God's understanding is like that. He can know everything we can know with our intelligence (and much more), but he does so with the same ease with which we take in a landscape with our eyes (or with greater ease).

As one translation has it, Aristotle once called god "the supreme and everlasting animal". He could have said "the supreme and everlasting intellect"—in fact, he did say it and could have left it at that. Apparently he felt that sounded too dead to the human ear. *Intellect*. The very word sounds bookish and dusty. God is intelligent, but his intellect has the same effortless, vivid immediacy of eyesight. The two halves of our own nature, mind and sense, resemble him in complementary ways, it seems. By our minds, we have the power to understand (to some degree) the universe, and all things in it, to penetrate beneath the surfaces of things, and to transcend the limits of the here and now. By our senses, we have a taste of crisp knowledge without toil. Together, they make a more complete and worthwhile life for us than either would make by itself. Together, they paint a fuller portrait of god than either could do alone.

Here, we discover afresh that man is a microcosm. As the many parts of the universe imperfectly express the divine perfection that they imitate in distinct and particular ways, but together and as a unified whole they express the divine more fully, so do the rational and animal natures in a human being. What perfections we find apart in ourselves, residing in our distinct faculties, coalesce in the single and unlimited perfection of god.

8

Intractable Minds

Whereas unbelief is in the intellect, the cause of unbelief is in the will.

— Thomas Aquinas, *Summa Theologiae, Secunda Secundae*

Is Theism Boring?

Years ago, when my children were little, they expected birthday parties and other similar events involving whole armies of kids. At one of these events, a particularly rambunctious group of boys took it upon themselves to reenact various scenes from the movie *The Lord of the Rings*. Their soprano war cries and their running to and fro made me nervous, but I managed to hold my tongue and not spoil the fun. For a while. When a particular member of the Fellowship jumped up onto the coffee table, I felt the time had come to intervene. I could see the table rocking and hear the sand under his shoes grinding as he twisted this way and that to fend off imaginary orcs. I addressed this "Frodo" gently but firmly. "My dear Frodo," I said, "you really must stay off the coffee table and off the furniture generally." (Bear in mind that this particular Frodo had hardly seen more than five winters at the time.) Rather than hop off the table, however, this hobbit-size adventurer glowered at me, clenched both fists at his sides, and (this is true) threw out his chest as he demanded to know: "*Why?*"

I was taken aback. It was my house. My coffee table. I was the host, he the guest. That should have been enough why. But I gave him reasons anyway. I don't mean I gave him what for. I just mean I explained that jumping on furniture was bad for the furniture, as well as dangerous for the jumper. Did the explanation help? It did not. Hot, angry tears rolled down his cheeks. He leapt off the table and ran out of the room, fists still clenched at his sides, to inform on me to his mother, who was in our kitchen.

Now it is the why part that interests me. How should we understand such a why? It came not from a desire to learn but from a wish to defy. Our exchange had been a contest of wills, not of intellects, and he was angry that I had won. But the assertion of his contrary will had nonetheless taken the form of an inquiry—"Why?"

We grown-ups are not always as far above this kind of thing as we think. We too can dress up what is really an attitude as though it were a reasoned stance. We too can feel the urge to defy authorities who gainsay our will. Perhaps you have seen the old "Question authority" bumper sticker. There can be good reasons to question authority. But if someone questions every authority simply because it is an authority, there's a bit of the teenager in that—or of the rambunctious five-year-old.

In prior chapters, I concentrated on purely intellectual problems concerning the existence of god. Here I turn to problems that involve the human will in one way or another. One source of hesitation about god is what we think. Another is what we want. In the next chapter, we shall see how the existence of evil in the world can make god unappealing to many people and can even form the basis of an argument against his existence. In this chapter, we shall see that aside from the manner in which god governs, some people find it distasteful to conceive of anyone governing the world at all. To them, cosmic anarchy seems best. The very idea of god offends such people's intellectual sensibilities. They feel that life in general, and intellectual life in particular, is more fulfilling without a god than with one. Let's begin by examining that idea.

Richard Dawkins thinks it possible to be an intellectually fulfilled atheist. In one sense, that is clearly impossible. Consider the questions "What is the first cause? And what is so special about it that it does not need a cause?" There are no truly satisfying answers to those questions for an atheist. An atheist can deny that there is any first cause at all, postulating instead an infinite regression of presently acting causes producing any given effect. But that is practically the definition of intellectual frustration. There is no ultimate answer. Infinite causal regression of that kind is impossible anyway, as we saw back in chapter 1. Or an atheist can substitute another first cause in god's place—matter, for example. But then he cannot supply any good reason why matter gets to exist and act without dependence on a cause, while other things do not. All matter involves combinations of distinct parts and properties, and all kinds of potentials, and those are the very things that require combiners and actualizers before them. And what exactly about the concept *matter* makes it impossible for it to have a cause? To remain satisfied with atheism, there are many questions one simply mustn't ask.

If atheism is intellectually frustrating in the sense that certain ultimate questions must be carefully avoided, there is another way of gauging it. Theism can feel like a cramp in one's intellectual style insofar as it posits a single cause for all things. Where atheism allows for a whole pantheon of causes at work in the universe, theism, or at any rate monotheism, would seem to allow just one—god. "God" becomes the boring monosyllabic answer to all interesting questions. Why do birds have wings? "God made them so, my dear." Why do stars burn longer than forest fires? "God, in his infinite wisdom, saw fit to make them that way, and it is not for us to question him." The Richard Dawkinses of the world, meanwhile, regale us (or at any rate, promise one day to regale us) with a feast of reason: there is a special cause for each special effect, a fascinating and unique genesis for every creature under the sun, a symphony of cooperative powers required for the production and maintenance of the humblest bacteria; the world itself, instead of hanging there, passive and limp, is a powerful, productive, fertile mother of all things. The theist, meanwhile, is in danger of admiring god not just more than the universe, but instead of it. The universe gets demoted to a mere stage equipped with pulleys and props, with god the lone actor upon it. A dull play.

Would that this were only an unfair caricature of theists drawn by the atheists. Unfortunately, some of the "creation science" books do more to destroy the credibility of theism than any atheist could ever do. To read some of these, one would indeed think that god alone causes things, and the world is populated with no real causes at all, but with mere puppets inside of which the divine hand alone is at work. One might as well say: "Fire does not burn paper; *god* burns it. To make fire a true cause of burning would be to detract from the divine causation! Molecules and natural forces are all very well, so long as we don't allow them to *do* anything."

The truth, though, is quite the contrary. Were god thus incapable of producing anything genuinely productive, unable to cause a real cause, powerless to confer power, then his causation would sink beneath our own. We can make powerful things, things that really do things: space shuttles, pacemakers, computer-operated railroads. All the more can god do so. Since he is the supreme cause, he must possess supreme power to make other causes, to confer upon things other than himself the dignity of causation. And he is perfectly willing to do so. He is not jealous or afraid of his own works.

If god produces true causes, then he cannot be "the cause of all things" in the sense that he creates every single thing solo. Of course, he does make *some* things in that way. Whatever his first product is—say, the first and most fundamental material underlying everything—he must produce all by himself. Perhaps others, too. But there are scads of other causes at work in the world besides the first cause. Parents cause their children. Builders cause their buildings; poets their poems. Planets cause eclipses. Pathogens cause diseases. Doctors effect cures. Teachers educate. Acknowledging these causes, studying them, admiring them, and, when appropriate, extending our gratitude to them is not to deny their derivation from still prior causes, or from the very first cause of all. Conversely, acknowledging the first cause of all things is not the equivalent of annihilating all other causes. Recognizing the military genius of a general is not the same as denying the role of those under his command. True, the general does not supply his soldiers with their whole substance and power of action, as god does for created things. The cases are nonetheless analogous. The soldiers truly receive from their general things without which they could not gain a victory. They receive instructions and information about the disposition of the enemy, and perhaps they take the necessary courage for action from the general's stirring exhortations. The general himself, therefore, in some sense acts within his soldiers as they march and fight, seeing as it is his words and his passion within them that direct them and urge them on. Be that ever so true, the knowledge and will that he has given them to make war are now really theirs, really within them, and they really act by means of them. All the more must god be capable of communicating causal power to other things, while they truly depend on him. God is therefore not the replacement of other causes, but the cause of them. Our understanding of god does not replace our understanding of other causes, but completes our understanding of them.

The existence of god, therefore, does not eviscerate intellectual life. That might follow were it impossible for the very same effect to have many causes—but that is not impossible. It is not that my pencil is writing some parts of this chapter and I am writing the other parts. The pencil is writing the whole chapter, and so am I. Two causes for the entirety of the same effect. This is possible because the pencil's power to write the words comes from me. When god makes natural causes, he does something similar, although in the measure that he is a superior cause to me, the power he gives to other causes is correspondingly more real, more intrinsic to them, and more abiding. The acorn has a real power within it to become an oak, whereas the pencil lying on my desk has no inherent power to write a specific sentence, and I can give it none. Nonetheless, neither the acorn nor its power would exist if it were not for god's action conserving it in its being, just as the pencil would not write were it not for my action of writing by means of it.

It seems to many people that if god does something, then nothing else is doing it, and if something else is doing it, then god is not the cause of it. This thinking is in part responsible for the creation of the "god of the gaps"—the stand-in "god" who gets hauled in to explain effects in the world only when no better cause seems to be available. Once he explained lightning, but then we found a better cause for that, and the god of lightning was retired. Another time he explained the growth of the crops, or the rain, or earthquakes, or fertility and infertility, or recovery from illness; when other causes for these were found, god's scope for action shrunk still further. Anyone can read the writing on the wall. The god of the gaps will soon become the god of rare, strange events with conveniently few witnesses and eventually the god of nothing at all. Napoleon Bonaparte once asked Pierre-Simon Laplace where god fit into his mechanical model of the solar system, and Laplace famously replied, "I have no need of that hypothesis." And really, who does? Even Christians, who believe that god is the cause of rare and strange events, to be sure, also believe that he is the cause of all things whatsoever, which means they do not believe in a god who gets put out of a job as soon as other causes come into play. Rather, he is the cause of such causes.

There is no competition between the carpenter and his tools in order to take credit for the house being built. It is not as if the carpenter causes some little bit of the house over here while the tools and materials cause a different bit over there. Whatever the tools and materials cause to come to be, the carpenter does too, and vice versa. And there is no redundancy in this. He is not superfluous, because he is a cause of an altogether different order from that of his tools and materials. All the more is this true for god, who is not a cause of natural or human effects in the same manner as the particular natural or human causes involved; rather, he is a cause of those causes themselves. God is the cause of all things, of everything, not by replacing the other causes at work in the world, but by producing them and sustaining them in being in accord with the laws of being, of coming to be, and of ceasing to be, which he has established.

A particular sticking point for some people is that god is supposed to be an immobile cause of all things, whereas many things change, or begin to exist and then cease to exist after a while. Doesn't it follow that god is causing this right now, and later he is not causing it, and so he has changed from causing to not causing? Does it follow that he is a changeable being after all? That *would* follow if his causing required some reality added to him and not just a new reality in his effects. For god to cause something does not really require a change in him. His causal power is like the knowledge of a teacher, which can be entirely unaffected by causing similar knowledge in others. It is true that a teacher sometimes learns by teaching, but that is true only in an incidental way; it is not precisely in virtue of the student's increasing in knowledge that the teacher also does, but only by the teacher's noticing new things while explaining something. And often that does *not* happen while a teacher teaches, but his knowledge comes away entirely unaffected by its communication to another. It is also true that a teacher has to choose to teach now and then choose to stop teaching later, and his knowledge is sometimes "asleep", stored away in his mind in habitual, accessible form, and other times it is "awake" in actual use. But if his knowledge were *always* in use and awake, like god's, that would only mean it was always ready to communicate itself to others. The teacher himself also exists and operates by means of motions and changes taking place in time, and he is in these ways unlike god. In fact, god must be the cause of time itself, since time, whatever it is, is not god, but seems to be something tied up with space and change. Nothing prevents god from willing that change and time exist, by an unchanging and eternal act of will. Why, even we can get up in the morning and will that various events take place in some temporal order during our day, without changing our minds as the day goes on.

The Will to Atheism

I have said that atheism cannot possibly be intellectually satisfying insofar as it cuts short certain investigations. But there is a special sense in which atheism is more "intellectually satisfying" than theism. I mean that the atheist can afford to believe that he pretty much knows the whole basic story of reality or at least that this is possible in principle. Not all atheists think that way, of course. Einstein comes to mind. While he refused to call himself an atheist, he was certainly a disbeliever in any "personal" god endowed with mind and will. He called the notion childish. But he believed that the world, or something underlying it or immanent within it, was fundamentally and permanently incomprehensible to us, and that the proper attitude toward it was one of humility. That is an option for the atheist, albeit a rather "mystical" and perhaps not entirely consistent one. It allows for a kind of reverence for reality as something essentially "bigger" (in an intelligible sense) than we are, and not just "bigger for now". But that is not atheism in its purest form. The unadulterated atheist thinks of all reality as intellectually conquerable. We don't have the whole of it in the palm of our hand just yet, but that should be our goal and our hope. At least that is another option for the atheist, and one that probably suits him best.

The theist has no option like the second. The god discovered by the reasonings in this book cannot have a mind just like ours, or just like anything we can imagine, experience, or comprehend. He is forever and in principle beyond our encapsulation, so far as our human faculties (or any finite faculties) go. The step from man to god is greater, incomparably greater, than the step from beast to man. A toad would stand a better chance of fully comprehending a man, and of appreciating the whole life of that man, than a man would have of comprehending god, of knowing him through and through. The gulf is unbridgeable, at least from our side. The theist has no choice but to acknowledge that he is profoundly ignorant and to admit that what he does not know about reality permanently and infinitely surpasses whatever he knows. God's knowledge of the universe, and of you or me, must infinitely surpass our understanding of the universe and of ourselves.

So there must forever be truths about all things, including ourselves, of which we are ignorant, and the best we can hope for by sailing on our own steam is continuous finite progress into the infinity of truth. Experience confirms this. Who would dare lay claim to a perfect and exhaustive understanding of anything? Who fully understands everything that is true about a triangle, for instance? The mathematician has not lived who dared to claim that. Now, a triangle is a relatively flat and shabby thing compared with living beings such as ourselves, let alone compared with god.

In this respect, the atheist has available to him a "satisfaction" that the theist does not: the satisfaction of regarding himself or his clique or at least his species as unsurpassed possessors of wisdom—that is, of a knowledge of all things that is in principle thorough and complete and in principle as good as anyone else's (be he human or alien). Not every atheist takes advantage of that opportunity. Plenty of atheists are modest people. But atheism opens the door to believing that human enlightenment, or one's personal enlightenment, is supreme. No theist is free to think of himself or his kind in that way. On the other hand, there is a difference between *satisfied* and *self-satisfied*. The only way to rest in the intellectual self-satisfaction specifically available to the atheist is to neglect to pursue certain questions to their end and to take care to read only the lowbrow theists, or better still, none at all. Anyway, that is the manner of intellectual satisfaction available to him and not to the theist.

Theists are, of course, quite capable of being intellectually arrogant asses. But a theist of that variety seems to keep god at a safe distance, locked up in the realm of unreal abstractions, as though he existed for the sole purpose of enabling the theist to be right about something. Such a person might even be a practical, if not a theoretical, atheist, assenting in a purely intellectual way to the existence of god, but in no way letting that remote fact muck up his life. A theist who is alive to what he is acknowledging, who thinks of god as being quite as real as and no more abstract and ideal than his own wife and kids, will suffer a more or less continual awareness of his own inferiority. And his very knowledge of god, since it is tediously reasoned out and not vivid and immediate, will impress on him its anemic and abstract quality. The reasonings such as those found in this book, be they ever so rigorous, exact, and correct, are nonetheless reasonings, possessing none of the immediacy and vitality that are to be found even in plain sensation. It is one thing to read about the blue whale; it is another to take a ride on its back. It is one thing to know the meaning of "a regular polygon with five trillion sides" and to know that there is no impossibility in such a figure; it is quite another to form a distinct and vivid image of it. So too it is one thing to know, as the result of tedious reasoning, that this statement is true: "There is a being possessing all positive perfections in itself, and simultaneous knowledge of all things, without any composition or confusion of these, all in a single and simple actuality." It is altogether another matter to be able to form a simple and positive conception of what it is like to be such a being. We simply can't fit such a thing into our heads. John of Damascus once called god "the infinite ocean of substance". The image is apt. The ocean has parts, of course, and god does not, but both contain an inexhaustible wealth of life. And there is this further parallel: as an infinite ocean has no limits to its size by which we could circumscribe it and see it all at once, so god has no limits to his perfection by which we could define him and encapsulate him in a single, adequate conception. "Knowledge of stars" is true about god, since he has—or rather is—such a knowledge. But so too "knowledge of numbers" is true of him, and "knowledge of animals" and "knowledge of languages", and these are true of him not in virtue of different thoughts he occasionally forms one after another, but in virtue of one and the same unlimited, uncircumscribed divine thought, through which he knows all things at once, without discourse or confusion. We ourselves can form no such thought. The true nature of it lies forever beyond us, however sure we are that it must exist.

Another source of satisfaction for the atheist that no theist can hope to enjoy is moral autonomy. If we demand our autonomy—if we hold dear the notion that we (as individuals or as a race) are entirely self-determining, that we can become what we please without further consequences than those that follow logically and physically upon our choices, that we should finally be answerable to no one—atheism sits well with that. A god, however, throws a giant wrench into that machine. True, a god might be imagined who was rather indifferent to our behavior—although why such a laissez-faire god would bother to make and sustain things other than himself would be difficult or impossible to say. A god necessarily introduces the possibility of an external measure and standard, so that we have to satisfy not just ourselves anymore, but another being with (only too likely) standards and an agenda quite different from our own. That is potentially unpleasant. To find ourselves indebted, by our very existence, can come off as rather unflattering, even oppressive. Christopher Hitchens once wrote that he could never find it consoling to believe in god, since to do so is to believe in a sort of benevolent dictatorship.

Certainly a benevolent dictatorship is an obnoxious thing (and hence never altogether benevolent) because a dictator, in the usual sense of the word, is someone who robs us of many decisions we are better off making for ourselves. God, however, does not seem bent on robbing us of any decisions. He bestows upon us our decision-making power in the first place, right along with our nature and our existence. Surely he wouldn't give us decision-making power just to squelch it, but more in order that by it we might move ourselves toward happiness and (some say) especially toward a share in his happiness, which is infinitely better than any of our own design. But he does not insist. Quite undictatorlike, he will, it seems, let us choose to flick him away like a nasty bug, to sneer at him and call him a dictator, if we like—although we can hardly fault him if he does not come crawling back to us every time we do this, but eventually leaves us to our own devices.

If anything, it might seem that god is far too indulgent with us. A wayward child of the very best parents will sometimes regard them as dictators, and not even as particularly benevolent ones, though that is no fault of theirs. The child is narrow-minded and egocentric and incompetent to govern himself, unassisted, toward a more mature and more worthwhile life. The child's parents accordingly behave far more like benevolent dictators than god does. Seeing their beloved toddler's incompetence in self-governing, they will *not* take his no for an answer, will *not* leave him to shift for himself, as far as they have anything to say about it. And they insist upon their rule even though their headstrong toddler is much nearer to being their equal than any human being is when compared with god. Some of us, blessed with good parents, grow up wishing that our parents had been less strict with us. Once we have grown up enough to appreciate their superior wisdom, we are amazed that we used to regard them as impediments to our freedom. All the more might we wish that god were less tolerant of our mistakes in life. As it is, he is no dictator, however obnoxious he might have seemed to Hitchens.

A superior alien race is a much less annoying prospect for the atheistic will to perfect autonomy. However superior to us they might be in intelligence, we could always hope to catch up by our own evolution one day. They would be like the older siblings we could look forward to outgrowing. Or they might even go extinct and we needn't worry about them. But with god, it is all unilateral benefit giving and entirely irreversible superiority on his side, with permanent debt and dependence on ours. One might say the idea of god offends our democratic sensibilities. But atheism makes room for our perfect autonomy. As Nietzsche's Zarathustra put it: "To reveal my heart entirely to you, friends: *if* there were gods, how could I endure not to be a god! *Therefore* there are no gods."[1] Clearly this is an expression of will and not proof. I have known atheists all my life and have been and continue to be friends with many, but it was not until graduate school that I met one who showed me that it can be, and perhaps usually is, a willful disposition. The person I have in mind was another graduate student, a friend of a friend, who drew me into arguing for god's existence over beer and pizza one night in the house in which I was renting a room. We went on and on, exchanging arguments, counterarguments, objections, replies, distinctions—it was exhausting, though not exactly unpleasant. It was after three in the morning when I thought I had him. He conceded to me that he saw no flaw in my positive arguments and now perceived the defects in all the objections he had formerly presented to the existence of god. Victory? Not at all. He told me plainly that he was not in the least moved or disturbed by this outcome, that he

---

[1] Friedrich Nietzsche, *Thus Spoke Zarathustra: A Book for Everyone and No One*, trans. R. J. Hollingdale (New York: Penguin Books, 1969), p. 110.

would certainly remain an atheist, and that he was not likely to give the matter any further thought after we parted ways. My jaw dropped, and I asked him something to this effect: "Don't you realize that if your position cannot be altered no matter how you come to regard its rational merits, then your atheism is not rational, but simply willful?" For the first time in our conversation he appeared to be deeply moved, and again I thought maybe I had him on the ropes. But he said, with perfect calm and raising his eyebrows a bit as if appreciating some truly important insight, "You may be right." I got no sense that this was embarrassing to him—only interesting. He had not learned anything important about reality at large, but only about himself. And he gave every appearance of being content with what he saw in himself. Rather than rouse him from his atheism, I had inadvertently helped make him a more self-conscious atheist.

Understand that I am not suggesting here that every atheist is someone who really just wants to live a life of dissipation and therefore decides not to believe in an inconvenient god. To that same end, a person might as well believe in an indulgent god (such people are not difficult to find). The grad student whom I just described was certainly not inclined to reckless living. On the contrary, he was remarkably principled—perfectly sober, perfectly honest, and by all accounts perfectly faithful to his girlfriend (later his wife). He even reprimanded one of our mutual friends for his attachment to pornography, which he regarded as degrading to women. He was also remarkably erudite and generally cultured. Only, his atheism was not a reasoned thing; it was a preference. He simply didn't *like* the way the world looked to him with a god in the picture. It made the picture ugly to him. He would have nothing to do with it. I am not sure why. No doubt he had encountered many of god's unpleasantly self-appointed representatives (who hasn't?) endowed with an exquisite combination of ignorance and arrogance. Certainly he had studied the histories of the ungodly things people claimed to have done in god's (or rather in God's) name. Probably the intelligent and cultured people he had met had, for the most part, been atheists with little interest in god one way or another, and the god-fearing people he had encountered had largely been uneducated, uncultured types with coarse sensibilities and with whom he had little in common. However it was, his atheism was a matter of preference, not a rational conclusion.

And it seems to me that this is the only sort of atheism that really sticks. If there is nothing of will in it, nothing of personal distaste for or indifference to the idea of god, if it is purely a matter of drawing proper conclusions from sound premises, one's atheism is in grave danger. That's because sound reasoning finally goes only one way. The rational, even if unwanted, conclusion is that there is a god. Now, even an honest and intelligent person can fail to see this for quite a long time, even when face-to-face with the right arguments. Reasonings to god's existence that proceed by deducing inevitable consequences of self-evident truths, reasonings such as the ones in this book, can easily appear as mere probable arguments. If the presentation is particularly poor, or the audience ill disposed, the same can look like mere rhetorical arguments, or even question begging. Their proper force cannot be seen, cannot be felt, until one devotes time, thought, and energy to their foundational principles. Like an unknown challenger in a prizefight, good theistic reasoning needs to be given a chance to show its real strength. If it is dismissed the first time an objection is lodged against it, the first time it takes a hit, if one does not stay and see whether it really goes down for the count, then one will never see its power to withstand objections. Or one can watch some theistic reasoning defeat the reigning atheistic champion and conclude that it was a lucky punch—or at least that one day it too will be dealt a knockout blow.

There can be many causes behind this kind of unimpressed response to a genuine proof. One such cause is inexperience with the mode of reasoning used in proofs. In college I once presented the whole argument for the Pythagorean theorem to a friend, but he still wasn't convinced it was true. He said he didn't see why someone couldn't come along one day and raise a problem with the proof that no one had ever thought of before. He himself didn't see any problem with the proof. He just had that vague concern. Such concern is reasonable when the evidence presented rests on hypotheses or guesses or probabilities, or when the mode of argument does not guarantee the truth of the conclusion just because the premises are true. On the other hand, when a pure deduction starts from premises such as "Equals added to equals make equals", that settles the matter. But if someone is unaccustomed to deductive reasoning, he tends to mistake it for a weaker form of reasoning with which he is more familiar and responds to it accordingly. So someone can walk away from a proof unfazed.

This is truer still when the deduction is the target of many objections. To see how the back-and-forth all plays out, to get to the real bottom of things, demands that one stay focused on such arguments. This sort of staying, however, is incredibly time-consuming, especially in the case of reasonings about god. Few have the patience for it. Antony Flew is a rare example; he was a contemporary British philosopher who scrutinized arguments for and against god for over fifty years before abandoning atheism in favor of theism. His was an extreme case, and it is not my contention that it takes fifty years to get the argument, if one happens to begin with the right arguments—such as those found in Aquinas. Nonetheless, one must be willing to read a book or two and do so with care and attention. Such committed self-application requires very strong desire. If, then, someone is not terribly *interested* in whether there is a god, it will be impossible for him ever to see the force of genuine theistic reasoning. It will always appear to him silly, or nitpicking, or at least dismissible and indecisive. And if someone would rather that there *not* be a god, he finds nothing in his immediate experience that forces him to take any other view, and his atheism has the appearance of something self-evident. Perhaps he can be made to see that atheism is not self-evident and that he cannot prove it—but then he finds it still quite possible, without effort, to look at the world in the way that he would rather have it be. And so he does. And he cannot be induced to give himself over to some arduous course of study when the only incentive is that he might be released from what he in fact finds to be a rather congenial arrangement.

It should come as no surprise, then, that atheists and materialists in their most honest moments make no pretensions about establishing their view by rational means. The idea that atheism can be somehow proved by science is particularly lame. In an oft-quoted passage from "Billions and Billions of Demons" (which appeared in *The New York Review* in 1997), evolutionary biologist and atheist Richard Lewontin wrote:

It is not that the methods and institutions of science somehow compel us to accept a material explanation of the phenomenal world, but, on the contrary, that we are forced by our *a priori* adherence to material causes to create an apparatus of investigation and a set of concepts that produce material explanations, no matter how counter-intuitive, no matter how mystifying to the uninitiated. Moreover, that materialism is an absolute, for we cannot allow a Divine Foot in the door.[2]

The truth is that modern materialism is a choice made prior to reasoning about the question, before evidence is brought in, and it dictates what sorts of evidence will be admitted in court henceforth.

"Finite Goods Only, Please"

Atheism is not particularly fulfilling intellectually and philosophically. Could it nonetheless be described as better than theism? Is it preferable? Does it present a rosier picture? Let's consider: Which should we prefer to be true—that there be in existence, or that there not be, an infinite good, a perfectly happy and everlasting being, whose life we might ourselves come to share? The question should answer itself. Even if we prescind from the possibility of our entering into god's life, it seems to me the answer as to which truth is "better" remains the same. If there were an entity more complete and perfect than the universe itself, that would be exciting, not boring; thought provoking, not stifling. And are we any worse off for finding ourselves dependent upon a god who made us? We are already dependent for practically everything on each other and on the universe—both for our coming into existence and continuing in it, for our being well off and for our being at all. What difference does it make to add one more benefactor to the long list?

Ah, but the answer is obvious: there is the unpleasant idea that we might be judged by god, subject to him, answerable to him. Nor is that all. Unlike the authority of human societies, his authority might well come equipped with omniscience and omnipotence. Which of us would be pleased to discover that the manner of living we had hitherto thought purely our own, free and clear, was in fact being conferred upon us quite conditionally by some elderly stranger in a

---

[2] Richard C. Lewontin, "Billions and Billions of Demons", *New York Review*, January 9, 1997, p. 31.

far-off country, who had expectations of our devoting ourselves to acts of gratitude and obedience—who watched our every move, and who expected us to live by his arbitrary standards, on pain of having our income withheld or of being punished in horrible ways? Which of us would, in short, be happy to learn that his whole life was in the hands of someone like Bertie Wooster's meddlesome Aunt Agatha, only with a good deal more knowledge and power?

Admittedly an abhorrent image. It arises, however, not out of rational reflection on what god is, but from anthropomorphic think-ing or else from the doctrines of one or another of the purportedly revealed religions or from some misrepresentation of them (deliberate or otherwise). Particular revelations aside, there is no sound reason to think that the first cause is a silly being with ill-conceived ideas and unfair demands. Quite the opposite. It is beyond the scope of this book to investigate the moral qualities of god (although I will get into these somewhat in the next chapter). Here it should be enough to observe that anyone who finds infinite goodness and infinite knowl-edge to be dull or disgusting things in themselves, things that would be better not to exist than to exist, is an odd duck, to say the least.

Nor is there anything repellent about an external moral standard for us. Rather it is the person who truly wishes to be autonomous—to do whatever he darn well pleases without consequences and to indulge whatever desires might happen to dwell in the darkest recesses of his heart—who is repellent. And what if the external standard is patient, wise, just, merciful, and morally *helpful* and not merely a judge? Show me someone who has never engaged in weighty moral struggles and occasionally lost or come perilously close to losing, someone who claims never even to have felt the temptation to do something that would embarrass him to have published to all his family and friends, and I will show you someone who lies to you, if not also to himself. Show me someone who has never come to realize that some of his former views about what is right and wrong were goofy, and I will show you either a teenager or else an old fool.

It should not be the mere existence of moral authority, of the external standard, that we shun. It should be only the incompetent, intrusive, malignant, and unhelpful one. We have all seen, in life and literature alike, the legalistic, pharisaical authoritarian who feels the need to make his greatness felt. He enjoys inspiring fear and shame and inflicting punishment for its own sake. And he never fails to excite our contempt. He reveals in himself a pettiness, a meanness, a smallness of soul. He is ugly. We are his moral superiors, and we know it. He bears every sign of someone testing his own greatness, so that he might be sure of it. God, surely, is nothing like that. Such shriveled motives require uncertainty of oneself, hence weakness or ignorance, or both. God is immune to these.

We have also encountered the sanctimonious moral prig, who has warned us time and time again, who loves to say, "I told you so", who is vociferous in condemning, eager for our next slipup, who shakes his head, but who never stirs a finger to help us out of our troubles. That is just another form of the same pettiness, born of the need to feel bigger than someone else. If we mortals are sometimes susceptible to it, that is no reason to think god could ever be. As Aristotle said, god cannot be jealous. Hence, neither could he be petty or mean. All of those things imply neediness.

As to which scenario is more flattering, more consoling to the self-complacent, more agreeable to the indolent, there can be no question. The godless universe is "better" in the estimation of such souls. As to which would be better absolutely, surely infinite goodness wins that contest. Besides, it is rather a heavy condition of our self-satisfaction that we be satisfied with our condition, with no more happiness (and no less misery) than our own wherewithal can guarantee. A frightful prospect, especially for those of us less fortunate. Surely the picture brightens if there are greater goods available to us than those we mere humans can supply for ourselves? We have motive to think otherwise only if our moral inertia outstrips our desire for great things. Not believing in anything better means we don't have to do anything about it.

Why We Wonder

Let's return, for a moment, to intellectual fulfillment. Some of the New Atheists are driven by a sense of wonder—the desire to understand, for its own sake, mixed with a certain awe of, or admiration for, the magnitude, the ancientness, and the splendor of the universe that it is their desire to understand. This desire to understand, this sense of wonder, implanted in all of us, stronger in some of us than in others, and quickly educated out of most of us if we take no special precautions, is in the strictest sense significant. It is a sign that the first cause of things, the author of our natural desires, is an intelligence who made the universe for the sake of provoking wonder and for moving minds such as ours toward deeper and deeper understanding, which is to say, toward himself.

Those who see natural selection as the sole author of intelligence must see intelligence as a mere tool. It is *for survival* (albeit in a weak and nonpurposive sense of *for*). As with any other excrescence, intelligence is not worthwhile in itself, but only because it is somehow useful for the continuation of our species. That is all. Understanding for its own sake cannot produce even a blip on natural selection's radar. Only the understanding that produces survival results can be of any "interest" to it. But it is an odd fact that many of the things that provoke our admiration the most, and on which we bend the efforts of our understanding, are also the most useless to survival. We want to know whether there is intelligent life on other planets just to know this, not so much because we are in search of survival advice or better real estate. For that matter, bacteria are more adept at surviving than we are, quite without the superfluous appendage of scientific intelligence and philosophical wonder. Perhaps it is just our bad luck that our particular evolutionary path requires us to survive by our wits; that is our peculiar niche, as it were, relatively inefficient though it may be. At any rate, it is entirely a fluke if our naturally selected intelligence should happen to cause us to delight in anything objectively delightful and worthy of admiration in itself. It might even be a fluke if our minds are well formed for discovering truth; truth is often not particularly relevant to survival, and many an illusion proves useful.

Accordingly, the atheist must endorse a rather stunted and incoherent theory of wonder. He must, on the one hand, insist on the pursuit of truth for truth's sake, wherever it may lead, in order to maintain his credibility. He must praise wonder and denounce intellectual indifference, self-serving thought, and lazy credulity. More than that, he has to praise the beauty of the universe if he is to avoid looking like a curmudgeon. He must subscribe to the wholesomeness of science and literature for their own sakes, not merely for political ends, if he is not to appear an insensible, thuggish bureaucrat. On the other hand, his principles do not permit him the luxury of any convincing genealogy for the spirit of wonder. It can only ever be the freak side effect of pragmatic survival instinct. It cannot really have been honed by natural selection, since *wonder* means the true love of knowledge for itself, precisely not just for its utilitarian results (just as truly loving a woman means loving her for herself, not for her money or her connections or the use of her body). But natural selection is not supposed to be able to encourage anything apart from what is useful for survival, never mind something that is altogether apart from any utility. And yet such are the things we wonder about most. We wonder how many stars there are, and how many galaxies, and how old the universe is, and whether it comes to a stop anywhere, and what that would mean. We wonder about these apart from any utility the answers might bring. And there is little hope that they will bring any.

Truth be told, our speculative interests often run against immediate practical concerns. They say curiosity killed a cat. Archimedes was murdered by a soldier because he refused to look away from the circles he was drawing. A servant girl laughed at Thales for falling into a well while he was gazing up at the stars. Such devotion to truth for truth's sake could earn someone the Darwin Award. It is anything but survival minded. If, unlike the servant girl, we admire wonder, it is not because it brings us nifty gadgets and adapts us to our environment. It is because our wonder is what enables us to rise out of ourselves, above our petty concerns, and to catch a glimpse of greater, grander things, to take them in, and in some way grow more like them, and participate in the divine. If there is anything natural selection could not give two shakes about, that's it.

Atheism, in sum, does not allow for a very satisfying explanation of the desire for satisfying explanations. According to the atheistic view, moreover, if the universe is as wondrously beautiful as we perceive it to be, this can be no more than a bizarre cosmic coincidence—both that it should *be* wondrously beautiful and that we should perceive it to be so. Atheism can admit no beauty-producing causes.

The moment god is allowed on the scene, wonder makes perfect sense. No longer is it a mere freak of one mammalian species' drive to survive, however useful it might occasionally be to that end. Instead, wonder becomes an internal compass intentionally bestowed upon such creatures as can follow its pointer. The beauty of the universe, too, becomes significant, and not an inexplicable piece of serendipity. The world becomes both a thing in its own right, and also a beacon to beings such as ourselves who are sensitive to meaning and look for significance. The world is real. But it is also really saying something.

Faith and Satisfaction (and Dissatisfaction)

Since my general topic in this chapter is god and intellectual fulfill-ment, it might seem negligent of me to ignore the question of reli-gious faith. I must excuse myself from any attempt here at apologetics for my own faith. That project is not especially relevant to the one I have undertaken in this book. But while I will not here defend my particular faith, I will offer a word in defense of religious faith in principle.

I am a Catholic. That is my faith, my belief, not a body of conclu-sions about god deduced from self-evident starting points. I cannot defend the claims unique to my faith as I have set out to defend the main thesis of this book—that is to say, by reasoning with inescapable logic solely from premises that are equally accessible to every honest, willing, and capable mind. I can offer no like procedure by which to arrive at the Trinity or the Incarnation or the Eucharist or any other distinctively Christian (or Judeo-Christian) articles of faith. No one can. And no educated Catholic would pretend to be so capable. My faith affords me a great many answers, albeit on a type of trust, which the method of this book simply could never yield.

My faith and the results of thinking about god from self-evident first principles nevertheless harmonize. I could hardly hold the contents of both theistic philosophy and of my faith to be true if I did not think them compatible. But they are also in some measure independent of each other. Were I, for whatever reason, to lose my confidence in the particular reasonings in this book, my faith, not based on them, would remain. Probably I would go in search of new arguments, hopeful, because of my faith, that such could be found (see Romans 1:20 and Wisdom 13, for instance), since I find myself driven to pur-sue the greatest questions as far as I am able. But my faith would not depend on the results. Conversely, were I (God forbid) to lose my faith, my confidence in reasonings such as those found in this book would remain. I might become a seeker among other religions purporting to be of divine origin; but I would carry my little share of philosophy before me like a lamp, and whatever religion ran afoul of it would hold no particular attraction for me.

It is possible to maintain the existence of god, even to know it as the result of sound reasoning, and to take the matter no further. Such, I suppose, would be the plight of someone who had no faith in any of the world's religions, but who saw the need to admit a god in a purely rational light. But that is not a very satisfactory state. Many crucial questions remain unanswered. Does god listen to prayers? To what extent does he care about me individually? What does he expect of me, if anything? Is there a life after this one? The very best philosophy can give only generic responses to such questions, not thoroughly satisfying and practical answers.

I once heard of a certain philosopher who, on his deathbed, when asked whether he would become a Christian, admitted his belief in Aristotle's "prime mover", but not in Jesus Christ as the Son of God. This sort of acknowledgment of the prime mover, of some sort of god, still leaves most of our chief concerns unaddressed. Will X ever see her son again, now that the poor boy has died of cancer at age six? Will miserable and contrite Y ever be forgiven, somehow reconciled to the universe and made whole, after having killed a family while driving drunk? Will Z ever be brought to justice, having lived out his whole life laughing at the law while another person rotted in jail for the atrocities he committed? That there is a prime mover does not tell us with sufficient clarity. Even the existence of an all-powerful, all-knowing, all-good god does not enable us to fill in much detail. And so it seems reasonable to suppose that god has something more to say to us, in explicit words, and not only in the mute signs of creation. Perhaps he is waiting to talk to us, biding his time for the right moment. Perhaps he has already spoken, but we have not recognized his voice.

When we cast our eye about by the light of reason in this way, it seems there is room for faith in general, even if no particular faith can be "proved" true in precisely the same way that it can be "proved" that there is a god. I do not mean that there are no arguments in favor of the truth of one religion over another. It is my own view that of the religions claiming to be of divine origin, only the Christian religion fully squares with what reason can know of god, of human nature, and of history. Be that as it may, reason is more capable of paving the way to religion than of driving us into it. It is friendly to religion in general, though not to all particular religions equally, and to some not at all. And it is reasonable to expect that god, were he to say something to us in words, would not limit himself to saying things that we can dream of in our philosophy. Probably he would add certain other things surpassing our powers of verification, which he would expect us to take on his word. It is reasonable, in other words, to expect that god would ask us to have a little faith in him.

Some, such as Sam Harris and Richard Dawkins and the late Christopher Hitchens, have said that even this is not true. If god is a mind, an intellect, say they, he would love the good of reason, of intelligence—namely, truth and evidence and vision, not a blind trust of the word of others. So god would never ask us to believe anything but would only show us things, or prove them to us, when the time was right. He would not ask us to abandon our minds in order to follow him.

There is some truth in that. God loves the good of reason, since he is the author of reason, the ultimate good of reason, and the most intelligible and interesting being there is to contemplate. He imbues the universe with its intelligibility, its rational order, making it beautiful in itself and communicative of its author. He speaks to us through reason, that divine spark in each of us. He gave us, and whatever other rational creatures call this universe their home, the drive to truth, thus steering us back to him as though by a homing instinct. It can be no desire of his that we choose which authorities to trust in divine matters more lightly than we decide which brand of fabric softener to use. Nor would he see much point in asking us to believe anything if our belief could never, in this life or some other, be turned into knowledge. But why would he demand belief at all? Why let us see some truths in the light of reason and evidence right now and show us others only after a lifetime of trust? Why would that ever be reasonable?

Well, is it not reasonable, on general principles, to offer some goods unconditionally, but others conditionally? We do this with our own children. One reason for offering certain goods conditionally is to provide an incentive for self-improvement, to present an opportunity to earn, and in some sense deserve, a further and superior good. It is better to receive a good deservedly, when possible, than to receive it purely because someone has been generous toward us. And when the further good in question surpasses our natural deserving, it becomes absolutely necessary for us to earn it and somehow rise to its level.

Suppose, then, that god presented us with two lives: (1) the first one here and now, in which to possess a happiness and a knowledge of him and all other things so far as in us lies, and also (2) a subsequent life in which to receive a happiness and a knowledge of him such as lies only in his power to give. The first is given without condition, since we cannot merit anything without first being alive in some way. Also, since this present life is commensurate with human capacities (and weakness and mortality), it does not really stand above us as something we must improve ourselves for in order that it be fittingly given to us. And if it is unequally happy for different people, and for some mostly miserable, it may at least present equal future opportunities for all and is in any case mercifully short. But the second life is god's own private life, as it were, his own blessedness, his own untouchable immortality and perfect knowledge. That is above us and is something god has no obligation to share—and, one might say, he has every reason not to foist it upon the undeserving. He will bestow his life upon those who prefer it to the living that they can scrape out for themselves by their own poor powers. He will confer it, then, upon those who prefer to trust his judgment over their own and who esteem his promises over all those of purely human origin. The superior good will be given to those, in short, who acknowledge its superiority, who appreciate it, who live accordingly, and thus deserve some part in it.

If some such arrangement as this were in the divine plan (and it does not take a Christian to think so—even Socrates, Plato, and Aristotle believed in something very like it), it would make plain sense for god to reveal to us certain things that we could not in this life verify for ourselves and regarding which we would have to trust him. On this supposition, god would be extending to us an invitation into his own life without yet drawing us fully into it.

Accompanying the invitation, presumably, would be some explanation of the means by which to grow in the divine favor, to become worthy recipients or heirs of his superhuman and eternal life. Being humanly good is not enough. That is sufficient for deserving a human happiness, perhaps. If we are to deserve the divine happiness, we must somehow become divinely good. But how? God alone can provide the means. Since his goodness is itself spiritual and invisible, the means of our conversion into it would also no doubt be spiritual and invisible, even if our access to those means were through visible actions, instruments, or vessels. Accepting the divine invitation would therefore require our belief in particular spiritual remedies and qualities, things of an invisible order that we must either accept on god's word or reject. God could openly reveal these spiritual things to all our minds if he wished, so that we could see immediately for ourselves their reality and nature, but in so doing he would deviate from the original course; he would now be granting us immediate vision and perfect possession of the things of his life rather than an imperfect possession by which to earn the perfect one. If he holds to the set course, he must instead tell us what to do in order to begin our interior configuration to him but not show us the spiritual reality of it just yet. We must take his word for it.

The arrangement itself, then, requires god to ask us to put a little faith in him. It is fairer than fair for god to demand of us some show of confidence in his wisdom and goodness before granting us full access to them. It would be an unspeakable injustice to grant divine wisdom to those unwilling to take god's word for anything, particularly things concerning him. If god is willing to make his creatures little gods, as it were, sharers in his own life in some degree, he must first hold them to certain standards and let them prove that they love the divine life as he himself does, as a life more worth living than all others combined. Faith in his word would be a minimum standard.

And so the expectation of faith would appear to be quite reasonable after all, at least in a general way and as a temporary measure. If god is to let us take hold of his eternal life and mind, we must first let him take hold of our temporal life and mind. That would be better than fair—a bargain infinitely in our favor. God could not be as closefisted as Nietzsche and say to himself, "Since I am god, how can I suffer others to be gods? Therefore there shall be no other gods!" He is too great to be so small-minded. He would rather communicate his divinity so far as possible, although none could ever be made quite his equal. Nonetheless, he could not very well thrust his divine life upon those who show contempt for it, like a self-disrespecting woman casting herself into the arms of every man she meets. Out of love for the goodness of his own life, he must pledge it only to those willing to prove they think it something worth waiting for and something too good to acquire without his help. He must pledge it, in other words, to those faithful to him.

Whether we venture down the path of some revealed religion or not, once we know god exists, we are bound to a moral response. At least we must come away impressed with a sense of our inferiority to the first mind and at the same time with a sense of our superiority to creatures incapable of thought. This sense of awe differs qualitatively from the variety found among the atheists. Carl Sagan (who was perhaps not exactly an atheist) had a gift for stirring up quasi-religious emotions about the universe. He and others like him have exhorted us to adopt something like a grateful attitude toward it for its thoughtless act of originating us. Or, if it is not exactly gratitude we are meant to feel, perhaps it is humility. We scratch out our little lives on this one speck called Earth. We once thought it sat at the center of the world, and that its sun was the prince of the stars. We know now that our planet and our sun are just one instance each among billions more, some just like them, some quite unlike them. Many of our race once thought the age of the world spanned little more than sixty human lifetimes. Now we know better. Should we not feel dwarfed by the vastness of space and time? Obscured by the multitudes of stars? Perhaps we should.

But it is a shallow humility if it conceals a note of self-congratulation. Are we perhaps proud of being the only things capable of self-recognition, of humility, of appreciation of grandeur? Do we take pride in our courage to face an indifferent, even a hostile, universe and to shake our fist at it even as we acknowledge its greatness? That manner of deference leaves untouched our true egos, our intellectual and moral selves. We are more capable of happiness than the great slumbering cosmos. Its very grandeur is in a sense more ours than its own. We see it and rejoice in it. Meanwhile, it is comatose. Its stupendous past is no longer, except as it lives on in our minds. And we know it. We are lords and masters of the universe—if it produced every mind and none produced it. The truth, however, is both more uplifting and more humbling than that. The universe is a sign to us, and its fantastic dimensions, dwarfing us and our whole solar system into nothing by comparison, are a symbol of the corresponding superiority of its cause. Knowing that, we cannot but feel a thrill of reverential fear. On the other hand, we should also be consoled to learn that the universe is at bottom neither hostile nor indifferent to minds such as ours, but is indeed addressed to them, bearing a hopeful message. The human soul is at once made smaller and bigger for having discovered that infinite ocean of substance.

9

What a Lovely Thing a Rose Is

> But it is hard for me to explain all these things as if I were a
> god. Nor indeed is it permitted to man to grasp by his mind
> or unfold in his speech all the devices of the divine work. Just
> to have seen this clearly should be enough: that the god who
> puts forth all natures is the same one who disposes all things,
> directing them toward the good.
>
> —Boethius, *Consolation of Philosophy*

The Problems of Evil

When my daughter Evelyn was less than a year old, she had a terrible
ear infection. The doctor put her on amoxicillin. It came in the form
of that familiar bubblegum-pink milky stuff that you have to keep
in the fridge. But Evelyn was a nursing baby, unaccustomed to the
bottle. How could we get her to take the medicine? We tried the
direct approach first. Mom holds the baby; Dad brings the measuring
spoon to the baby's mouth, brimming with the pink stuff. It worked!
Evelyn opened her mouth, in went the stuff, and she closed her
mouth again. And then she stuck her tongue out, and all the medicine came dribbling down her little chin. The look on her face said,
"Well, that was interesting, but certainly not worth swallowing."
We went through this process several more times. She was always
willing to take the medicine, never willing to swallow it. The bottle
was noticeably less full than when we had begun. Great. Now what?
Somehow we had to trick her into swallowing. Then I got an idea.
I readied the spoon with another dose, and she quite willingly took
that one into her mouth again, but before she could spit it back out, I
blew into her face. She involuntarily blinked and swallowed—and

then cried a bit in protest. I imagined what was going through her mind afterward: "What did I do to deserve this? Why did they subject me to all that? Are Mommy and Daddy unable to help themselves? That seems unlikely. Are they completely unaware of how gross that stuff tastes? I thought I had made that plain enough. Do they perhaps not care about me? Or not as much as they should?" Happily, the doses were far enough apart that she fell for the same trick every time and got over the infection.

Determining whether there is a god is difficult enough. Yet even after settling that question in the affirmative, it is not everything we wish to know. What is the attitude of this being toward us? The former question, not the latter, has been my principal concern in this book. The two are nevertheless intimately connected, and it is possible to reason from statements about the sort of thing god is to his relationship to his works, and conversely. If, for example, it is true that god is infinitely powerful, wise, and good, this implies that he would be a perfect governor of the universe. If, on the other hand, the world is in anarchy, then either god is indifferent to it—and not so "good" after all, or not to us—or else he is incompetent to govern it and lacks something in power or knowledge. And there are further consequences. It would seem that any of these options is incompatible with the idea of a god who produced the whole universe and each thing in it by his wisdom—such a god could not have limited knowledge of his own works or limited power over them, nor could he be indifferent to them. In other words, if the world is manifestly not perfectly governed, it will spell trouble for god's very existence. It is for this reason that I have devoted this chapter to the problem of evil.

The problem of evil is actually many problems. This becomes clearer if we say instead the "problem of bad things". We tend to think right away of morals when we hear of good and evil. But if instead we say *good* and *bad*, the terms include many more things than virtues and vices. *Bad*, for most people, means something more general than *evil*. Everything called evil is also bad, as an evil man is also a bad one. But not everything called bad is called evil as well, except in an antiquated sense. A flat tire is a bad tire, but it is not an evil one. Some people think that *good*, similarly, must always mean morally good. But then the term would have no use outside of human affairs. Very little reflection is required to see that this is untrue. Even within human affairs, *good* does not always mean morally good. If I have one flat tire, then I still have three good ones—and I don't mean they are morally good or that they make me so. And when I say that meat is good for my dog, but chocolate is not, I don't have to bring human beings into the picture to give meaning to what I'm saying.

Now, it is not just evil—that is, moral depravity or wickedness—that is hard to reconcile with divine providence, but other bad things, too. In fact, moral depravity itself presents little difficulty. When human beings are bad by their own choice, we might be content to blame the human beings and not the god who gave them the power of choice. Most of us, anyway, are glad to have the power of choice and are ready to accept the blame when we make poor use of it—or at least we think other people should be ready to take blame when they deserve it. It is mostly the bad things that happen to people without their choice, against their will, that cause anxiety about the justice of divine providence. We worry about the victims of the morally depraved, for example. Why is it that bad things are allowed to happen to good people? Why do innocent children starve to death?

For convenience, I will chop up the problem of bad things into four distinct problems and sketch out a general solution for each, as far as that is possible within the confines of this chapter. The four problems are (1) the problem of the cause of evil actions, (2) the problem of bad design, (3) the problem of great white sharks, and (4) the problem of permanent injustice. I will give short shrift to the first three, since they are not nearly as difficult or as important to people as the fourth.

Is God Responsible for Evil Actions?

If god is the cause of all causes, is he also the cause of evil causes and of their evil actions? Is god the cause of a murderer's act of murder? Is he even more to blame than the murderer himself? Many people are content to say that god is the cause of the murderer's existence and free will, but not the cause of his murder; only the murderer causes that, by badly using a freedom that god gave him to use well. I think the truth is a bit more difficult than that, but perhaps not in a way important enough for the present purpose to merit any detailed discussion.

The difficulty I mean is that god is continuously causing the existence of every positive being—including this man, this action, this movement, and so on. If god withheld his causal power from the bullet moving through the air, it would cease to exist. Hence, the positive realities in which the murderous act consists are things caused and sustained in being by god. Still, it is not right to call him a murderer. The disorder in the purpose behind firing that bullet is entirely in the will of the murderer, and that disorder does not come from god, since a disorder is not a positive thing, but the absence of some right attitude toward things. And an absence, like darkness, does not need an active and productive cause. If there is something amiss in my leg, I will limp. This limp, a defect in action, cannot be blamed on my brain, even though everything positive in the movement of my leg comes from my brain. The case is similar to that with god and the murderer. Unlike the brain, however, god could positively intervene and put a stop to the defective action, or heal up the defect in the defective agency. That he does not always choose to do this pertains to the final problem, concerning injustice. I will address it there.

The Problem of Bad Design

Richard Dawkins, Stephen Jay Gould, Christopher Hitchens, and many others have followed in Darwin's footsteps in propounding an argument against design in nature from the supposed ubiquity of "poor design"—organs that are needlessly fragile, foolishly bestowed, stingily assigned double duty, encumbered with pointless features, or just plain useless. The human back, for instance, seems to be a botched bit of engineering—too much strain on the lower end of it, you see, which is always fighting the enormous leverage of the inadequately supported upper body (similar complaints could be lodged against human knees). Other animals, inferior to us, receive superior strength or speed or agility or longevity. We also find inferior species—say, eagles—given eyes superior to man's. Our eyes are "wired backward". All the fibers from our photoreceptors protrude into the body of the eye itself and then jut back out through the blind spot, where they are bundled into the optic nerve—it would obviously be much better just to put the fibers on the back of each receptor and have them shoot out the back of the eye, with no need for a blind spot at all, as our inferiors the octopuses have it. Certain whales develop teeth while in utero, which dissolve before they ever get used. Some moles have eyes completely covered in skin and fur. This fascinating list goes on.

The list of amazingly efficient and obviously useful organs, however, is far longer. And those that seem to be inefficient or even altogether useless often turn out, upon more careful investigation, really to be efficient or useful after all—such as the human appendix, which seems to be a safe house for benign bacteria. For the sake of argument, though, I am willing to suppose that some appendages are as useless as they seem to be. Most of these are probably vestiges of things once very useful, but no longer so, that in their disuse are somehow beginning to atrophy. In that case, they are not instances of bad design, but signs of transition from one well-adapted state to another.

That an intelligent god would design living things to adapt to their environment presents no special problem to my mind. He might do so by enabling individuals to form useful habits by experience. He might also do so by enabling the genetic endowment of races to present future options so that environmental factors could "select" the most viable ones. The presentation of new future options for the design of the organism might result from mere genetic copying errors. Or they might result from some as yet unknown internal mechanism that is specifically responsive to environmental cues. An intelligent god might employ both these techniques, and others besides, in the measure that they get good results.

In any such scenario, what is shaping the organism is not god alone, but also the nature of the organism itself and the condition of its environment. And it is not god, but the secondary cause—whether it be the flailing trial-and-error method of random mutations plus natural selection, or something else—that is responsible for the "oddities" we find. As I observed in chapter 6, a good teacher of a foreign language can do a better job of translating in class than his students can, but he is a better teacher if, instead of doing all the translating himself, he gives his students what they need to do it themselves. They will make mistakes, and introduce needlessly circumlocutory translations from time to time. But if they are never allowed to make their own translations, they might as well drop the class. The intermediate causes are fallible, and therefore to some extent fumbling, and this is manifest in their work.

I suppose someone could complain that a perfect creator should never make imperfect creatures. But there is some equivocation in that. *Imperfect* has at least two meanings: (1) missing some of its natural parts and (2) not yet in possession of its ultimate good. A newborn baby without arms and legs is imperfect or incomplete in the first sense, while even a baby with all his fingers and toes is incomplete or imperfect in the second sense, not being a fully grown, well-raised, educated, and fulfilled person. All living creatures, or at least the superior ones, start out imperfect in that second sense, precisely so that by dint of their own natural powers, they might move themselves toward their own perfection or fulfillment, in whatever that might consist. Creatures are nobler things, better creatures, for being able to perfect themselves in some way. Certainly they are better manifestations of the power of their Creator, who not only has power to produce things, but power to give them power. Accordingly, a perfect Creator will indeed make imperfect creatures, but enable them, at least in sufficient numbers, to reach their perfection.

The world also includes birth defects, of course. Many animals and plants simply don't come out "right". They lack the proper equipment for making a living in their own species-specific way. These are imperfect in the first sense. But this is due to the fallibility and mutability of the natural causes themselves, not to bad design. If *good design* means that failure is impossible, then by definition material beings cannot be well designed. Material beings are changeable, destructible things, and it is not compatible with their nature to be incapable of failure. If the mere possibility of failure means they are simply bad and ought not to exist, then we are not finding fault with god for making them as he did, but for making them at all. We are wishing ourselves out of existence. God seems to have seen it in another light—mortal and destructible beings are still good, still worthwhile, despite their fallibility and impermanence. He even found a way to impart to them a kind of immortality—namely, perpetuation of their species through reproduction.

This observation also goes some way toward answering the "problem" of the human back and other like difficulties. If the goal were to make man naturally indestructible and immortal, certainly god foozled it. But if the goal were instead to make man durable enough, for the most part, to live a life humanly worth living, and perhaps in some instances to discover another life even more worth living, the human back seems quite up to the job. At any rate, it hasn't stopped us from climbing Everest or going to the moon. (And if those who insist that our back is not sufficiently well made for an upright posture have begun living by their own doctrine and going about on all fours, I can't see that they have gathered much of a following.)

Then there is that other notion: if only god knew what he was about, he would have given the most perfect animal the most perfect version of each kind of organ. That is just ridiculous. The purpose of an organ is not to be the best organ it can be, regardless of whom it is meant to serve. Its purpose is to serve well the specific needs of the user. To give an eagle merely human eyes would mean its starvation and death, given the lifestyle of that particular animal. To give a human being eagle eyes would be to make an already predominant sense overwhelming and too attention absorbing. For an eagle, there is no drawback to having its visual life dominate its attention, since it does not have much more life than that. But a human being is supposed to be a rational being with an interest in grasping the world by means of every sense, even if by some more than by others. If the noblest and most godlike thing in a human being is reason, then the "right" organs for a human being will be those that make the most reasonable life possible. The human nose need not, then, be the most sensitive sniffer. Dogs and bears can discern thousands of nasty smells at great distances from their sources. Very useful to them, I'm sure. As for us, we can appreciate and enjoy (and even put to our use) the canine sense of smell without having to be burdened by it ourselves, thank god.

It is a general principle that one cannot judge a governor without knowing toward what good he is trying to govern things. Most Darwinist critics of god's designs rush on to finding fault with his arrangements without so much as bothering to ask what god's purposes might be—as if there could be no difficulty about that question. Obviously (they seem to think), if there is a god, and we are his special darlings, then he would wish to soup us up with all the best attributes. We should be the fastest animals and the strongest and the longest-lived and the tallest and, heck, while we're at it, why shouldn't we expect also to have the best wings, the best claws, the best horns, the best scales, the best fur, and so on? There's design for you! As if any competent artist or engineer cared more about the bits themselves than about how they contributed to the whole. It is a poor artist who pays equal attention to everything on his canvas, and who paints the faces in the background with as much detail and vividness as the main figures in the foreground, or who lays equal stress on every note in the symphony. It often happens that a part that is "best" in an absolute sense is not best for a specific purpose. The best nose is not necessarily the best nose for man.

Aristotle observed that some people think man is the worst designed of all the animals. Man is among the slowest moving, most vulnerable, most helpless of animals, least equipped with weapons and armor, lacking sufficient survival instincts at birth. Aristotle saw this as a misunderstanding of mankind's superiority. We can possess the speed of the horse by riding the horse, and we can get off it when we please. The horse, on the other hand, can never take off its "shoes", that is, its hooves. It must forever wear its running clothes, and this places severe limitations on the kind of life it can live. Thanks to our native nudity, we can clothe and equip ourselves in an infinity of ways, a condition befitting the infinite conceptions of our minds and contrivances of our hands. The human mind is in a way capable of doing all things, adopting all modes of life, so that it might experience everything. God would not imprison so free a spirit in a hyperspecialized body. The human hand, unlike a claw or a fin or a wing, is not specially adapted to any of the purposes of those organs, but precisely for that reason, it is not restricted to any of them; it can instead become all things by grasping this tool now and then putting it down again and picking up another. The hand is now a hammer, now a saw, now a violin; and none of these extensions of our bodies would be possible if we had, instead of our unspecialized hands, organs specially adapted to one specific purpose instead.

The Problem of Great White Sharks

Individual organisms aside, it appears to some people that the world is under general mismanagement. Much of the natural world is patterned on the relationship of predator and prey. Is this not needless cruelty? Wouldn't a wise and gentle god have made all the animals vegans? Does he care nothing for the pain and terror of animals? Even if it were somehow reasonable, what excuse can be made for the peculiar atrocities we discover in the animal kingdom? Many insects eat their own mates during the act of mating. Sibling sharks devour each other in the womb. Dolphins torture and kill porpoises, I'm told. Horrible parasites and diseases cause needless suffering to their hosts. Can the tapeworm really be part of a divine plan? Its very appearance and way of making a living are hideous. Worst of all, we human beings are supposedly his special creatures, since we alone on earth can recognize his existence; and yet he has placed us in this most singularly inhospitable of worlds. We, too, are subject to parasites and diseases and occasionally get limbs bitten off by great white sharks. Our very planet suffers devastating earthquakes and storms and fires and droughts.

It is for reasons such as these that the Manichaeans believed the world was evidently the battleground of two gods—Good God and Bad God. Good God was looking out for us and was doing his level best to make this world a beautiful, comfortable place for all, while Bad God did everything in his power to uglify it and make it more dangerous and unpleasant. So Good God made things such as puppies and butterflies, while Bad God made things such as poisonous snakes and spiders. Good God sent us sunshine and gentle rains, while Bad God sent us volcanic eruptions and crop-destroying hailstorms. Neither god has been able, so far, to get the upper hand.

That philosophy, however, is untenable, tempting as it might be in a world of good and evil. It is not possible that the two gods each enjoy perfectly independent self-existence. One of them must give being to the other, or else they both derive their being from something else, and neither of them is a first cause. The reasons for this were brought out in previous chapters. Besides, badness can never be a self-sufficient cause, since badness consists in the absence of something good in a thing that itself is not bad. Blindness, for example, is the absence of sight in an eye, making the eye "bad". But the blindness itself is not a self-sufficient cause, both because it is an absence and not a positive power and because it cannot be at all without the eye. It is impossible, then, for badness itself to be a first cause or a god. The two-god solution will not do. How, then, can we solve the problem of great white sharks?

Some have solved the apparent nastiness of predation by supposing that animals have no sensation, but are like mere windup toys. They only *seem* to feel pain. I don't think anyone saying this can have paid serious attention to or spent much time with dogs or horses. Even worms obviously experience something like pain and fear. It could be, though, that when a zebra is finally taken down by a pride of lions, it goes into shock and in that state does not feel much pain in its last moments. Probably it feels less pain than it would by slowly dying of some disease instead. So there seems to be no special difficulty about predation in the animal world—the problem is just that there is death and pain. A world without death, however, would mean a world without mortal creatures, without creatures made of alterable stuff. That is simply another world altogether, not a "more peaceful" version of a world of alterable, mortal natures. Would it be a better world if no living thing ever killed and ate another one? If plants and animals believed all others to have an inalienable right to life? Then the only animals would be things like autotrophic bacteria and rot-eaters and carrion-eaters. There would certainly be nothing like dogs and cats and horses and whales. It might be possible to have a world in which there were only plants, and hence death but no pain. But would that be a better world? It seems to me a far poorer one. Some goods are worth the prospect of pain, and a world of mortal creatures with awareness and self-motion seems to be one of those worthwhile goods. But you can't have such creatures without pain. Since they can sense attractive things, and move themselves toward them (which is all to the good), they will also encounter destructive influences now and then and would quickly perish if they felt no fear or pain. They are, remember, mortal, destructible beings made of changeable stuff.

Predation does not introduce pain and death then. Those things are entirely prior to great white sharks and their ilk. And it is far from clear that the animals that become prey suffer more that way than they would by death in some other form. Would the world be a better place if, over and above the autotrophs and recyclers, we made room for the vegetarian animals and plants, leaving out just the meat eaters? There are some who suppose that all animals were vegetarians in the prelapsarian times. They would have it that the lion's teeth and claws came from the devil. I cannot agree with them—partly thanks to all the scientific evidence that carnivores have been around for longer than sinners have been. But there is also something in me to which the lion's ferocity is profoundly appealing. I don't wish to be mauled by one any more than the next fellow does, but I would be deeply saddened—nay, disgusted—if a troop of busybody genetic engineers had found a way to turn off the hunting instincts of all lions in the world and to make them into well-behaved vegetarians, all for the good of the zebras. I don't want to get eaten by a great white. But I'm thrilled that those amazing animals exist. The world, to my mind, would be a dull place if it were not so wild, if every animal made its living by "peaceful means", as it were. I have never hunted animals myself and have hardly ever gone fishing, but the world strikes me as much more alive, much more real, and much more dramatic as it is, with bears catching salmon, and spiders catching flies, and even (so wonderfully improbable and bizarre) anacondas constricting sheep, than it would be if the high-minded among us could have their way and put a stop to it all. I don't really fit into the wilderness, exactly, and I don't wish to be subjected to it, but I am mighty glad it's there. The universe is filled with things that could kill me, from waterfalls to supernovas. I would not have them expunged to increase my safety.

It is quite conceivable, then, that god is responsible for the world much as we now find it, with death and pain and predation, even very odd or shocking forms of predation, and that these are not from the devil, much less from no intelligence at all. Such a world serves the purpose of showing that even a mortal existence can be worthwhile and can present a type of beauty not to be found in immortal realms—a harsh, violent, fierce beauty, like the severe beauty of a desert or the furious and powerful beauty of a storm. Only in such a world could we find nature's crafty survivors, cunning thieves, bloodthirsty murderers, and brave warriors weaving their endless and fascinating tales. If this world seems at times too hostile for our own fragile frames, a spectacle not worth the risk, it is entirely possible that this is not the original state of things—that the human race was initially gifted with a special security and comfort in this world, a security it has since lost or cast aside. However that may be, I would still rather live in this world than in a boring but safe one.

The Problem of Seemingly Permanent Injustice

The main form of the problem of evil, the one that causes the most concern for people, is about bad things befalling the innocent. We could frame it as an argument against the existence of god, like this:

1. If there is a god, then there is a being that is all powerful, all wise, and all good.
2. If there is a being that is all powerful, all wise, and all good, then bad things would not happen to good people,
   (since the only reason anyone would allow that to happen is that
   he is unable to stop it, or
   he is unaware of it, or
   he is unwilling to do anything about it).
3. But bad things do happen to good people.
   Therefore, there is no god.

Why this argument fails will become clear in a moment. But first a disclaimer. Those who have suffered something horrible, and who have subsequently become angry with god or ceased to believe in his existence, cannot usually be helped by any such considerations as I am about to make. That is because the considerations needed to answer this argument in general are themselves very general, and hence are of no special use to someone who is suffering from some quite particular evil, and also because rational considerations are rarely sufficient to help someone whose thinking is influenced by powerful emotions. But this book is not about how to be a wise and understanding friend to those who are suffering or to those whose suffering is interfering with their thinking. It is simply about thinking correctly. None of what I am about to say, in other words, is intended as counsel or consolation for anyone who is suffering some pain or loss. I am only responding to the argument made above.

The main difficulty is how to reconcile evil with an omnicompetent governor of the world. Before tackling that problem, it is worth noticing that atheism has its own version of this problem, and it is utterly unsolvable. The problem of evil is not just that we have a hard time seeing why a decent god would allow it. The problem is we hate it and want it taken care of. Given a god, the injustices done to innocent people in this world, and never righted in it, still stand a chance of being righted in a future world. Without a god, the injustice is permanent and unfixable. In many cases, evil pays and righteousness doesn't, and that's that.

To answer the argument above now, it is not sufficient to suppose, as some have done, that anyone who suffers anything must have deserved it. If that were so, then indeed it would be easy to explain the suffering in the world and to reconcile it with divine providence and justice. Certainly some people deserve some of the bad things that happen to them. If a man rapes a child and goes to jail and doesn't particularly enjoy his life there, few of us will lose sleep over his plight. Certainly, too, among the people to whom bad things happen, and who richly deserve what they got, there must be some who nevertheless seemed not to deserve anything except rewards and admiration, who had everyone fooled about their real character. In many cases, in other words, it merely *appears* that bad things have happened to a good person, because the person only seemed good but wasn't really good after all. Those are easy cases to understand in principle. What, now, about the case of the young boy who starves to death? Or who is tortured to death for fun by enemy soldiers? Or the poor young mother who accidentally runs over her own four-year-old in the driveway? The world is filled with horror stories. No need for me to supply more.

The difficulty of the truth clearly goes beyond our mere failure to fathom the depths of every sufferer's moral turpitude. There can be no doubt that the evils that befall some of us surpass our deserving. What then? Does the argument above make its case?

It does not. As many others have noted, it effectively assumes the very thing to be proved. How so? It assumes that there is no reason other than weakness, ignorance, or bad will for tolerating bad things that happen to good people. In other words, it assumes that there is no good that is *good enough* to make the tolerance of such a state of affairs worthwhile. This is the way that Dostoyevsky's Ivan Karamazov thinks. If he were invited to be part of a universe that would be made ecstatically and perfectly happy at the sole price of torturing one innocent little girl, he says, he would respectfully return the ticket. That is his way of showing he has the moral high ground over god. Of course, there is something a bit wrong in his hypothetical

scenario, since the innocent little girl is left permanently uncompen-
sated and unavenged; Ivan calls her suffering "unrequited" and leaves
it at that. But the unrequitedness of innocent suffering and its utter
meaninglessness are precisely what god, and god alone, can remove.
(By the way, if the goodness of god can make all evils worthwhile
and put them right in the end, that does not mean evil deeds are not
really evil. Blowing up a bus full of people is evil, especially if done
in the name of god. The same goes for burning people at the stake.
What god wants and what we decide for ourselves he must want are
not always the same thing.)

Ivan also makes this further assumption: there are certain evils that
are so evil that no good is good enough to make bearing them worthwhile. If this assumption were correct, then the argument from evil
would follow as night follows day. The assumption, however, is rather
curious. The evils of this world are finite, are they not? They last only
for a limited time, or, if they are the permanent loss of something, and
so last for infinite time (which would be difficult to verify), they are
nevertheless the loss of something finite. Would not an infinite good,
if it were one in which the innocent sufferer himself were somehow
made a partaker, be well worth the tolerance of the finite evil? If we
assume that there is no infinite good, then we are assuming the very
thing the objector's argument was supposed to prove.

God himself does not perpetrate evil deeds to bring good out of
them later. He permits them, though, or else they wouldn't happen.
Besides the three cited in the objector's argument, there are in fact
other possible reasons, conceivable at least in a general way, why god
would permit terrible things to happen to perfectly innocent people.
It is conceivable, for instance, that god never permits the loss of any
important good by any innocent person except when he has in view
a much greater good for that very same person, a good that could
not be attained, or not nearly so well, without the prior loss of the
previous good. No one can know this is false without knowing pretty
much everything, including the entirety of the future. There are many
goods, after all, that cannot exist without certain evils. Generosity
cannot exist without need. Courage in battle cannot exist without
war. It is tempting to deem poverty and the ravages of war too high
a price to pay for the opportunity for a few people to practice generosity and courage. But these moral perfections cannot really exist, let

alone be known to exist, without opportunity for their action. And that we have so low an estimate of them as to place them beneath wealth and comfort has more to do with their invisibility and our poor grasp of their worth than with their true measure. Socrates, at least, thought human life worthless apart from moral excellence and thought it worth trading everything else for the sake of it.

Still, if the poor or those living in war-torn places make it possible for others to be generous or brave, what's in it for them? It seems to me that a just god would look very favorably upon those who undergo such trials and by their sufferings make possible certain great deeds that reflect his own perfections. His universe, his project, is improved (in the manner described) to no little extent at their expense and without their having signed up for it. If that is the end of the story, I for one do not understand how such a god can be said to love his creatures. His love for his creatures would seem inferior to my own ineffectual sympathy for them.

Ah, but we needn't say that an unhappy death for innocent sufferers in this world *is* the end of their story. Why not say instead that this life, which is natural to us and shaped by our own shortcomings, is both an opportunity to learn what sort of happiness we can cobble together by our own efforts and also a time to strive for a life better than any we could contrive for ourselves? In that case, the severe limitations to our happiness here, and even the unmitigated misery of many, should not remove our hope for something much better, but only cure us of the idea that we are all doing quite fine without divine assistance. If god had in store for us another life that is everlasting and purely good, a life in accord with the immortality and goodness of our souls and with his justice rather than in accord with the mortality of our bodies and merciless fortune, a life we ask for by the manner in which we live this life we did not ask for, then there is no *general* difficulty in understanding why god allows terrible things to happen to innocent people.

He makes the universe, after all, not out of personal neediness, but out of generosity, in order to communicate his goodness to creatures, both by making them good themselves in various ways and by enabling some of them to see that the goodness of creatures points to a far superior goodness in himself. It is all too easy for us rational animals to stop at the goodness of the universe and not to see it as reflecting another and infinitely superior goodness, the divine good itself. Even after seeing that there is an infinite good distinct from the universe, even after coming to believe that we might share in that good ourselves one day, depending on our merits, we can still prefer the finite goods already within our grasp. If this life were a perfect paradise by human standards, probably most of us would desire nothing further and give god no particular thought. One might say the misfortunes of the innocent, like an unpleasant medicine, are a blessing in disguise—a strong way to wean us off the idea of resting in this world, of making it our be-all and end-all. Since the needed lesson comes at the expense of some, one would expect divine reward to be particularly lavish and divine mercy to be particularly indulgent in their case. In light of that, one might be concerned more for the fortunate. It is easy to become complacent about or forgetful of our moral condition when we are comfortable in most external ways. Perhaps, too, those given much in this life will find more is expected of them when being recompensed in the next.

If deserving an immortal and divine life depends, as it seems it must, on *loving* that life, and loving it above other modes of life inferior to it, it follows that we cannot deserve immortal happiness in the next life without showing in this life how much we prefer it. And while it is possible to live a life of innocent pleasure and comfort while giving glory to god for it, it is much clearer that one loves god and thinks his life worth waiting for if during the wait one is sometimes beset with trials and sufferings. In fact, this fits in very well with the divine purpose—to show forth his goodness and to give others the opportunity to love it for its own sake. Were the world all puppies and rainbows and peaches and cream, one extremely compelling way to deserve the divine goodness would have been left out—namely, the enduring of intense suffering while still trusting in god. The power of his goodness shines forth especially when we see it able to move hearts so and to become an object of unswerving loyalty despite calamity in this short life.

God allows innocent suffering at least in part to answer the challenge of the Ivan Karamazovs among us. Many of us think that some horrors, some outrages, are so great that nothing good is good enough to make them right again. And that is true about the finite goods of this world. It is untrue about the infinite good. God's universe cannot fulfill its purpose, or not nearly as well as it ought, without accepting that challenge, and he cannot accept that challenge without allowing the conditions of it. He cannot show that his goodness is more potent than any and all evils when it comes to determining our ultimate fate unless he lets evils do their worst. And so he sometimes does. Or at least he permits truly terrible evils, even if he spares us the worst ones without our knowing it.

Such general reasons are some, and only some, of those for which god might allow evils, even unspeakable atrocities, to befall the innocent, including those who love him. I should say especially those who love him. Love, after all, is itself one of the greatest goods, the greatest manifestations of the divine goodness, which cannot exist, or not so well, without some suffering to prove its truth. I love my wife. Suppose I am never called upon to do or have done to me anything on her account that I do not also find entirely agreeable to myself. Then how will it ever become clear that I love *her*? And that I wish *her* happiness, *her* good, not just my own? A condition of truly proving my love is the occasional separation of what delights me from what delights her, so that when these conflict, my choice can show forth what lies invisibly within me. This is what motivates lovers to desire to suffer and to labor for their beloved—to manifest the purity of their love. Those who love god, and who therefore wish this love to be tested and manifested, will accordingly desire the opportunity and fortitude to suffer and labor for him.

Suffering, even innocent suffering, in this life makes sense in a general way as a means to a happy end for the innocent sufferers. It is reconcilable with the goodness of god and with his purposes. This is a far cry from saying we can make sense of it in the details. A married couple, friends of mine for many years, had twin girls. One of them died of SIDS. Why? Why that particular death? Why that particular suffering for her twin sister, for her siblings, her parents? Why the one twin rather than the other? I have no idea. And anyone who does not know them personally and would profess to know the answer based on general principles alone is a fool. Unless god reveals it, no one can know the answer fully on this side of the grave. God alone knows what lies in the depths of every soul, how all souls affect each other, and what the entire future holds. Far be it from me to profess to know any such things.

We ourselves sometimes permit our children to learn lessons "the hard way", but there are certain points at which we must draw the line. My two-year-old is screaming for a piece of the lemon I am juicing for my guacamole. At first I resist, knowing that he does not really want what he thinks he wants. After much screaming on his part, I relent and give him a wedge, which he greedily shoves into his mouth. The result: a lesson for the child and an amusing memory for the parents. No one thinks I should be reported to a social worker for that. Now my two-year-old is trying to stick a fork into an electric outlet. I take it away from him, and he screams at me, demanding it back. After much screaming on his part, I relent and give him back the fork, to let him learn the hard way. If I do that, I deserve prison time. The difference, of course, is that in the first case, no great harm comes to the child, just a momentary discomfort, whereas in the second case, great and irreparable harm does, or could, come to him. We do not think we are allowed even to permit horribly bad things if it is in our knowledge and power to prevent them.

Why, then, should god be excused? If I knew that my next-door neighbor had abducted someone's little girl and had her tied up in his basement and was abusing her in various ways, but I did nothing about it, did not even phone the police, people would be right to want me locked up. That is depraved indifference. But when god allows it to happen, then what? Why is his case different? Precisely because of his unlimited knowledge and power. I must act in accord with my limited knowledge and limited power and authority. In my limited knowledge, I see with some degree of probability that some very, very bad things might happen if I let my son play with the electric outlet. I cannot with any degree of probability see anything worthwhile coming of his electrocution—that it will prevent him from becoming a future Hitler, for instance, and hence, he will await me in heaven rather than end up in hell. I see nothing of the sort. I must act out of my knowledge, not out of my wild and unfounded imaginings. Will god rectify my son's untimely death, after I let him stick his fork in the outlet? Certainly. That hardly excuses me, since part of the rectification of the evil will involve my answering for it. God is the author of human reason and parenthood and their attendant instincts. He made me able to prevent the evil of the fork in the outlet. He will fix the evil—and maybe fix me—if it occurs, but it is no will of his that it occur except in the sense that he might permit it for now.

God owns human life in a way that we do not, since he produces it, fashions it in likeness to himself, and, even if he takes it away, has the power to give it back. As for me, I am only too conscious that the world is not mine, nor even are my own children mine, such that I can do as I please with them, answerable to none, or such that I need never worry about consequences, as though I could always undo them.

God cannot be held to the same standards that ought to measure us. He is simply more competent than we are. It would be wrong for me to set up a private practice at my house and offer people fifty-dollar appendectomies. It is not therefore wrong for *everyone* to cut patients' abdomens. For god to permit suffering and death and any number of atrocities falls within his purview—he is capable of making absolutely sure that all wrongs are righted in the end, and made eminently worthwhile, so that even those who suffered most miserably, but whom he had brought to a safe and better place, would insist that they wouldn't now change anything about how they came to be where they are. I have no such power and can give no such assurance. In other words, to govern a universe, to keep it on its divinely appointed course, to bring all things to a good end, so that all horrors (and sometimes horrible people) might be turned to good, or at least be made to serve a worthy purpose, is all above my pay grade. That is no reason to think the job surpasses infinite knowledge and power, too. And so here we have another way of expressing a general reason for tolerating evils. If god simply did not permit evils, or not especially bad ones, it could appear as though his providence were incapable of dealing with them.

If I have lapsed into what-ifs, my excuse is that I am not attempting here to settle the truth, to figure out exactly what god is up to, as much as I am answering an objection to god's existence based on the existence of evil. The objection says that *if* there is a god, *then* there can be no evil, since the only possible reasons for allowing evil are powerlessness, ignorance, and indifference. To overthrow that objection, I am not obliged to find out exactly what the story of the universe is; I need only supply other plausible reasons, or even just possible ones, for the existence of evil, besides a lack of power or of knowledge or of goodness in god. A single alternative is sufficient to show that the objector's conclusion does not follow.

But I can hardly fault anyone for wanting something more, some little indication that the divine being who does not need us, and who so often refuses to intervene in our affairs in the ways that we would wish, is not in fact indifferent to us. I have already suggested that it is unthinkable that he should be indifferent to us since we are his own works and since we resemble him in the measure that we have any sort of reality and desirable quality. We are the offspring of his mind, and furthermore, like him, we have minds by which to contemplate him. But there are other hopeful signs of the divine benevolence. Among these I count the predominance of beauty in the world. In a charming passage in Sir Arthur Conan Doyle's *Memoirs of Sherlock Holmes* (in "The Naval Treaty, Part 1"), Watson relates a little episode in which Holmes made a pertinent, if somewhat uncharacteristic, observation on the subject:

"What a lovely thing a rose is!"

He walked past the couch to the open window and held up the drooping stalk of a moss-rose, looking down at the dainty blend of crimson and green. It was a new phase of his character to me, for I had never seen him show any keen interest in natural objects.

"There is nothing in which deduction is so necessary as in religion," said he, leaning with his back against the shutters. "It can be built up as an exact science by the reasoner. Our highest assurance of the goodness of Providence seems to me to rest in the flowers. All other things, our powers, our desires, our food, are all really necessary for our existence in the first instance. But this rose is an extra. Its smell and its colour are an embellishment of life, not a condition of it. It is only goodness which gives extras, and so I say again that we have much to hope from the flowers."

Even a cruel god who delighted in our suffering would have to provide us with the necessities of life. But with beauty? As a man gives flowers to a woman not to keep her alive, but as a sign of his love, of how beautiful he finds her, and of his wish to make her happy, so it would appear god has given all flowers to all of us. What about the ugly things of the world, then? They exist in the service of beauty, too. They are relatively rare. Often they are hidden things, useful ones doing the dirty work necessary for the upkeep of the flowers—and even when the ugly ones do not help the beautiful things to be, they help them by contrast to be seen and to be cherished.

10

Hecklers

> Some things really are made of silver, others of gold, while others are not and only appear to be so.... In the same way both deductions and refutations are sometimes genuine, sometimes not.
>
> —Aristotle, *On Sophistical Refutations*

Trouble Brewing

I have long enjoyed fine wine. I do not profess to know much about it, except what I do and do not like. Nor can I boast a remarkably discerning palate or a broad experience of high-end wines. But I love a good bottle with a good friend over a good meal. And I also love to hear others talk about wine when they really know their stuff. I am particularly interested in how it is crafted. There was even a time when I toyed with the idea of making my own, but one look at a serious book for do-it-yourselfers cured me of that. Far too involved. Far too difficult for the likes of me. There are "recipe" wines that are easy enough to make at home, but I have never tasted one I liked.

Then I discovered home brewing. Beer, it turns out, is much more within reach of the do-it-yourselfer than wine is. I bought some books and equipment and ingredients. With the help of an experienced friend, I brewed up my first ale and fretted over it while it fermented in a dark, cool spot under the stairs. Whenever I grew anxious about its progress, I did some online research. I discovered a whole world of home brewers on the Web. It was all very friendly and encouraging, but it soon became clear that many brewers disputed what I had been taught about proper brewing procedure. How much hops to use? When should I steep it in the water and malt syrup, and for how long? What yeast is best for such and such an ale? Is it acceptable to use one's mouth to siphon the wort into the fermenter? Is a secondary fermenter really necessary? Every question had several, sometimes quite opposite, answers. Despite the intimidating avalanche of occasionally contradictory information, I managed a decent first batch.

Not too much later, I ran into another interesting response to my home brewing procedures. A student of mine somehow got me talking about my little operation. I described to her the entire process in minute detail, and when I had finished, she said, "Sounds like a lot of trouble for a bottle of beer." Well, that deflated me. Here was a whole new kind of objection not only to my home brewing process, but to anyone's at all. And indeed many outsiders scorn the whole hobby. Why brew your own when it costs practically as much as a commercial beer, takes forever, eats up space in your house, carries a high risk of yielding a ruined batch, and when there is such a great variety of fantastic brews available right now just down the street?

Just so are there two sorts of objections to the project of this book. One type kept showing up throughout—the "You're going about it all wrong" type. This type objects to the conclusion that god exists, or else to an argument, distinction, definition, or premise along the way. Another type attacks the whole undertaking as impossible or a waste of time. Reasoning can get nowhere on this sort of question (says such an objector), or, even if it can, it is not worth getting there by such means.

Confronting this second type of objection is logically prior to the procedures in this book, and for that reason it might have been the business of the first chapter. I have chosen instead to relegate the matter to this final chapter. I had a few reasons for doing so. One was that arguments about whether arguments can or should be made about something can get a book off to rather a coughing start—better just to start making arguments about it and decide in retrospect how successful the project was (do we really need a meeting to decide whether it would be worthwhile to hold a meeting?).

Another reason was that disdain for argumentation about god is a bit out of vogue these days. In the time of the German philosopher Immanuel Kant, things might have been different. He claimed to have shown, once and for all, that the existence of god lay forever beyond proof or disproof. Educated readers at that time might have expected an author of any there-is-a-god book to come out swinging at Kant on page 1. Today, however, the more popular view is that we *can* more or less settle the god question, some authors saying "exists", others saying "almost certainly does not exist". It has been my chief goal to show the shortcomings, in fact the impossibility, of that latter view.

But now, for the sake of completeness, I will briefly handle the other sort of objection in its principal manifestations. The main objections to the possibility or desirability of the very enterprise of reasoning to the existence (or nonexistence) of god are as follows.

1. *"No proof convinces everyone."*

Anyone attempting to prove the existence of god must either be a super-duper genius, more brilliant than all previous thinkers, or a mere crank, boobishly unaware of the universal failure of all such arguments up till now, one of which he will naively present afresh. If any of the arguments of the past had been any good, it would have convinced everyone, or at least the logicians and scientists and philosophers. As it is, none has succeeded in convincing everyone, or even a significant majority. Hence, none has been worth a hoot.

2. *"Kant proved there can be no proof one way or the other."*

Read his *Critique of Pure Reason*, and you will see a carefully worked out proof that it is impossible for reason to prove, or disprove, the existence of god. Kant is famous for having done this.

3. *"The existence of god is a matter of faith."*

Everyone says so. And it wouldn't be a matter of faith if it were a matter of proof. Hence, it cannot be a matter of proof.

4. *"Anyone who attempts to prove the existence of god has an agenda" and hence cannot weigh evidence impartially, but really he is just gathering rhetorical support after deciding in advance what the truth of the matter must be.*

An honest inquiry must begin instead with the assumption that there is no god, since the prima facie evidence weighs heavily in that direction—just as it does in the case of the tooth fairy. Whoever pretends to begin an "honesty inquiry" into whether the tooth fairy exists, starting with the idea that the odds are fifty-fifty, is dishonestly

ignoring the fact that almost certainly there is no reality corresponding to so fantastic a notion. Atheism, then, is the starting point, and
one must persevere in it until something forces him out of it.

5. *"A god who needs his existence proved cannot possibly exist."*
What motive would he have, after all, for hiding himself? Why
would he tolerate all the atheists out there who defy him to prove
them wrong?

6. *"The principle of verification implies that proof of god's existence is
impossible."*
A.J. Ayer is famous for proposing the principle of verification,
which goes roughly like this: *Every statement that can be known to be true
with certainty is either a fact of immediate experience* ("I am sitting right
now"), *or else a tautology or an analytic statement* ("Bachelors are bachelors" is tautological; "Bachelors are unmarried" is analytic, because
the predicate is part of the meaning of the subject), *or else is deduced
from statements such as these.* But anything deduced from tautologies
or analytic statements will still be itself tautological or analytic, and
anything deduced from premises expressing immediate empirical data
will itself be something empirically verifiable. For example:

Every unmarried man has no wife.   = analytic
Every bachelor is an unmarried man. = analytic
Every bachelor has no wife.   = analytic

This sitting person is brown eyed. = empirically verifiable
I am this sitting person.   = empirically verifiable
I am brown eyed.   = empirically verifiable

Accordingly, if the existence of god can be deduced with certainty,
the statement "God exists" must be either analytic (or a tautology)
or else empirically verifiable. But it is neither. Therefore, it is not a
verifiable statement.

7. *"There is no proof outside of mathematics."*
In mathematics we find real proofs, which is why everyone agrees
about those things. Outside of math, we find no proofs, but only

probabilistic arguments. Hence, it is silly to try to "prove" god's existence, unless one were to do so mathematically—which is even sillier.

8. *"Proof in general is impossible, since we must trust our brains."*
All our knowledge depends on trusting our senses and our brains. For all we know, each of us is just a program in a computer, or a brain in a vat with evil scientists subjecting us to a virtual reality of their own creation, or we might in some other way be victims of a "Matrix"-like prank. To have perfect certainty about anything (which is what *proof* implies), we would first have to be sure that our senses and brains are trustworthy organs of knowledge bringing us real information about real things, and we would have to come to this knowledge without relying on our senses and our brains, which is impossible.

9. *"Proof of god's existence is either useless or impossible."*
It is useless if it proves only that there is some sort of divine being without identifying it with any particular god known to us through some religious tradition; impossible if it means proving that the god of some particular religion really exists as described by that religion. For example, if someone proves that there is an intelligent first cause of all things but does not prove furthermore that this being had special dealings with Abraham, Isaac, and Jacob and sent his only Son to redeem mankind from their sins et cetera, that is useless knowledge, since it does not tell us how we might be saved or gain eternal life or become in any way better off. On the other hand, it would be impossible to prove that such a being had special dealings with Abraham, Isaac, and Jacob—it is not even possible to prove, in any strong sense, that Abraham existed. Such statements are bound up with the inaccessible past, which we can know, if at all, only by very tenuous inferences and with a good deal of trust in certain authorities.

10. *"Proof is useless in general, being incapable of moving the heart."*
Even if someone became convinced of the truth of the Jewish faith, or the Christian, or the Islamic, or some other, it remains that the manner in which he becomes convinced by "proof" leaves him

cold and indifferent—merely assenting to statements and not yet willing to devote his life to the things assented to. And that will not do
him any good. A living and ardent faith is what is needed to please
god. And where there is faith, there is no need for proof.

11. *"Proof is unnecessary, since god's existence is accessible by the much surer
means of religious experience."*

Anyone who comes to love god and to converse with him regularly in prayer receives in return over the course of a lifetime some
degree of experience of the presence of god and becomes as sure
of god's existence as he is of the existence of his other friends. This
experiential knowledge is surer and more intimate and better than
any cold, logical "proof" that reasons from effects to causes.

12. *"Proof is unnecessary, since god's existence is self-evident".*

It is impossible to think god does not exist, given what the word
god means: a being whose superior cannot be conceived. If such a
being existed only in our minds, then we could easily think of a
superior—namely, such a being existing outside our minds as well.
Consequently, having thought of a superior, we would have to say
that "a being whose superior cannot be conceived" turned out to be
also "a being whose superior *can* be conceived". But that is a contradiction and is plainly absurd. Hence, it is entirely unthinkable that
god does not exist. Accordingly, no argument from effects to causes
is needed.

13. *"God clearly cannot exist, since his attributes contradict each other, especially omnipotence and omniscience."*

It would be silly to try to prove god exists if *god* names a self-
contradictory thing. And some of the divine attributes immediately
appear mutually contradictory. Omnipotence is a case in point.
Comedian George Carlin, for example, used to ask whether god can
make a rock so big that even he can't lift it. If not, well, *there's* something he can't do—but if so, there is still something he can't do,
namely lift the darn rock. (My son Ben, at the tender age of eleven,
thought up basically the same question on his own.) Dawkins, too,
argues that god's omniscience is at odds with his omnipotence, since
his omniscience requires that he already knows what he will do in

the future, which means he is powerless to change his mind, which means he is not omnipotent.[1]

14. *"The specific line of argument in this book has been debunked."*

My last and final heckler is someone who thinks the whole project of this book is ridiculous because it amounts to resurrecting the argument from first cause, which has been done away with by competent modern logicians and philosophers. Bertrand Russell is a famous and eloquent example of such an objector. In *Why I Am Not a Christian*, he summarizes the argument of the first cause—the chain of causes cannot go back forever but must terminate in a first cause which we name god—and then debunks it in several ways. First, he explains, the whole idea of causes has practically been discarded by modern philosophers and scientists. Even aside from that problem, he goes on, the argument is entirely invalid. As a young man he had accepted the argument of the first cause until one day, when he was eighteen, he came upon John Stuart Mill's autobiography in which Mill wrote: "My father taught me that the question 'Who made me?' cannot be answered, since it immediately suggests the further question 'Who made God?'" Russell then remarks,

> That very simple sentence showed me, as I still think, the fallacy in the argument of the First Cause. If everything must have a cause, then God must have a cause. If there can be anything without a cause, it may just as well be the world as God, so that there cannot be any validity in that argument. It is exactly of the same nature as the Hindu's view, that the world rested upon an elephant and the elephant rested upon a tortoise; and when they said, "How about the tortoise?" the Indian said, "Suppose we change the subject." The argument is really no better than that. There is no reason why the world could not have come into being without a cause; nor, on the other hand, is there any reason why it should not have always existed. There is no reason to suppose that the world had a beginning at all. The idea that things must have a beginning is really due to the poverty of our imagination. Therefore, perhaps, I need not waste any more time upon the argument about the First Cause.[2]

[1] Richard Dawkins, *The God Delusion*, p. 101.
[2] Bertrand Russell, *Why I Am Not a Christian* (New York: Touchstone, 1957), pp. 6–7.

Whew! Now a brief reply to each of these, one at a time:

1. *"No proof convinces everyone."*

This objection is perhaps the most prevalent, and the cheapest one to make, yet a complete answer to it involves several components and is also interesting in its own right. For these reasons I will take a bit more time with this response than with the subsequent ones.

This objector presents me (and others like me) with a dilemma: either I must pretend to be a supergenius like none the world has ever seen, presenting new and amazing arguments for god's existence that will, for the first time ever, convince everyone and bring hordes of atheists to their knees, *or*, less flatteringly, I must countenance the possibility that I am a hack with prodigious ignorance of the failures of past thinkers and arguments concerning this matter.

Well, I freely confess I am no supergenius. The arguments in this book, convincing as I take them to be, are not my own inventions. Practically all of them come from a great tradition of thinkers that began with the pre-Socratic philosophers and acquired fresh vigor with Socrates and Plato and Aristotle, then continued through Boethius, the great Arab Aristotelians, and Aquinas, and lives on today in various universities around the world.

But if any of these arguments is truly a proof, then why has none been universally accepted? Why do so many smart people continue to reject them all?

Before I answer that question, it is only fair to note that since the time of Aquinas, if not since the time of Aristotle, there has always been a significant number of philosophers in the world who have accepted arguments like those in this book as successful proofs. That is roughly twenty-three centuries of measurable success. Somehow such reasonings persist down through the ages, convincing thousands of great minds in every generation along the way, some of whom were originally atheists. It is simply a matter of fact, in other words, that the arguments do convince many smart people and have done so since they first saw the light of day. That still leaves us with the unconvinced philosophers to account for, of course. Some who go by the name philosophers are quacks, and we need not concern ourselves with what they think. Many others struggle with a willful attachment to atheism, as illustrated in chapter 8. Unlike any mathematical truth, the truth about god's existence or nonexistence is profoundly relevant to everyone's conception of goodness and happiness and purpose. Not only god but many other things considered by philosophers and not mathematicians possess this potentially life-altering character—a fact perceived most keenly by the philosophers themselves. Hence, there is a possibility of desire influencing thought in philosophical questions where there is no correspondingly strong element of desire in mathematical investigations. We should not expect, in other words, that even the most solid and genuine proofs of philosophy will enjoy the same universal convincing power as those in mathematics. In philosophical matters, even genuine proofs can be surrounded by obstacles nowhere to be found in the world of mathematics.

But if we continue scanning the people who have been called philosophers, after leaving aside quacks and those whose thinking is unduly shaped or inhibited by desire or prejudice one way or the other, we will still find a number of them left to be explained. There are many philosophers in the world who do not go about promoting arguments like those in this book and are nevertheless neither quacks nor particularly attached to atheism. What can be said about those?

It seems to me that most of them simply have never heard the arguments. This might at first sound incredible. Practically everyone who can read has heard of Aristotle, and most people have heard of Aquinas. Then how can there be nonquack philosophers who have not studied Aristotle's or Aquinas' arguments for god's existence? The answer is not far to seek. We must remember that philosophy is an enormous enterprise with a history spanning well over two thousand years and that modern education encourages specialization. That is a recipe guaranteeing significant lacunae in every philosopher's intellectual formation. I believe it was Konrad Lorenz who said, "Every man gets a narrower and narrower field of knowledge in which he must be an expert in order to compete with other people. The specialist knows more and more about less and less and finally knows everything about nothing." Not every philosopher winds up as bad as all that, but some degree of specialization is necessary, and consequently a generous dose of ignorance of one's own general field is inevitable. Much the same is true in science. A particle physicist might be as ignorant as I am about the Krebs cycle of respiration or of the chemical formula for caffeine. A Kant expert might hardly have read two words of Aristotle. Even an expert in Aristotle's logical works might know next to nothing about his ethical and political writings.

There are also powerful academic disincentives for anyone who might be tempted to study Aristotle or Aquinas at all with a view to finding out the truth. One of these is that Aristotle and Aquinas are both thinkers from the distant past. That is sufficient evidence for most people, even most of those who go into philosophy these days, that their thinking is in all ways outmoded. It doesn't help matters that they were geocentrists. The result is that the study of them is widely regarded as an exercise in the history of thought, not so much a properly philosophical enterprise. But if we do bother to read them, we find in their writings more than geocentrism and similarly outdated ideas (which, by the way, they themselves regarded as hypotheses and distinguished sharply from philosophical truths that they considered absolutely certain and timeless). In 'Aquinas we find that the statements emphasized and insisted upon are not those like "Earth is at the center of the universe" but those of another type. I mean self-evident statements, such as "Nothing gives what it does not have" and "Among things actually existing but unequal, one must be the maximum" and also the necessary consequences of these. Such statements remain as true as ever. They are not time sensitive. And they have nothing to do with geocentrism.

Nonetheless, a thoughtlessly inherited prejudice against reading "ancient" and "medieval" thinkers for genuine insights into reality persists in modern universities, as it has now for at least a century or two. And so indeed the god-philosophy of Aristotle and Aquinas is read by a bare minimum of today's philosophers and read with any degree of care and open-mindedness by far fewer still. That is why Christopher Hitchens (who was not a philosopher) could mention the word *geocentrist* and consider Aristotle and Aquinas quite dispatched by it. It is also why Richard Dawkins (also not a philosopher) can grossly misrepresent Aquinas' five ways while provoking hardly a squawk from any but a handful of philosophers. And it is also why Bertrand Russell (who was a philosopher) could set up a mere straw man and call it the "argument of the First Cause".

Now let's sum that all up. Unlike most mathematical questions, the god question is among those that affect human desires, and so it inevitably becomes the object of prejudices, intellectual fashions, educational policies, social trends, laws, obnoxious religiosity, and other cultural phenomena that can skew our thinking about it in either direction, for or against a god. That philosophers do not all agree about it is therefore no proof that it lies beyond the sphere of inherently decidable (and decided) questions. The disagreement is instead largely due to other causes, such as those I have been describing. To suppose that the failure of an argument for god to convince some thinkers is necessarily the fault of the argument, before even identifying such a fault, is therefore a lazy assumption valued only by those who would avoid having to understand the argument itself.

2. *"Kant proved there can be no proof one way or the other."*

When Kant attempted to prove there can be no proof of god's existence, he did so by assuming a theory of knowledge that dictates that you cannot know that any person exists besides yourself. (In fact, the principles of his *Critique of Pure Reason* do not even allow that you know yourself to exist, in any ordinary sense of *yourself.*) I regard any such theory as fatally and fundamentally flawed. (Explaining here how he lapsed into such a theory would take us too far afield.) We cannot agree with Kant without also agreeing to the tenability of solipsism. And if we are willing to do that, we are not ready for an argument to convince us that god exists. We need first to know that there is a "we" to be convinced. And I did not write this book with such a delusional audience in mind.

3. *"The existence of god is a matter of faith."*

In my experience, most of those who believe in god take it to be "a matter of faith" because they have been expected to believe in god's existence all their lives, and no one has expected them to prove it or has told them that proving it might be possible. I do not pretend to know what authorities in other religions have to say on the subject, but any Christian should be willing to listen to Saint Paul:

> For the wrath of God is revealed from heaven against all ungodliness and wickedness of men who by their wickedness suppress the truth. For what can be known about God is plain to them, because God has

shown it to them. Ever since the creation of the world his invisible nature, namely, his eternal power and deity, has been clearly perceived in the things that have been made. So they are without excuse. (Rom 1:18–20)

It sure sounds as though Saint Paul is saying the existence of god is not always and necessarily a matter of faith—that is, a truth beyond the power of rational verification—but is instead something that can be "clearly perceived" by understanding the need for a cause of the effects we see. So it is that men are "without excuse" if they try to "suppress the truth" about god.

Aquinas distinguished between the "preambles" to faith and the "articles of Christian faith", and it seems to me that this distinction is very helpful here. The articles of the Christian faith are those statements that it believes to have been revealed by god and that surpass the power of reason to verify or disprove. The preambles are those truths to which we must assent if we are to have faith at all and which at least some people can come to see by the natural light of reason. Without assenting to the preambles, we could not possibly assent to the articles. That god exists, for instance, is a preamble to the articles of faith. It is possible simply to believe it, to trust in the word of people wiser than we are about it, or to assent to it because of an interior prompting from god himself; but it is also possible to come to know it from "the things that have been made". That god is a Trinity of Persons, however, is necessarily an article of faith (or a mystery), since it is beyond the power of reason to determine its truth or falsity. And although it is possible to believe that god exists without believing that god is a Trinity of Persons, the reverse is impossible. Hence, the existence of god is a preamble to faith in the Trinity.

4. *"Anyone who attempts to prove the existence of god has an agenda."*

Well, anyone who attempts to prove *anything* has an agenda— namely, the establishment of a particular conclusion. No mathematician proceeds just by gathering known facts at random and trying to click them together to see where they might lead. That goes nowhere. What comes first, before any discovery of a proof, is the suspicion that statement P might just be true. Only then comes the search for proof. Besides, I don't pretend to be the discoverer of a proof or to be recounting my own thought process by which I transitioned from uncertainty to theism.

The comparison of god to the tooth fairy (which I first learned about from a teacher when I was in high school) certainly puts god in a bad light. But the comparison is hardly apt. The idea of the tooth fairy is altogether silly. No serious thinker ever believed in such a thing. Socrates, Plato, and Aristotle believed in god, or in gods—or both, actually. Are we supposed to think they were silly children? Presumably the aptness of the comparison is this: just as we are told about the tooth fairy as children to make us feel good, so we are told about god as children to make us feel good, and therefore we should judge alike about both cases. But that is hardly compelling. In all cases where the parents tell the children about both, the parents themselves do not believe in the tooth fairy but do believe in god. They tell their children about god not just to make them feel good, but because they think that what they are saying is true. And many parents tell their children that if they misbehave, god will punish them, which does little to inspire good feelings.

The argument amounts to an accusation: "You believe in god just because it makes you feel good, comforts you, reminds you of your safe childhood, allows you to continue to identify with your parents, and enables you to look forward to eternal bliss." Even if that is true in some or many cases, it proves nothing about the actual truth of the matter. It does not prove there is no god, or that his existence is in itself implausible, or that the arguments for the existence of god are failures. It simply imputes psychological motives to all believers in god, although those motives clearly do not apply to all cases and certainly not to serious and thoughtful theists. The same sort of argument can be made against the atheist: "You deny the existence of god only because all your friends think that way and you want to be just like them, and because you want to live a guilt-free debauched life." Even if that is true in some or many cases, it is hardly a sound reason for rejecting atheism in principle. Neither, then, does this sort of argument work against theism.

5. *"A god who needs his existence proved cannot possibly exist."*

God does not hide himself, but has revealed himself to human reason in every single existing thing known to us. Hence, it is not quite accurate to say that god is hiding. It is true that his nature is hidden from us, that he is incorporeal, and hence he is inaccessible to human eyes and imagination, but he is not inaccessible to reason. The beauty of the universe, especially, is a sign, an expression of the divine, and not a concealment.

It might also be that god has spoken to the human race in words, and hence more distinctly and explicitly. But it is beyond the scope of this book to address that question.

As to why god would put up with atheists who bad-mouth him, I suppose it is because he is not as impatient with them as they are with him.

6. *"The principle of verification implies that proof of god's existence is impossible."*

The late Ralph McInerny, in his book *Characters in Search of Their Author*, presented a delightful demolition of this objection.[3] I will content myself, however, with pointing out that Ayer's principle of verification cannot possibly be verified, according to itself. It is neither a tautology nor an analytic statement nor an expression of some immediate, here-and-now, empirical fact. Therefore, even if the principle were true, one could never know it to be true. One could never verify it. Abstracting from whether it is true or false, one can innocently ask: "How can I *know* that it is true? Is it supposed to be self-evident? Because it isn't, to me. Has someone proved it? Then where is the proof, huh?" But no one pretends to prove it—how could you prove it, since according to it, you would have no premises available to you except here-and-now empirical facts and worthless tautologies?

Well, then, since it is impossible to prove it, and since it does not appear to be self-evident, I make bold to say *it is completely false.* And the facts are with me. There are plenty of general statements, nontautological statements that are not just about the empirically verifiable here-and-now, that are nonetheless perfectly true and of which we can be perfectly certain; for example, "Equals added to equals make equals." The equals in the predicate are not the same equals as either

[3] See Ralph McInerny, *Characters in Search of Their Author* (Notre Dame, Ind.: University of Notre Dame Press, 2001), 21, 74.

pair of equals in the subject. Hence, the statement is not a tautology. Nor do the equals mentioned in the predicate enter into the definition of either pair of equals in the subject. Hence, the statement is not analytic either. Nor again is it about some particular here-and-now fact, but it is altogether general. And it is true. And anyone who is not a nincompoop knows it. Ayer's principle of verification is false, then, and poses no threat to theism or to anything else.

7. *"There is no proof outside of mathematics."*

I will concede that there are no proofs outside of mathematics that enjoy the same degree of precision, certainty, and rigor as the proofs found in mathematics. But people still speak of proving something in a court of law, even of proving it "beyond all reasonable doubt".

I have aimed at something between these—that is, between mathematical proof and legal proof.

Mathematical proof causes certainty of the conclusion by reasoning, with inescapable logic, from prior premises known with certainty, starting from first principles known to everyone, or readily known by anyone sufficiently intelligent and willing to take a little time to conceptualize them.

Proof in a court of law falls short of that exact standard. It does not usually argue by means of inescapable logic, but by multiplying probabilistic arguments. Nor are most of the first premises things known with perfect certainty, such as "No number is both even and odd", but instead they are things taken on good authority, things that it would be silly to doubt, such as "Johnson was at the corner of Fifth and Elm on Saturday, June 10, at 11 P.M.", in view of the fact that a video, thirty eyewitnesses, and his entire family placed him there. It is *possible* that they are all mistaken or lying; it is just exceedingly improbable.

The proofs I have endeavored to provide in this book are more like the mathematical than like the legal. They reason rigorously from their premises to conclusions that must be true given only that their premises are. They are deductions, in other words. Also, the first principles on which they rest are evident to all people from their own experience, or else from an adequate understanding of the terms in them. No outside witnesses are needed.

The principles at the foundation of theistic deductions are nonetheless a different story from the principles of mathematics. The very first principles of mathematics are typically not difficult to grasp and acknowledge, although enormously lengthy reasonings go forth from them. The difficulty in mathematics is the argumentation itself, more than the vetting of its first principles. Or, in cases in which the mathematical principles begin from terms that are themselves somewhat sophisticated and require a good deal of thought (for instance, an integral might be such a thing, or a field or an abelian group) and we are faced with obviously foreign and technical terms, we readily see that we would be fools to deny the legitimacy of the principles or proofs based on these, when we so plainly understood nothing of them. In the case of the terms and principles in this book, however, they are almost always refinements of things we have all encountered in life—of the ideas of "cause", "effect", "one", "many", "whole", "part", "actuality", "potential", "before", "intelligence", "perfection", and so on. The effect is that we feel we are talking about things we know quite well.

The truth, though, is that before giving them any special attention, we know these things well enough only to have a rough sense of them adequate for our daily affairs. Without careful reflection on those concepts, most of us would be unable to distinguish their subtly distinct meanings and to enunciate the axioms concerning them, or to defend these from objections. This is the potentially *offensive* thing about philosophizing, about getting precise and exact answers to very universal questions everyone has encountered; thanks to the generality of the things under discussion, and to their consequently universal familiarity, we all tend to regard ourselves as experts about universal questions much more than we really have any right to. And consequently we are put off by those who would try to help us into being more exact about these things. Socrates never got in trouble for his teaching of mathematics to slave boys. But he got into enormous trouble for trying to explain to people that their conception of courage or wisdom or friendship was seriously inadequate.

In short, if *proof* means "what will convince anyone when it is presented to him", then I am not sure there are any proofs, even in mathematics, and I readily admit there are no proofs of the existence of god. If, on the other hand, *proof* means "a form of reasoning based on unalterably true premises, whose truth is naturally evident to all who correctly conceive the meanings of their terms, and from which a conclusion follows with absolute necessity", then there is indeed proof of god's existence, and instances of it are found in this book. Out of willfulness, or due to some confusion, a person can still refuse to admit that he knows this or that premise in a proof for god's existence. He might deny the statement "There is truth", for example. But in denying this statement, he thinks he speaks the truth and thus shows that he somehow sees the truth of the premise—he just fails to see that he sees it.

8. *"Proof in general is impossible, since we must trust our brains."*

Like Ayer's principle of verification, this idea self-destructs. Can we trust this reasoning, which leads the objector to think that we must first run our brains through a thorough certification process before we can trust our own reasoning? If so, we can reason in a trustworthy manner before any such process after all. If not, then we needn't bother about the objector's conclusion.

This objection is also similar to the Kantian one raised under item 2. Whether on the grounds that he cannot give a reason to believe he is awake rather than dreaming or on the grounds that he has seen *The Matrix* or seen *Star Trek* or read about phantom limbs, or read Descartes, anyone who seriously thinks that our brains and senses and reason might not be in any way trustworthy until we find a way to establish their trustworthiness independently of trusting them is beyond the help this book aims to provide. I openly and unapologetically presume an audience of readers who think they know they exist, that the world exists, and that many other specific things in it exist.

9. *"Proof of god's existence is either useless or impossible."*

I admit it is impossible to prove (in any sense of *prove* outlined above and perhaps in any legitimate sense of *prove*) that there is in reality a being to whom all the divine predicates found in the Bible belong. I also concede that proving the existence of a divine being in a general sort of way, such as I have done in this book, is, at least by itself, grossly inadequate for winning anyone a place among the saints. But that is a far cry from saying it is altogether useless. Such arguments could help prepare the way for faith in someone who has been hitherto struggling intellectually with the idea of god. They can help believers answer much of the ridicule of atheists. And aside from any apologetic purposes to which they might be put, they are incredibly interesting things in themselves. Were they ever so useless for compelling other people to admit their conclusions, I would still want to understand them for myself.

10. *"Proof is useless in general, being incapable of moving the heart."*
See the reply to objection 9. Otherwise, I will add only this: A pastrami sandwich is generally useless for banging in a nail. That doesn't mean a pastrami sandwich is generally useless.

11. *"Proof is unnecessary, since god's existence is accessible by the much surer means of religious experience."*
Anyone who truly enjoys an experiential and personal connection with god possesses a certainty about god's existence that is superior to and independent of the kind afforded by the reasoning in this book. Possibly, to such a person, this book will appear dry, cold, and abstract. But I am not in the business of offering people a personal connection with god. Without denying or disdaining such a thing, I am up to something else. And the something else (up to which I am) is of more use to those who have intellectual struggles with the idea of god, or who simply wonder about the rational path to god, than any religious experience of mine could ever be.

12. *"Proof is unnecessary, since god's existence is self-evident."*
The thought presented in the objection is that of Anselm of Canterbury, or very like it. While Anselm was not exactly trying to prove god's existence to himself, this particular thought sequence of his is one of the many (and quite different!) arguments brought under the confusing and showy label "Ontological Proof of God's Existence". Ever since the time of Anselm, there have been people who believed in the soundness of this thinking precisely as a proof of god's existence or of the self-evidence of his existence. Even today there are plenty of logicians who find the argument compelling. (Would that they were right! It certainly is short and sweet.) A surprising amount of literature exists on the argument, and probably there will always be erudite people who are convinced by it. There are several important insights connected to it. Nonetheless, insofar as it is supposed to be a

proof for god's existence, or for the self-evidence of his existence, I side with those who consider it a failure.

One reason for its failure is that "the being to which no superior can be conceived" might simply be the universe, for all the argument shows. If someone says, "Ah, but an intelligent creator would be even better than that!", we have to wonder how we know that an intelligent creator is better and also how it is even possible. Perhaps a creator is impossible; perhaps the universe is self-existent and is the supreme sum of all things, and hence, nothing truly possible and truly conceivable could be better. Or, if an intelligent creator would be superior to the universe, why not ten or fifty intelligent creators? Wouldn't that be ten or fifty times better still? If that is not possible, or not better, the Anselmian argument does not tell us why.

And then there is that premise: *if* a being whose superior cannot be conceived does *not* exist in reality, then we can think of a superior— namely, a being whose superior cannot be conceived *existing in reality*. Ah, but would this really be superior, if it is in fact an impossibility? How do we know that this weird formula does not contain a hidden self-contradiction, as "greatest prime number" and "thirty-sided perfect solid" do? It seems we need to supplement the argument with quite a bit of information about what makes something better than another, and what makes a thing of some given description truly possible and conceivable rather than a mere agglomeration of words.

There are other shortcomings in the argument, but it is not worth getting into them here. Were the Anselmian argument quite sound, after all, it would just mean that my main theses in this book are entirely correct; I just took a lot more trouble than was strictly necessary to establish them. I took the long way around. The scenic route. I could live with that, were it so.

13. *"God clearly cannot exist, since his attributes contradict each other, especially omnipotence and omniscience."*

Some believers in god have tried to avoid such problems simply by denying divine omnipotence. God has his limits like the rest of us, that's all. But something is amiss there. If god is the first cause, the only uncaused cause, and hence the cause of all other things besides himself—at any rate, of anything positive and real in them (as opposed to privations and absences and the like, which as such need no cause)—then how could any positive effect lie beyond his power? If it were something that some other cause can produce, then he can produce it, too, since he would be producing its cause.

It is thus necessary to admit that god is almighty, omnipotent, able to produce any effect. But what ought we to mean by this? What does it mean, exactly, to say that god can do all things?

Does it mean that god can do anything that can be spoken in words? For instance, can he make a perfect circle that is not a perfect circle? Can he make it so that the number three is an even number? Can he make a triangle that has no sides? Can he make himself never to have existed? Can he sin? Can he forget or make a mistake or catch a cold? Can he make a creature to exist independently of himself? Or make another god who is infinitely better than himself? Plainly there are many things he cannot do. What, then, does it mean to say that he can do all things?

It means he can do all things that are possible.

But how are we to understand *possible things*? Does this mean those things that are possible for human beings to do? In that case, god's power is limited to what human beings can do, which would hardly deserve the name omnipotence. Does it mean those things that are possible for creatures to do? That is similarly absurd, since god can do many things his creatures cannot, such as exist and act independently of any other cause. Does it mean those things that are possible for god to do? But then when we call god almighty, we would be saying nothing else than "God is able to do all the things that he is able to do", which is circular and does not bring out what is distinctive of his power.

We must, then, understand the word *possible*, in this context, not in relation to any particular power (as in possible for human power), but absolutely, in which sense anything is possible that does not involve a contradiction, and only something that does involve a contradiction is impossible.

Accordingly, whenever we say, "God can make [or do] X", we say something true, as long as there is no contradiction involved in X.

God cannot make a circle be also a square at the same time or make three be both an even number and an odd one at the same time since these things involve contradictions and for that reason are in themselves unable to exist. Nothing real is subtracted from the divine power by saying that god cannot do these "things", since these are not really things at all, but empty words, signifying no reality outside the mind—in a sense, these "things", being unthinkable, are not even really in the mind. Can god know that three is an even number? Of course not. Why not? Because three is *not* an even number. *Knowledge* does not extend to things that cannot be (except in the sense that we can know they cannot be). Likewise *power* is not measured by things that cannot be, but only by things able to be.

Sometimes, however, the thing in question involves no contradiction in itself, but only as said of god. God can make a mind change, for instance. But he cannot make his own mind change. For a mind to change is not a contradiction. But for god's mind to change does involve a contradiction, since this would imply potency, mobility, imperfection, and other things that cannot possibly be found in god. (I am not speaking here of any incarnation of god, but only of god purely in his own divine nature.) Similarly, there is no contradiction involved in walking, or in being mistaken, or in learning, or in growing old and dying. Yet all of these involve terms that *are* contradictory with respect to the divine perfection, and so god cannot make himself walk or make himself sneeze or make himself be mistaken or make himself sick or anything of the sort. But in our saying that god cannot do these things, nothing is subtracted from the divine power either, since we are saying only that god does not have the power to make a mistake or the power to get sick and so forth; in such expressions the word *power* seems to be abused. A true power is for something positive and perfect, not for something negative or a defect. The "power" to make a mistake is an inability, a disability, a want of power, rather than a power.

It is in this way that one should answer the goofy objections sometimes made against the divine omnipotence. "Can god change his mind?" No, that involves a contradiction, i.e., that a being with perfect knowledge also has imperfect knowledge so that he will be able to reconsider things in case he missed something the first time. God's inability to change his mind, then, is just like his inability to make a mistake; it is really a power, not a disability at all. "Can god make a rock so big that even he can't lift it?" No, that involves a contradiction, i.e., for him to produce an effect that exceeds his own causal power. But this is something he cannot do in the same sense that making a mistake is something he cannot do. We humans can, in some way, produce effects that we cannot undo or control, but this is because of our lack of foresight, because of our dependence upon other causes (not fully in our control) in making anything we make, and because of our limited power. To call our ability to bring about such a state of affairs a power is laughable. Far be it from god to have any such "power".

It has escaped the notice of Carlin, Dawkins, and the logicians to whom Dawkins refers that the only things that god can be said to be unable to make are nonsense beings (i.e., self-contradictory verbiage) and disabilities in himself, neither of which subtracts one iota from the divine omnipotence.

14. *"The specific line of argument in this book has been debunked."*

Anyone who has read the first four chapters of this book, or even the first two, can see that Bertrand Russell has thoroughly misstated the "argument of the First Cause", as he calls it. Probably he had run into nobody in his particular circles who knew any more potent arguments about the first cause than the version he put forward. But it is only a straw man. Here are some of his misrepresentations (I do not presume they were deliberate, only ill informed):

a. He says that the philosophers and men of science have "got going on cause", implying the whole idea of a "cause" has been called into question.

In fact it has been, but never reasonably. Those, such as Hume, who have called it into question or tried to whittle it down to a purely mental association, as opposed to a real relationship between things, did so on grounds so general that they would (and did) also call into question the existence of their own selves and a great many other obviously real things, a procedure that even most philosophers would think absurd. There are many such theories floating about that can be entertained only while we adopt an artificial "Let's try to doubt everything" attitude, which is sometimes taken to be the proper attitude of a philosopher. I beg to differ. I do not think that is thinking, but more like playing a game, or something rather less honest and wholesome than that. At any rate, I have made it part of the method of this whole book not to sweat blood over any objections that entail such ideas as "I have no notion whether I have ever caused anything [say, this book] and whether I even exist."

I similarly dismiss Russell's idea that "there is no reason why the world could not have come into being without a cause." I do not have any rigorous philosophical proof that the world began to exist— nor do I suppose a temporal beginning to the universe anywhere in this book. But if the corporeal, mobile world *did* come into being, I take it as evident that something must have preexisted it and produced it. We can imagine "something popping into existence" without imagining a cause. That is not the same as imagining "something popping into existence without a cause". The second is impossible to imagine (in any way that would be distinct from, say, imagining something popping into existence due to an invisible cause), whereas the first does not prove that things can pop into existence without a cause. If I can imagine A without imagining B, it does not follow that A can happen or exist without B. I can imagine my seeing and hearing without imagining my brain; it doesn't follow just from this that my seeing and hearing can be without my brain. Besides, if it were a real possibility for something to come into existence without any sort of cause, there could be no reason why it doesn't happen, or start to happen, for every kind of thing, everywhere and all the time. But that doesn't happen. So it isn't a real possibility.

b. Russell says that if anything can exist without a cause, "it may just as well be the world as God."

He says this as if no one ever thought to give reasons why the world could not be the first cause. But nothing composed, mobile, extended, or unintelligent can be the first cause, as we saw for the reasons given in chapters 2, 3, 4, and 6. And all those reasons were to be found in very famous books that were in print long before Russell himself popped into existence and remain accessible today.

c. Russell's rendition of the argument seems to depend on the premise that the world had a beginning in time.

(Stephen Hawking is guilty of this same misrepresentation, incidentally.) This betrays his confusion about the expression *first cause*, as though this meant a cause operative far back in time, which got everything going. On that reading, the argument for the first cause would rely on the idea that the universe had a beginning in time and came into existence after previously not existing. That is not how I understand the argument for the first cause, nor is it how any of its heavyweight proponents understood it. Aristotle thought that there was a first cause and that it was eternal, but he also thought the world had never begun to exist but had always been. Aquinas thought that there was a first cause and that it was eternal and intelligent, and that this could be proved, and he also thought the world had a temporal beginning to its existence, but he did not think it was possible for us to prove this latter point. So neither he nor Aristotle ever, ever, ever used as a premise, in arguing for a first cause, that "the world must have begun to exist." Following in their footsteps, I also have made no use of the premise that the world began to exist. The material and mobile and corporeal world, whether it began to be or not, needs a cause even just to *be right now*, as long as it exists; and whatever uncaused agency, currently existing and acting, is responsible for that, *that* is the first cause.

Bertrand Russell has mistaken a popular argument about the first cause for the real deal. Accordingly, he has destroyed no important argument for the existence of god. Leaving aside some of his groundless assertions, he has at best found certain shortcomings in an argument made off the cuff by some of the less informed theists in the world, an argument bearing only the most superficial resemblance to the sort presented in the foregoing chapters. It will always be possible to lump together arguments that are only grossly similar under a single label and, by finding flaws in one of these, to give everyone to understand that every argument dragged under the label has been dispatched. It is not always done on purpose. But it can always deceive a significant number of people, since we are all prone to seeing broad likenesses more readily than subtle differences, however essential they might be.

d. Russell's amusing anecdote about the world resting on an elephant, and the elephant on a tortoise, et cetera, is not so much a criticism of the real argument for a first cause as an appeal to it.

It is absurd to suppose that everything needs support. But some things do need support. Therefore, there must be some kind of unsupported support—at least one, such as the earth itself. So too it is absurd to suppose that everything needs a cause. So there must be an uncaused cause, a first cause. Why can't this be just the universe? Russell would have discovered the answer, had he read the greatest minds on the question.

EPILOGUE

The Shoulders of Giants

The existence of God would pass with me as at least as certain as I have ever held the truths of mathematics (which concern only numbers or figures) to be.

—René Descartes, *Meditations on First Philosophy*

All our knowledge has its origin in sensation. But god is most remote from sensation. So he is not known to us first, but last.... If anyone wanted to see divine things in themselves and to grasp them with certainty in the manner that sensible things and mathematical demonstrations are grasped, he could not take hold of them in this way because of the insufficiency of his understanding, even though those things are, in themselves, intelligible in that way.

—Thomas Aquinas, *Super de Trinitate Boetii*

Night Safari

In 2009 I took a new teaching job at a small college in southern California. That meant uprooting my family from a well-established life in Connecticut. My three children were not exactly ecstatic about the news. When my wife and I explained to them that we were moving to California, we might as well have said "to the moon". Our oldest, Max, could not remember that he had lived the first two years of his life in the Golden State. Evelyn and Ben had never known life anywhere outside New England and had never been on a plane. It didn't help matters that we had lived for ten years (the entirety of my children's conscious lives at the time) in the same house. It was a beautiful old colonial. It came with plenty of old-house headaches, but none of those had bothered the kids. They just saw the charm of the place and knew it was home.

I had serious doubts about being able to afford anything comparable to it on the West Coast. In the summer of 2009, well into the national housing crisis, banks were still refusing to let go of foreclosed properties at their current values, so there were very few houses on the market once we had flown west and begun looking. We were living in a trailer on campus. It was all I could do to keep a smile on my face and to try to find the bright side of everything for my poor homesick kids. I tried to devise special tactics to help each child adjust and learn to see good things about California.

Ben was the easiest, even though he was only nine. He had a keen interest in nature and was always my fellow explorer. In fact, the day we arrived on campus, straight from the airport, everyone was exhausted from the flight and went right to bed in the "double wide"—everyone, that is, except for Ben. He had worn a backpack for the entire plane ride and again for the car ride from the airport, intent on exploring the moment he set foot on college property. He was especially insistent once he saw the place. He could see that the campus vegetation and wildlife was unlike anything he had ever seen before. So he kept his backpack on, filled with his essential survival gear. When the rest of the family were pretty much settled in, and it was already getting dark outside, I took him for a quick tour by flashlight. And that was the beginning of a nightly routine we carried on for the three months we lived in that trailer.

We chose to explore at night for several reasons. During the days, I had to teach or go house hunting. And it was September, the hot time of year, with daytime temperatures frequently soaring over 100 degrees. That meant more comfort after sundown for us and for many of the bugs and animals we hoped to see. Most critters other than lizards and ants hole up somewhere during the day, venturing out only by night to find water or prey. The campus is nestled in the foothills of the Topatopa Mountains in the southern reaches of the Los Padres National Forest, so there are critters aplenty. A mountain stream wanders through the lower portion of campus, feeding three ponds and watering the roots of a great variety of trees, but mostly live oaks and sweet gums and giant redwoods.

Here, on one of our nightly safaris, I would march in front, Ben close behind, my flashlight's faint circle of light dancing fitfully before us. The world seemed larger by that little light—the circle of visibility itself was small and monochrome, devoid of detail, painted in broad, dim strokes, but by it the surrounding blackness seemed all the blacker and more imposing. And it was plainly full of *things*, though we could not see them. Out of that blackness exhaled the exhilarating nighttime smells of the chaparral terrain, carrying notes of earth and wet hay. We could hear the noisy stream percolating nearby, spilling into one of the ponds, and the night songs of hundreds of crickets and frogs.

Later, on the way back to our trailer, where the others were already asleep, Ben would always want to review everything we had seen and how well we had seen it. We had seen five deer at a distance, but they had run off into the darkness when they heard a twig snap under my feet. The eyes of an owl, perched silent and still on a branch way up in a tree, gleamed back at us from afar when we had pointed the flashlight upward. In mason jars we had caught and released a Jerusalem cricket, two black widows, a bluish-black tarantula, and an enormous beetle whose name we did not know. It had been a good night. This review process was important to Ben, partly so that he would be ready the next morning to tell his siblings and his horrified mother what we had encountered. But mainly the review was for himself. He wanted to see all in one mental glance everything he had added to his experience and to begin to anticipate what we might find on our next tramp. Maybe some night we could get a better look at the deer, if we walked more quietly. Or maybe next time we would find a scorpion or the elusive bobcat.

The apple must not fall far from the tree. After the long trail we have followed together in this book, gentle reader, I too wish to take stock of the sights we have seen along the way and to reflect a little on the kind of seeing we have done.

As to what we have seen, it is easy to summarize: we have seen the answers to the questions that launched our whole investigation. Must there be such a thing as a first cause? There must, as we saw in chapter 1. How many first causes are there? Just one, as chapter 2 revealed. And what kind of thing is that first cause? It is an unchangeable, nonbodily, perfectly actual intelligence—as we saw in chapters 3, 4, 5, and 6—and hence, it is a "who", a god, and the designer of all nature. And why isn't this designer himself designed? Doesn't everything complex need a composer? Yes, but the divine mind, although it is perfectly intelligent, is for that very reason also perfectly simple, and so it is impossible for it to need any cause, composer, or designer before itself.

Where Credit Is Due

So much for the things we have seen. As to the light in which we saw them, there are many things to say.

First, we saw these things by reasoning from what we know, not from what we take on religious faith. I have no quarrel with religious faith. I am a man of faith. But there are advantages to knowing some things about god independently of faith. For one, you can communicate reasonings, but not faith, to other people. A reasoned understanding of god's existence also enables its possessor to answer the attacks of atheists—sometimes even to their satisfaction—and thus to pave the way for faith.

What we have seen, we have also seen with certainty. The reasonings of this book are not merely probable (see appendix 1 to get a synoptic view of them). They all work by deducing the logical consequences of timelessly valid principles. It is not by chance that those principles have arisen in the thoughts of great minds again and again down through the centuries. They are the common heritage of the human mind. "Nothing comes from nothing." "What is put into action depends on what acts by itself." "Nothing is before itself." "Nothing gives what it does not have." "Some things are nobler than others." And on and on. Such are the laws of being, expressed in terms too universal for science to employ, let alone refute. We are free to ignore them, since the explicit recognition of their truth is in no way necessary for our daily business. We can even land on the moon without putting them into words and nodding. They just quietly await our notice. The conclusion that god exists, when deduced from principles like these, is true and hard-won knowledge, worthy of the name. It has a careful rigor about it, keenly responsive to certain contours of reality that all of us experience. The same principles show that matter cannot be self-existent or purely self-moving, and so these fundamental assumptions of atheism are thoroughly demonstrated impossibilities.

The certainty of these deductions, however, falls somewhat shy of mathematical certainty. At the heading of this epilogue, I quoted Descartes and Aquinas saying quite contrary things. Descartes was a mathematician and is the acknowledged father of modern philosophy. Aquinas was a Dominican priest and later a canonized saint. Given no more information than that, one would expect Descartes to have been the one touting the superiority of mathematical certainty over all reasonings about god, with Aquinas piously saying the opposite. Surprise! Descartes says the existence of god is at least as certain to us as the truth that two and two make four, and it is Aquinas who says that that could never be.

I must agree with Aquinas. Descartes denied the primacy of sensation in our knowledge. He sought to emancipate our intellectual knowledge, at least in its beginnings, from any dependence on sense experience. In fact, he made sensation itself dependent on our intellectual knowledge, attempting to prove the truth of the senses from the existence of god, their author. If this were the proper order in our knowledge, we would have to be sure there was a god before we could be sure there were dogs and cats. Descartes was brilliant, but he was misled into a backward theory of knowledge by certain genuine difficulties about how sense knowledge and intellectual knowledge depend on each other.

We need not go into his views in detail. But it is interesting to note that atheists happen to agree with Aquinas on this point—the certainties we have of sensible things (such as cats and dogs) and imaginable ones (as in mathematics) are greater than any our minds could attain about god. It does not follow from this, however, that god's existence is a little bit uncertain. I like beer, and I like wine more. It doesn't follow that I *dislike* beer a little bit. But if god's existence is not a little bit uncertain, how can it be "less certain" than our certainties about the things we can sense or imagine? Answer: our certainties about sensible and imaginable things *cause* the certainties we have about other things, such as god. We argue from the existence of causes familiar to us in sense experience, causes such as carpenters, to the existence of a first cause who is unfamiliar to us. We argue from the properties of mobile things we can see to the existence of an immobile thing we cannot see. From our own experience of understanding, we glean certain principles about understanding that lead us to discover that the first cause must be intelligent. And so on. But the first certainties from which we derive other certainties are the most certain of all. So the certainties we have about sensible and imaginable things will always be stronger than the later certainties we derive from these.

There is something else about the truths you have considered in the foregoing pages. You did not have to take my word for them. All of them were things you could see for yourself. Every premise was one of those perennially valid principles, such as "What begins to be needs a cause" and "Nothing gives itself something except by one part giving and another receiving." Truths like that are common property, accessible to everyone. The truths of cutting-edge science, by contrast, are things the layperson must simply take on a kind of faith.

Scientific approaches to god have certain advantages, to be sure. But even they must eventually avail themselves of the more universal principles of philosophy, since the subject demands it. God is not a force or an energy in any sense that can be neatly packaged in the relatively narrow terms of science. A philosophical approach, on the other hand, need not avail itself of any cutting-edge science. I am not aware of having wandered over into science anywhere in this book, for example. I answered some science-based objections and drew examples from the sciences now and then, not because the arguments of Aquinas depend on science, but because it is important to see that they don't depend on overthrowing science either. Like the truths of mathematics, the principles of Thomistic philosophy are quite friendly to well-crafted scientific theories but remain standing no matter which side of a worthy scientific dispute wins out. Whether the world had a beginning in time or not, whichever side you take in that big bang dispute, there must still be a first cause, possessed of all the attributes we have discovered. I did not even pick a side in the polemics over evolution. The general arguments I have been at pains to present are indifferent to whether one species somehow gives rise to another and to how great a role random mutations and natural selection have played among natural causes in the grand drama of life. The first cause has to be intelligent precisely because it is the first cause; this attribute rolled right out of everything a first cause had to be. It was not a hypothesis introduced to explain the fact that things appear to be intelligently designed. Science gets into the details of things in a way that universal principles by themselves never could. But genuine universal principles are true independently of how they play out in the details. And we are all capable of grasping the truth of universal principles without the assistance of science. They are prior to science.

It would be going too far, though, to say that all of us can, without assistance, discover the right universal principles and how to put them together to arrive at god's existence. I certainly could never have done it without assistance—lots and lots of assistance. Even Isaac Newton (echoing a sentiment attributed to Bernard of Chartres by John of Salisbury in the twelfth century) famously said, "If I have seen further, it is by standing on the shoulders of giants." He made earth-shaking discoveries but still thought he owed his success mainly to others. I have not made any discoveries. Aquinas and Aristotle deserve the main credit for formulating the principles and deductions I have labored merely to present. Aristotle himself gave credit to his predecessors for making his contribution possible. Although he thought none of them had found the whole truth about the first cause, each of them had found important bits on which he relied, and even their mistakes taught him to look for truth in places he might otherwise never have thought to look. I am similarly grateful—not only to Aristotle and Aquinas, from whom I have shamelessly stolen the real goods, but also to those with whom I disagree. Many of these have made it plain that, to their minds, "god" is an idea fit only for flat-earthers, hillbillies, and cavemen. For my part, the disrespect is not really mutual. For all my criticism of them, I am grateful to Richard Dawkins, Stephen Hawking, Christopher Hitchens, Bertrand Russell, and many others for their strong and intelligent formulations of views opposed to my own. Were it not for their insistence upon certain points, the significance of many things in the thought of Aquinas would almost surely have passed me by.

The Trail Goes On

We have now reviewed the main sights along the trail thus far and evaluated the light by which we saw them. It remains to say a word or two about what sights might lie ahead. What further truths might these same lights reveal? Certainly more questions about god remain, and it is likely that many of these lie along the path of sound philosophy. The writings of Aquinas point the way. One might still hesitate to read Aquinas himself—he is not light reading, or even good reading in any literary sense—but our long hike has put us in a better position to appreciate his questions and his methods.

And god is not the only thing to see by the lanterns we have swung to light our way. The illuminating power of universal truths might also reach as far as the human soul and to the great question of its mortality or immortality. We have not trained their light upon that ancient question, but we have nonetheless seen some very suggestive things. God's goodness, knowledge, and power and his uncoerced authorship of each thing in existence imply his mindful care for every one of them, in proportion to its capacity to reflect his goodness. It is a lazy or incapable architect who has no interest in or control over the details of his work. This implies that matters of justice—especially the great ones but even the minute—will not go forever unaddressed. But perfect justice demands a hereafter in which it could be dispensed, since it plainly does not exist here and now. That is one hopeful line of inquiry, then.

And there are others. The very knowledge of god's existence should inspire us with a new assurance about the purposefulness of living. Given god, nature itself is his sign, beckoning us on to more perfect understanding and appreciation. The invitation is built into our own natures. What a custom fit this superabundant world is to the ten million curiosities of my little Ben, who would prefer to leave no stone unturned. An invitation to know all things, engraved in every nature and sent to each of us in the form of inborn wonder, written by one who can neither deceive nor disappoint, should inspire us with childlike excitement. The deepest truths, the underlying meanings of all things, and the final outcomes of all whom we hold dear might in the end prove possible to know and to be cause for rejoicing. Ever since they came into my life, I have sought to provide my children with what is best for them. How much more must he who conceived their life from all eternity do the same. And if nature continues to surprise us and to surpass our expectations, how much more must its maker.

ACKNOWLEDGMENTS

I never knew just how little justice is done in the acknowledgments of a book until I sat down to compose this one, my first. "Support and encouragement" and "advice", and other seeming intangibles for which authors are always being grateful, have become for me quite tangible necessities. And if there are people in this world who are born writers, needing no more than encouragement and inspiration, I am certain I do not rank among their blessed number. For me, writing is hard, lonely work that never comes out right the first fifty-seven times, and all fifty-seven times I need the help of others to see why I have failed, and even more to see why I should not just throw in the towel. I suffer much, and frequently become insufferable, during my "process". How does one "acknowledge", let alone repay, all the unrewarding work that others have put into one's pet project—all their patient listening and hand-holding? I can only extend my wholly inadequate, undying gratitude. For guidance, or reality checks, or consolations, or pity, or instruction, or encouragement, for reading, editing, critiquing, suggesting, insisting, granting permissions, correcting, illuminating or inspiring or goading, and for various other services and kindnesses, my heartfelt thanks to:

Tony and Suzie Andres, David Appleby, Joe Audie, Danielle Bean, Duane Berquist, Chris Blum, Steve and Mary Cain, Chris Carruth, Jeff Lehman, Chris Oleson, Paul O'Reilly, Elizabeth Reyes, Mark Ryland, Alistair Saldanha, Jim and John Sullivan, Ben Wiker, and to the late Ronald P. McArthur—may he rest in peace.

Special thanks must go to my father, Robert Augros, and my brother Paul Augros, for reading the book in its early stages and, by means of their penetrating, extensive, gently worded and hilarious observations, making sure it did not stay there.

I must also thank my children, who provided so much of the inspiration for this book and who have ranked among my best teachers in this world.

Finally, I wish to thank my wife, Amy, who rightly reminds me that she has devoted as much time as I have to this project, counting every hour I spent on it, hence not with her, as a contribution of her own.

God bless you all.

APPENDICES

APPENDIX I

Naked Proofs

If you were to strip away everything in this book that was not an actual step in some deduction, the remainder could nearly fit into this appendix. Most of the work in the preceding pages consisted not in deduction, but in making the premises digestible. Not all self-evident statements are created equal. Some are so evident that any explanation of them to a normal and fully grown person is an insult. "Five is more than three", for example, is of this type, as is "Equals added to equals make equals." Others require a little explanation, but not too much, for their meaning and self-evidence to come to light. "Nothing both gives and receives the very same thing at the very same time" rings true the first time it strikes the ear, and yet it doesn't hurt to consider a few examples to get it firmly in one's grip. Still others sound meaningless when they are first heard in an abstract formulation, or else incorrect and susceptible to many counterinstances. "Whatever is received is received in the mode of the receiver" is one, for example, that at first sounds like a nonsense tongue twister, and "Nothing gives what it does not have", to anyone who has not considered carefully, appears vulnerable to exceptions. Most of the self-evident statements on which the deductions in this book rest are of this latter, more troublesome type. For that reason, I have spent a good deal of time explaining the meanings of the terms in them, or considering objections against them, or presenting certain qualifications or paradigmatic examples of them, all in order to remove obstacles to their self-evidence.

That is why the book is as long as it is. Without all that illustration and explanation, most of us (including me) could not understand the meaning of such principles, let alone see the truth of them, be they ever so self-evident in themselves. On the other hand, due to the sheer length of all the explanatory material, it is possible to lose sight of the forest for the trees. Mixed in among examples, counterexamples, observations, inductions, distinctions, definitions, side notes, and introductory anecdotes, the central deductions do not always stand out, and their order and flow is more hidden than one might wish. There is something to be gained, then, in extracting them from their natural habitat of examples and other illustrative matter and putting them on display in naked form, all together in one place. To this end, I have rounded up not all the deductions in this book but the main ones, and placed them here in order. They will be intelligible to you if you have read the book, although possibly not if you haven't. Here you see them in much the same state as you would find them in the works of Aquinas himself. Where I might spend a chapter explaining one or two deductions, Aquinas will usually give us a short paragraph. He gave us in most cases the bare bones of arguments and left it to us to flesh them out and lend them color and life.

Here, then, are the central deductions:

Deduction 1 (chapter 1)

If caused causes could exist without a first cause, they would constitute a middle with nothing before it.

But it is impossible for there to be a middle with nothing before it.

Therefore, caused causes cannot exist without a first cause.

Deduction 2 (chapter 1)

Among all the causes acting together and in series to produce an effect, one is most of all the cause of it.

What is most of all the cause of an effect in some series of causes acting together is uncaused by any of the other causes.

Therefore, among all the causes acting together to produce an effect, one is uncaused by any of the other causes.

In other words, in any series of causes acting together, there is an uncaused cause.

Deduction 3 (chapter 1)

From either of these two deductions, it is evident that if causes exist at all, there must be at least one first and uncaused cause.

But causes do exist.

Therefore, there is at least one first and uncaused cause.

Deduction 4 (chapter 2)

Two first causes would have to share a common nature (that of a self-existing thing) and hence would have to differ by a combination of this common nature with some distinctive addition in the case of at least one of them.

The common nature itself would be indifferent to this addition, since it can exist with it in one case, without it in the other.

Where something is combined with a feature to which it is indifferent, there is a prior cause, a combiner.

Hence, one of our two hypothetical first causes would depend, for its distinctness from the other one, on a prior cause. This means it would depend for its very existence upon a prior cause, and hence, it would not be a first cause after all.

Therefore, there cannot be two first causes, but only one at most.

Deduction 5 (chapter 2)

There is at least one first cause (deduction 3).

There is at most one first cause (deduction 4).

Therefore, there is one and only one first cause.

Deduction 6 (chapter 2)

Since there is only one self-existing thing (deductions 3 and 4), all other things have their existence through a cause.

And all things that have existence through a cause depend on a first cause (deduction 1 or 2), of which there is only one (deduction 5).

Therefore, all things other than the first cause depend on the first cause for their existence (they might also depend on other causes as well).

Deduction 7 (chapter 3)

A change cannot exist without something else existing (namely, its subject).

The first cause can exist without anything else existing.

Therefore, the first cause is not a change.

Deduction 8 (chapter 3)

All change is other than the first cause (deduction 7).

What is other than the first cause is caused by the first cause (deduction 6).

Therefore, all change is caused by the first cause.

Deduction 9 (chapter 3)

If the first cause could change, it would be giving and receiving this change to and from itself (because of deduction 8).

But nothing can both give and receive a change to and from itself unless it is divisible into cause and effect, whereas the first cause is not thus divisible.

Therefore, the first cause cannot change.

Similarly, if the first cause had any potential for some further actuality than what it now has, then, when it was receiving it, it would be both giving and receiving it without any distinction between the giver and the receiver, which is absurd. So the first cause cannot have any potential.

Deduction 10 (chapter 3)

All matter can change.

The first cause cannot change (deduction 9).

Therefore, the first cause is not matter.

And, conversely, matter is not the first cause.

Deduction 11 (chapter 3)

All matter is other than the first cause (deduction 10).

What is other than the first cause is caused to exist by the first cause (deduction 6).

Therefore, the first cause is the cause of the existence of matter.

Deduction 12 (chapter 4)

Every body (i.e., every dimensional thing) is changeable and has potential.

The first cause is not changeable and has no potential (deduction 9).

Therefore, the first cause is not a body (i.e., not a dimensional thing).

Deduction 13 (chapter 5)

A principal productive cause precontains in itself (in a simpler and superior way) whatever actualities it causes in other things (turnip axiom).

The first cause is the principal productive cause of all actualities in all things (deduction 6).

Therefore, the first cause precontains in itself (in a simpler and superior way) all actualities in all things.

Corollary: Consequently (deductions 9 and 13), when some actuality that we can name (such as "exists" or "acts") need not include any potential or limitation in its meaning (as "changes" or "cat" must), then that actuality must be attributed to the first cause.

Deduction 14 (chapter 6)

When some actuality that we can name need not include any potential or limitation in its meaning, then that actuality must be attributed to the first cause (corollary to deduction 13).

"Intelligence" is an actuality that we can name that need not include any potential or limitation in its meaning (since what understands all things, not just some, and actually understands them and is not merely potential to understanding them, would still deserve to be called "intelligent").

Therefore, intelligence must be attributed to the first cause.

Deduction 15 (chapter 6)

If the world is made by an intelligence, then it is designed, and the appearance of purpose and beauty in it and many of its parts is not illusory but real.

The world is made by an intelligence (deduction 14).

Therefore, the world is designed, and the appearance of purpose and beauty in it and many of its parts is not illusory but real.

Deduction 16 (chapter 7)

A god is a supernatural intelligence who deliberately designed and created the universe and everything in it, including us (cf. Richard Dawkins' definition).

A supernatural intelligence who deliberately designed and created the universe and everything in it, including us, exists (deductions 1–15).

Therefore, a god exists.

Deduction 17 (chapter 7)

God without the indefinite article (i.e., *god* as opposed to *a god*) means an intelligent immortal who alone is uncaused and who gives existence to all other things besides himself.

An intelligent immortal who alone is uncaused and who gives existence to all other things besides himself exists (deductions 5, 6, and 16).

Therefore, god exists.

APPENDIX 2

Hume Causing Trouble

In its early stages, most chapters in this book were much longer than they are now. Wherever you find one deduction or objection, there used to be five or six, sometimes more. Even my most enthusiastic feedback readers unanimously suggested substantial trimming. A single argument, painstakingly presented, was preferable to an indigestible avalanche of tersely stated proofs, objections, replies, and distinctions, all flung down before a bewildered reader. They were absolutely right about that and about thousands of other things besides, and I can never sufficiently express my gratitude to those who gave me such wise and generous advice.

They conceded, however, that some fraction of that early material, while unworthy of occupying space in the chapters, nevertheless deserved a place here in the appendices. In the chapters themselves, I confined myself mainly to discussing those relevant questions and problems such as anyone might have: Is there a first cause? Is it intelligent? Is it simple or complex? Why is there evil in the world? How can a cause give motion while having none? Also relevant to my line of thought are certain other questions and problems that not everyone has—that, indeed, no one has before getting educated into having them. Some of these made a brief appearance in the final chapter, "Hecklers". But a few remain that demand longer and somewhat more technical discussion than I could justify inflicting on the reader in the main flow of the book. Discussion of these problems is not strictly necessary for understanding the force of all the foregoing arguments, but confronting them equips us to answer those who attack us with them and forces us to make certain distinctions illuminating in themselves.

The three problems I have in mind are (1) David Hume's calling into question our knowledge of the existence of any causes whatsoever, (2) philosophical doubts about the existence of natures in the world, and (3) Newton's first law of motion, which seems to contradict the idea that all motion needs a cause. These three problems are the matter for these final appendices. This present appendix is dedicated to the first one.

The whole argument of this book relies on the premise that there are such things as causes in the world. I have taken that as a self-evident truth that first becomes clear to us in ordinary experience—in early childhood. All philosophers and scientists use causes to explain things. And almost all of them admit it. Some, however, have tried to deny that they believe in causes, entertaining the idea that there might be no causes in existence at all. The eighteenth-century Scottish philosopher David Hume is most famous for calling the existence of all causes into question.

The tricky thing about causation is that we don't see causation itself in the same obvious way in which we see colors and shapes and motions. Instead, we just see the distinct things, one of which is taken to be the cause of the other. So Hume tried to give us a shave with Ockham's razor, proposing that maybe there are no causes in the world, really. Perhaps instead it is sufficient to say that one thing often follows another in our experience, and when we see such a constant conjunction of two types of things, we call the one that typically comes earlier in time the cause of the one that typically follows after it. He also observed that many of the things we think we know to be causes, upon careful reflection, turn out to be quite opaque.

Like a modern Socrates, Hume had a knack for pointing out to us that we very often think we know things quite well, just because they are somehow familiar, but really we don't understand them very well at all. One example he gave was our own will or desire. You think (he would say) that your will is the cause of the motions of your hand when you are writing. But do you know how your will to move it causes the motion of your hand? Most people unthinkingly imagine themselves to possess some immediate power of their will over their hand. But if the right nerves were severed, your will would be powerless to move your hand. There are intermediaries, then, between your will and the motion of your hand. And who understands all those intermediate links, eh? Here we are, centuries past Hume, and we still don't fully understand the brain, or electricity, or—heck, we don't *fully* understand much of anything. But without knowing the precise links between the brain and the motions of the hand, how can you be sure that the one is the cause of the other?

While Hume's observations are worthy in themselves, and they should temper our estimation of our knowledge of causes, they aren't grounds for doubting the existence of causes. It is true that we see the things that are in causal relations better than the causal relations themselves—I see the motion of the hammer and the simultaneous motion of the nail into the wood better than I see that the moving hammer is *causing* the motion of the nail—but to see one thing better than another does not mean the other is not seen at all. I do not experience causation the same way I experience colors and shapes and motions, but that does not mean I do not experience it at all.

Possibly Hume was too preoccupied with the sense of sight when he was thinking about causes. If instead we turn our attention to the sense of touch, which is the sense of *effort*, we immediately perceive that our own causation is something we experience, not something we infer or deduce or postulate. And the notion that we simply form a habit or custom of thinking of A as a cause of B simply because A usually precedes B in time does not do justice to our experience. I hear the cock crow before dawn every morning—but it has never occurred to me to think that the cock's crowing was *causing* the sun to rise. When I come home from work, I always see my front door opening first and then see the interior staircase, but never in my wildest dreams was I tempted to think that the opening of the door was producing my staircase. Or if I was, it was long before I was on solid food. And at least some of the things that I think to be causes I can only pretend to have doubts about. I think I am the cause of this sentence. I authored it. I think Hume authored his books and deserves credit (and maybe also a little blame) for them. Any other attitude is disingenuous.

One might genuinely wonder how we know when we have a case of cause and effect and not just a case of one thing after another in time. The answer is a fairly simple rule. When the thing that came afterward in time in some way preexisted in the thing that came before, then the prior thing is in some way a cause. For example, the house that exists after the carpenter finishes working also preexisted in the mind of the carpenter. That is not just a case of temporal priority, then, but a case of causation. On the other hand, we see that night follows day on a regular basis, but we do not see that the night is somehow contained in the day, or that the day makes some effort to produce the night. Instead, some third thing—the motion of the earth in relation to the sun—is the cause of the alternation of day and night.

In many cases, though, the preexistence of the effect in the cause is very obscure to us, so we must be careful. Sometimes we might be inclined to deny that A is a cause of B simply because we cannot see how B preexists in A. In some cases, it doesn't, as the night does not exist in the day. But in other cases, there is preexistence, but in an obscure form difficult for us to discern. When I push my broken-down car three miles to the garage, I know that the motion of the car was not just "after" my motion in some sense, but also that the motion of my own body is the cause of the motion of the car. I'm not sure in what form the car's motion preexists in my muscles (scientists could tell you much more about that), but I know it must, somehow, since my pushing the car takes something *out* of me. It costs me something. That would not be true if the motion of the car were a fact independent of me.

It is also true that I rarely or never fully understand causes. I don't fully understand how my wish to move my hand causes the motion of my hand. No one does. But that does not in the least cause me to doubt that my wish causes my hand to move. These are not the same thing: knowing *how* something is so and knowing *that* it is so are not the same thing. And it is possible to have the latter knowledge without the former. I am probably more ignorant than most educated people of how my eyes enable me to see the world. But that does not affect my certainty that they do so.

Another Humean variation on the theme that for all we know there might be no causes is one that even my students who have not yet read Hume come up with on their own. There is no reason to think that anything *needs* a cause, they say. Things might now and then just pop into existence without a cause. If that could happen, who is to say that it isn't happening every time something new happens? And then there might be no causes at all. Things happen, that's all.

I will not reply to this by insisting that everything needs a cause.
I could hardly afford to do so, since my conclusion in chapter 1 was
precisely that there is at least one thing that doesn't! But I do think
that everything that comes into existence needs a cause at least for its
coming into existence. When people defend the theory that things
might just pop into existence without a cause, they usually refer to
their imagination. The thought experiment is simple enough. First,
imagine nothingness—black, empty space. Next, imagine that there
suddenly appears in that space a giant blue newt, or the Chrysler
building, or Woody Allen. Easy as pie! Since we can imagine something popping into existence without a cause, it must be possible—
since it does not seem right that we can imagine the impossible. (Can
you imagine a circular square? Or a four-sided triangle?) So goes
the thinking.

This thought experiment is not really an instance of imagining
something coming to be without a cause, however. Really it is just
imagining something coming to be *without imagining the cause*. We
cannot positively imagine the factual nonexistence of a cause for
the event in question. We can only neglect to form any image of
a cause for it. And if there are causes that we cannot possibly imagine (elementary particles and basic forces such as gravity seem to be
examples), then the mere fact that we fail to imagine them when
we imagine a new event does not prove that the new event can be
without the unimaginable cause. It only fits with the fact that the
cause of the event might be something we cannot imagine. Really,
then, if we insist that something can pop into existence without a
cause by this appeal to the imagination, we must be relying upon this
claim: "If we can imagine A *without imagining* B, then A must be able
to exist without B." And that claim is simply not true. I can imagine
Kermit the Frog moving and talking without imagining a puppeteer.
It doesn't follow that Kermit the Frog can do those things without a
puppeteer. I can imagine water without imagining water molecules.
It doesn't follow that water can be without water molecules. I can
imagine my own act of seeing without imagining my brain. It doesn't
follow that my act of seeing can be without my brain. When I look
out my window to the bottom of the hill on which my house sits,
I can see cars moving on the highway, but I don't see their engines.

It doesn't follow that they have no engines or that their motion just *happens* without their engines.

Puzzles such as Hume's are interesting, then, and maybe worthwhile in themselves, but they are not a good reason to doubt the existence of causes.

APPENDIX 3

Mad Philosophers and the Natures of Things

Natures, essences, forms: three names for the same thing. Everyone knows in some way that there are natures in the world. A horse has a nature. You yourself have a nature. Reality is not a continuum of stuff but comes in discrete packages. There are definite things with definite distinctions from one another—one thing stops here, and another begins. But for various reasons we sometimes have difficulty telling where one thing stops and another begins. We sometimes have difficulty even telling whether the two things in front of us are of the same nature or not. (Are a zebra and a horse really of different natures? Or are they of the same nature, but exhibiting surprising differences that lie within the range of that one nature's possibilities?)

Many of the natures we name are nevertheless real things. Not all of them are pure fictions we humans have invented for our own convenient classifications. That fact is important to a true understanding of the world. It is also important to some of the deductions in this book, such as that of chapter 2, which proved the singularity of the first cause from the impossibility of two things having in common a self-existent nature. Modern philosophers have added to the difficulty of understanding the natures of things by raising problems about the very existence of natures. This appendix is meant to deal with these.

Plato is famous for having posited essences or forms of things existing apart from their individual instances. According to him, "horse itself" was an eternal entity, really existing apart from the human mind and from every particular horse you can ride. "Circle itself" too existed apart from individual circles and independently of our thought, in some invisible and immortal realm. We can see and imagine particular circles. But "circularity itself" we can grasp only with the intellect, in the form of a definition.

To those uninitiated in Plato's thought, this notion of his may sound silly. It is not. He had many serious reasons for saying what he said, and there is much truth in his understanding of essences or forms; this is why some philosophers and many mathematicians to this day think he was completely right. And with regard to god, he was completely right. At least, it is true to say that god is not only wise but is his own wisdom, so he is the nature of wisdom itself, existing separately from all participations of wisdom in creatures.

Nonetheless, I side with the majority of subsequent thinkers who learned to draw certain distinctions that dissolve Plato's proofs for the existence of his other separately existing forms, such as "horse itself". Aristotle himself, after being Plato's student for about twenty years, rejected most of Plato's ideas concerning the forms, but agreed that there are real forms and natures in concrete individuals; two horses are distinct individuals of the same nature, for instance. That sounds much less bizarre and even in keeping with the ordinary perceptions of nonphilosophers. So, in advancing the idea that there are forms or essences or natures in things, I am not advancing a foreign Platonic idea. Really I am defending a bit of common sense.

More recent philosophers, as I mentioned, have raised problems with this bit of common sense. For various reasons, many of them have tried to reject the idea that things have natures at all. I say tried to reject because it is not really possible to divest ourselves of the idea that there are *different kinds of things* in the world. Our very language is founded upon that perception. So it is in some ways not possible to deny that there are *kinds* of things in the world. But that is what many modern philosophers have tried to do. Put this way, it might sound as though I am attributing a form of madness to them. Who would deny that there are different kinds of things in the world? Perhaps there is a touch of madness in that. Zeno, too, denied that motion existed. That sounds like madness. And in a way it is. But when you learn the problems these thinkers discovered (and in my opinion they are worthy of being called *discoveries*), you find there is method to their madness. Zeno's motion paradoxes were not good reasons to deny the existence of motion. But they were genuine problems about motion, truly worth thinking about, not easily solved, and their solution necessarily and profoundly advances our understanding of what motion is. Perhaps we can learn from the

tragic mistakes of mad scientists. We certainly can learn from the
mistakes of mad philosophers.

It is not important for the purposes of this book to fend off every
attack upon the reality of natures in the world. I will limit myself
to three. These will be sufficient to illustrate the inescapability of
natures, and they will enable us to sharpen up our concept of a "com-
municable nature". There is nothing like an opposing force to exercise our understanding of a thing.

1. *Ockham.* Some would have it that natures exist only in our
heads. The argument for this can be found in the thought of the
fourteenth-century philosopher William of Ockham, but it goes back
centuries before him. Here it is in distilled form:

The natures we understand are universals.
Universals do not exist outside the mind.
Therefore, the natures we understand do not exist outside the
mind.

That is not a silly problem. Both premises are somehow true, and
the deductive form appears valid. Whenever I ask my students
what they think of this argument, they usually say the first premise is
false. They say we can understand individuals, too, not just universals.
But is that quite right? I can sense or imagine individual people or
individual circles, but can I sense or imagine the *nature* of a person
or of a circle? As soon as I try to express the nature, I start giving a
universal formula: "a rational animal", for example. I cannot state the
nature of this particular human being, Wainesly Ascot III, without
leaving behind what is unique to him and describing instead what
is common to him and all other human beings. That is because his
nature is not uniquely his but is one that he shares with all the rest of
us. His nature is nothing else but human nature. He is not his own
unique species. He is one instance of a species or nature that others
have too, just as much as he does. So the first premise in the argument
above appears to be true after all. And only a Platonist would disagree with the second premise. There is no such thing as a universal
"Humanity itself" in the world, an instance of humanity that is nothing but the pure nature of humans, existing apart from any individual
human being. The problem is not so easily solved then.

The real mistake is more easily seen if we look at a similar mistake in a less difficult matter. Your eyes do not have the sense of smell. Insofar as things enter into your vision, they get separated from any olfactory qualities they might possess in reality. This could lead to the following misreasoning:

> The things I see are in my visual perception.
> Things in my visual perception have no smell.
> Therefore, the things I see have no smell.

We seem to have concluded that anything we look at is odorless— plainly false. I see flowers and coffee and bacon, and all those things have smells. So where did we go wrong? There is an ambiguity in the subject of the first premise. Does it mean "the things I see, *considered in themselves*, are in my visual perception"? Then it is false. It is not true that the dog in the street, or his shape or his motion, just because of what these are in themselves, exist in my visual perception. They can exist without existing in my perception at all. Or does it mean "the things I see, *considered insofar as they are seen by me*"? Then it is true. Insofar as things are seen by me, it is necessary for them to exist somehow in my vision. If we take it *that* way, however, then we must take the conclusion in the same spirit, so that the conclusion now reads, "The things I see, *considered insofar as they are seen by me*, have no smell." This means that the things I see, considered in themselves, might have smell, but their visual aspects exist without their smells insofar as they are present in my vision. All true and nonproblematic.

The problem about natures being universal is solved in the same way. The natures we understand, considered as they exist in our understanding, exist in our mind and not in reality. True enough. It does not follow that the natures we understand, considered as they exist in themselves, do not exist in reality. Just as "being apart from smelly qualities" is a condition of things in vision, but not necessarily of those same things as they exist in a dog, so too "being apart from particular instances" is a condition of natures in our intellect, but not necessarily of those same natures as they exist extramentally.

2. *Nietzsche.* The nineteenth-century German philosopher Frie-drich Nietzsche is probably the most famous proponent of the next problem about natures. The problem is that there seems to be no

real *common* nature, no single thing truly found in many instances, but only many things that are sufficiently similar for us to give them the same name. For example, what is a leaf? If we try to define it by color and shape, we find that we mean no definite color and no definite shape, since leaves—even those on the same tree—come in an endless variety of colors and shapes. So it seems that each of us calls any of a multitude of things sufficiently similar in appearance a leaf. And *sufficiently* means "sufficiently to our personal taste". We only hope that the particular range of similar things we have chosen to call leaves is more or less the same range as for other people, so we can talk to them. This view reduces a common nature to a mere convention of speech.

This is a mistake, too, but again it is an instructive one. It is true more often than we think that our names reflect human conventions as well as the natures of things. Alcohol in sufficient quantities impairs human speech, as well as motor and cognitive functions. But is there an exact moment when someone becomes drunk? Is there an exact blood-alcohol content that constitutes the nature of drunkenness? If you say it is .08 percent, would you bet your life that someone at .0799999 percent is therefore not drunk? Our laws define intoxication with quantitative exactness for the sake of enforcement—to avoid such quibbles. And that is very reasonable in principle. But it is also a convention and not purely a matter of nature. The same goes for the speed limit. Why sixty-five? Why not sixty-six? Because it has to be some agreed-upon number within the right range, and sixty-five got picked.

The Nietzschean view is only part of the truth, though. True, some names signify not a nature or a purely natural thing, but only a conventional cutoff, or a conventional grouping of things. That is in many cases both inevitable and desirable. It even happens in the sciences. When we cannot quite settle on nature's classifications among the beasts, for example, we still have to agree on classifications of our own for the sake of convenient communication. It is salutary to reflect on these things. But if all our names signify nothing but our conventional groupings of things, that amounts to saying that reality does no grouping of its own—as though the world presented itself to us as a smooth continuum of qualities, and we chop it up into arbitrary segments, and that is all.

Clearly that is false. *Water* names a very definite thing, *iron* another. Nature, not man, draws the distinction. It seems extravagant, moreover, to suppose that each thing called a water molecule is one of a kind, just coincidentally very similar to trillions of others and strikingly dissimilar to the trillions of other things we call caffeine molecules. No, the water molecules are all the very same kind of thing, and what slight differences they exhibit are just the wiggle room permitted by the nature of water itself.

Why else would we find that natural unities, like water molecules, can tolerate a certain amount of abuse while still persisting, but when we stress them beyond a certain point, then *poof!* we get something radically new? If reality were a continuum of variable qualities with no underlying natures, no natural boundaries, there would be no limits to how much you could fiddle with a water molecule—you would just get more and more slight differences, gradual changes. Instead, we get sudden and dramatic change, as though we had crossed a definite line drawn not by us but by the water molecule. Again, if there were no definite borders in things, then electrolysis of water should not produce the *same* radically new things, hydrogen and oxygen, every time. There should be no discernible pattern to what comes next, whenever we force things to change. As it is, there is a definite "next substance" in line, if you push this one beyond its limits.

So things exhibit distinctly pronounced limits to the qualitative and quantitative changes they can sustain before they get replaced by the next thing. And it seems these limits become more quantitatively exact and uniform as we descend into the microscopic (water molecules admit of less variety than leaves do). None of this would be true if there were not distinct natures out there underlying the flexible appearances. There are, then, definite natures common to many individuals in the world. But because these natures underlie the surface qualities that signal them to us, and because they permit some variation in those qualities (within limits), we struggle in many cases to understand the nature. In some cases we struggle to tell whether two things have the same nature, or distinct natures, or whether the thing in the beaker is a single thing with a nature of its own or a multitude of things, each with its own nature. But these doubts leave untouched the certainty that there are natures. I see a number of cows on the hill in the distance. I cannot make out just how many there are, and in some cases I can't tell whether I'm looking at two cows, a white one and a black one, or a single two-tone cow. I am nonetheless sure there are cows out there.

3. *James.* The last problem about natures or essences I will mention here was made famous by the American philosopher William James, who lived in the nineteenth and twentieth centuries. It goes like this. To suppose that anything has an essence absolutely, and irrespective of human purposes, seems untenable. Consider a sheet of paper. What are its properties? It is white. It is rectangular. It is smooth. It is combustible. It is blank. It is 8½ inches wide. It is two inches to the left of this pencil. And on and on. Now, which of these attributes is essential? The answer depends entirely on the use to which the thing is to be put. If it is to be used as kindling, then its combustibility is the essential thing, and its being white or rectangular is neither here nor there. If instead it is to be written on, its being white is now essential, but its combustibility is a mere incidental. No thing, then, "has an essence" considered just in itself and absolutely—it has an essence only in relation to this or that human purpose, and it has another essence in relation to another.

As with Nietzsche's mistake, this one is an instructive half-truth. Our names for things often designate more about ourselves than about the things. I call a piece of metal a fork. There is a shape in the metal that warrants the name. But the shape is not all. There is also a reference to human use. It is essential to a fork that it be suitable for use as a utensil. So when I call the thing on the table a fork, I am not talking just about the thing. I am dragging human beings into the meaning of the word.

But it is still possible to consider this thing as it is in itself, irrespective of human purposes. I see that the metal does not give a hoot about helping me eat my salad. But I feel its weight; it has a downward tendency that no human art imposed on it. So it has an agenda of its own, so to speak. It is also malleable, conductive, ductile, shiny, and responsive to magnets. Deeper study reveals that it is made of atoms whose electrons are easily evicted from the neighborhood of their nuclei. These properties all come together in this thing for some reason, and human art seems to have nothing to say in the matter. Moreover, among its properties there is a discernible order. It is useful for eating because of its shape, but it holds its shape because it is made of hard material, and not the other way around. The material is also conductive, and that is because its atoms' electrons are easily transferred. Within the metal itself there must be a first cause of the properties inherent in it. This first and underlying cause is what is called the essence or nature of the thing. So understood, things do indeed have essences irrespective of human purposes.

APPENDIX 4

Musings on Newton's First Law

The argument of chapter 3 rested in part on the conclusion that every motion is an effect being produced by some cause for as long as that motion endures. That statement would raise eyebrows in pretty much every physics department in the world, but largely because the physicists, on first hearing it, would be likely to misinterpret it without some further explanation. The cause of their concern would be Newton's first law. In his *Principia Mathematica Philosophiae Naturalis*, Isaac Newton enunciated his famous three laws of motion, the first of which is usually called the law of inertia and goes like this:

> Every body perseveres in its state of resting or of moving uniformly in a straight line, except insofar as it is compelled to change its state by impressed forces.

By *state* Newton meant a condition in which a body seems to be continuing to do what it was doing before—that is, maintaining the same speed and direction it had before. Hence, the two possible states are (1) absolute rest (in which a body maintains a speed of zero and moves in no direction at all) and (2) motion in one direction along a straight line at a constant speed. If a body moves at constant speed in a circle, it might in some sense seem to be continuing to do what it was doing before, but Newton did not call that sort of motion a state, since we see that familiar bodies, such as rocks, don't "like" to keep moving in a circle of their own accord. If you shove them a bit and then stop shoving them, they like to go off in straight lines, not in circles. Even if you whip a rock around in a sling and then let it go, although you had been moving it in a circle, it will fly off along the tangent after being released and show no interest in continuing to move in its original circular path. So the only way to keep something moving in a circle is to prevent it from doing what it wants to do—namely, move in a straight line. All circular motion, therefore, requires a force. But when a body moves uniformly in a straight line in nonresistant space (if such a thing exists)—that is, when it moves inertially—no force is required to sustain that motion.

This law has often been cited as a counterexample to the conclusion that everything in motion is being moved by something. According to Newton's first law, it is said, once a body is put in motion, it will continue in that motion forever, by itself, without the influence of any outside cause whatsoever. So (goes the objection), it is simply not true that everything in motion is presently being moved by something. The inertially moving body is not being forced. And yet the argument of chapter 3 would have it the other way: that every motion, even inertial motion, is being caused by some mover or another.

How should one reply? For one thing, Newton's first law actually doesn't make the negative claim that there is no cause for the inertial motion. It insists only that the body already in uniform rectilinear motion will persist in it. It does imply that there is *no force* impressed upon it. But that is not saying the same thing. Force and cause of motion are not altogether identical concepts. Every force is a cause of motion, but not every cause of motion is a force. My knowledge of how to build a table and my desire to build one are causes of my building it, but it is hard to see that either of these causes is a force as physicists use that word. A force has a definite direction, and it always occurs in a pair of equal and opposite forces; these things do not appear to be true about my knowledge and desire. A force, moreover, by the definitions of physicists, always means a cause of accelerated motion, a cause of change of state—of speed or direction, or both. (It is possible for forces to produce a uniform velocity, too, but only as a result of several of them fighting with each other, like a jet engine fighting wind resistance.) But there is nothing in the expression "cause of motion" that requires that the motion be an accelerated one. "Cause of motion" is a more general and inclusive concept.

So it might well be that a uniform motion can take place without a *force*, yet there must be some sort of *cause* of that motion nonetheless. Physicists don't make it their business to investigate everything and anything that might be a cause of motion; they deliberately restrict themselves to certain kinds of causes that their preferred methods are suited to reveal. As one might expect, there have been disagreements even among physicists about exactly what counts as "physics". Quarks apparently compose protons but can never exist in isolation and hence can never be observed or detected, but only inferred or maybe deduced based on theoretical considerations of other observable things. Most physicists would say quarks, thus understood, are fair game for physicists, while some initially said that they are not verifiable by the methods of physics and therefore lie outside the science, belonging to another discipline that is willing to proceed purely theoretically, or else deductively, without observations of free quarks. Some physicists, in other words, had thought it is the business of physics to study only those causes that are in some sense observable. But "observable causes" and "causes" are not identical concepts. (The experience of pleasure or pain, for example, can obviously cause us to do many things, but there is no observing these experiences from outside the one having them; only their outward effects and concomitant conditions are thus observable.) Even today's physicists, who accept quarks as part of the business of physics, would say that physicists study only mobile causes and causes that possess or exist in certain dimensions. But "mobile causes" and "dimensional causes" and "causes" are not identical concepts. *Cause* means "an active producer of some effect", which does not necessarily imply any size or mobility on the part of the cause. The truth that seven is a prime number is a cause of my understanding of it, for example, and yet that truth is not in any way changeable, and it seems meaningless to suggest that it has some sort of size. The physicist does not ask whether there might be causes beyond mobile and dimensional ones—or if he does, he has doffed his physicist hat and donned another. By pretty much any definition, a "physics" about unchangeable things without dimension is no longer physics.

"Cause" is broader, therefore, than "the sort of cause a physicist would study". And "cause of motion" in particular is broader than "cause of accelerated motion". A sculptor is the cause of sculpting— that is, of a change of shape in some material. Where there is no sculpting, no change of shape, there is also no dependence on a sculptor. For instance, a shape's mere continuation in existence, after the sculptor has finished sculpting, does not depend on a sculptor. Does that prove that the shape's continuation in existence is independent of all causes? Of course not. The shape, even though it is not changing, depends at least on the cohesive action of the parts of the material. If it is an ice sculpture, for instance, we see what happens when those inner bonds break down. Absence of change in the shape proves only an independence from a cause of any change in the shape. It does not prove that the shape itself exists independently of any cause. Likewise, the absence of change in a motion proves only an independence from a cause of change in the motion. It does not prove that the motion itself exists independently of any cause whatsoever. Newton's first law, in other words, is compatible with there being a cause of inertial motion, only that cause could not be a *force* as physicists use that term. No one need choose between the principle "Everything in motion is being moved by something" and Newton's first law as it is stated.

That is more than enough to answer the difficulty, but even more could be said. The first law itself is of a stipulative nature, for example. Newton calls it a law and even an axiom, but really it is only a well-substantiated stipulation. We can never in the strict sense verify the claim experimentally. To do so would require us to verify that some moving body is not being acted on by any forces whatsoever, or else that all the forces on it exactly cancel each other out—and that is simply impossible to do, especially since there are countless forces in the world. It would also require us to watch the moving body forever—even more impossible. And it would require us to verify that the body's motion was *perfectly* straight (or *exactly* along a geodesic) and that it never slows down or speeds up even the littlest, tiniest bit. There can be no such direct verification of the law. Instead, we see that the law fits with and explains much of what we see, so far as we can tell, and we adopt it as though it were the exact truth and go from there. And that might be the only reasonable thing to do by the methods of physics. But that is a far cry from saying it is a self-evident truth, like "When equals are subtracted from equals, the remainders are equal." The opposite of that would be unthinkable. But it is not unthinkable that a body, once put in motion, tends of itself, apart from impressed forces, to slow down imperceptibly over long periods. I do not say that this is true or even likely—only that it is possible, so far as one can see just by examining the general concept of a body in motion.

That "every motion requires a mover", by contrast, is the result of deduction from self-evident statements. So it is not a stipulation. It is a necessary truth. We saw this in chapter 3 itself on the grounds that no motion can *be* the first cause, and therefore every motion must depend for its existence upon the first cause and perhaps on many other causes as well. Every motion is an effect, so long as it exists.

There are other reasons to say that every motion needs a sustaining cause outside its mobile subject. Aristotle and Aquinas gave several. Here is a sketch of one. Evidently motion exists, and it exists *in things*. I mean the motion of a waving hand exists in the hand, and not just off by itself, like the smile of the Cheshire Cat. Why, then, does motion belong to this or that thing? Is there never a reason for it? It just happens? Plainly that is not true. In many cases there is an obvious cause, as when the golfer swings his club. But can motion in some cases belong to its subject for no reason at all? If any mobile (subject of the motion), whether a pigeon or a proton, were in some specific motion for no reason at all, then the same would be true of all its parts. Why, then, do all the parts agree to move all at once with the very same motion—all with the same speed and direction? There is an infinity of coincidences in that, since within the mobile thing, there will be as many distinct sectors as we care to distinguish, each moving with the same kind of motion as every other one and at the same time. Why does the left half of the pigeon move the same way as the right half? "Because they are stuck together", someone might venture to say. Ah, but that is only relevant if the left (say) is pushing or pulling the right, which is to introduce a cause of motion for at least the right side, after all. We can now ask the same question about the left. Why do all *its* parts agree about which way to go? Unless we are happy with an infinity of coincidences, we must suppose there is a unifying reason why the one motion belongs to all the parts. This fits, too, with the natural association of certain motions with certain things. Pigeons move in certain pigeon-specific ways, while protons move in quite different, proton-specific ways. So there must be a reason why each thing is in the motion that it is in, so long as it is in it.

But this very association of certain motions with certain things might lead us to think motion can belong to things just as a natural property, as being even belongs to eight. Although there is a reason eight is even—namely, because it is eight—this "reason" is not an active cause. Eight does not make itself even. Much less does anything else come along and make it even. Could motion belong to a mobile that way, just as a natural property? This is in fact how many materialists think. Motion is simply a property of matter, and is not in it due to any active cause, not even within itself. This cannot be true, however. If our mobile still has parts, the motion of the whole arises from the motions of those parts, and not the reverse. There is a one-way dependence there. This is clearest when the parts can actually be split off; they can move without the original whole moving, or even existing, but the whole cannot possibly have its motion unless its parts have theirs. Even if the parts for some reason cannot be separated, the motion of the whole plainly arises from the motions of the parts, and not the reverse. In a similar way, eight could not be even if two were not, whereas two does not derive its evenness from eight. And two is the end of the line. It has its evenness first and of itself, as a natural property. But what about in our mobile? The whole does not have motion independently of its parts' having theirs. And the same is true of those parts, and so on ad infinitum.

Someone might think that pure geometric points, which have no parts whatsoever, are the fundamental mobiles to which motion simply belongs as a natural property. But that also cannot be so. Points cannot exist by themselves, but only as the endpoints or corners or tips of bodies—like the corners of cubes and the tips of cones. But what does not have its own existence cannot have its own motion. It is not my surface that falls down the stairs. It is I, or my body, that falls down the stairs. My surface cannot exist without the volume of which it is the surface. It cannot exist without me. And so it cannot move without me either. It moves only in the sense that I move, and it must always come along for the ride. If I throw a cube down the stairs, then, it is not the surface of the cube that falls, but the cube, and its surface just tags along. Much less can one edge of the cube (a straight line) exist by itself, apart from the cube, and move around by itself. No, the edge falls downstairs only in the sense that it exists in the thing that is truly falling downstairs. By the same logic, neither can a corner of the cube fall downstairs by itself. The corner, which is a point, is nothing but the end of the edge, which is a line, which is nothing but the end of one surface of the cube. Points can be mobile only in a secondary and derivative sense, then. There is therefore nothing in a mobile that is altogether independently in motion—neither the mobile itself (since its motion always depends on its parts' having their motions), nor the parts (since they similarly depend on their parts), nor its points (since they have no motion of their own, but are just the extremities of the true subject of motion). But if there is nothing independently in motion in the mobile, as two is independently even, then we must always look for a cause of motion outside a thing's mere mobility, and this means a mover. And so everything in motion is being moved by something.

INDEX